A GUIDE TO

ORCHIDS

of the

WORLD

MARGARET HODGSON ROLAND PAINE
NEVILLE ANDERSON

Angus&Robertson
An imprint of HarperCollinsPublishers

AN ANGUS & ROBERTSON BOOK
An imprint of HarperCollins Publishers

First published in Australia in 1991
Reprinted 1991 by
CollinsAngus & Robertson Publishers Pty Limited (ACN 009 913 517)
A division of HarperCollinsPublishers (Australia) Pty Ltd
25-31 Ryde Road, Pymble NSW 2073, Australia

HarperCollinsPublishers (New Zealand) Limited
31 View Road, Glenfield, Auckland 10, New Zealand

HarperCollinsPublishers Limited
77-85 Fulham Palace Road, London W6 8JB, United Kingdom

Distributed in the United States of America by
HarperCollinsPublishers
10 East 53rd Street, New York NY 10022, USA

National Library of Australia
Cataloguing-in-Publication data:

Hodgson, Margaret.

   A guide to orchids of the world.

   Bibliography.
   Includes index.
   ISBN 0 207 16035 X.

   1. Orchids. I. Paine, Roland. II. Anderson, Neville.
   III. Title

584.15

Typeset in Garamond Light by Midland Typesetters,
Maryborough, Victoria.
Printed in Australia by Griffin Press.
6 5 4 3 2
95 94 93 92 91

CONTENTS

PREFACE

Orchidaceae is one of the largest, most diverse and exciting families of the flowering plant kingdom, comprising more than 700 genera and some 35 000 species of orchids scattered throughout the world. Their diversity in shape, size, colour, habitat and perfume, seem to be of unknown combinations and range.

A Guide to Orchids of the World has been designed for the keen amateur and exacting professional grower alike. We intend this book also to be a useful buyers' guide. Throughout the world there is renewed interest in species for hybridisation, since more orchid enthusiasts have begun doing their own hybridising and breeding. This book provides information to assist them.

As a book for both the novice and the professional *A Guide to Orchids of the World* has a wealth of information ranging from an introduction to what an orchid is, to details of cultivation, and a selection of illustrated botanical terms showing orchid plant structures from one species to the other. The book examines pollination, breeding, propagation, tissue culture, pests and diseases and provides a detailed glossary. Each section contains illustrations and photographs. A comprehensive range of genera are described in detail. The genera are fully illustrated and are accompanied by distribution maps and a selection of 458 species, each photographed in colour and described. The species include epiphytic, lithophytic and terrestrial orchids from around the world.

ACKNOWLEDGMENTS

In the preparation of a book, authors depend on many people for their assistance in gathering information and supplying plant specimens for photography and illustrations. We wish to acknowledge the contributions of individuals throughout the world.

Thank you to the staff of the Royal Botanic Gardens, Sydney, Australia, especially John Firlonger, and the staff of the National Parks and Wildlife Services in Australia and Borneo.

In Australia, we thank John Reipon, Sydney; Ross Whittle, Copmanhurst; Peter and Anne Schardin in assisting with our overseas travel, and film processing; and Michael Healy also of Murwillumbah; Lorrie Friar, Grafton; Steve Clemesha, Coffs Harbour; Graham Gamble, Lismore; York Meredith and Barney Greer, Sydney and Neville Fenton, Port Macquarie. A special thanks to Alan Englert of Tucabia for his assistance. We extend an extra special thanks to Alanah Anderson, also 'Sandy' and Ollie Anderson, of Woolgoolga, Australia, for their long hours of help and for making many specimens available.

We express our deep appreciation to Tony Ila, Member of Parliament for Lae, and Michael Coutts, both of Port Moresby, Papua New Guinea; Jeff Dennis, Government Botanist Honiara, from the Solomon Islands; Kevin Weinert, Peter Makuyike and Simon Daka, all of Madang, Papua New Guinea; Dick Phillips, Suva, Fiji; Som Sakdi, Bangkok, Thailand; and Elias and Alicia Javier, Manila, Philippines.

We extend our appreciation to our guides who assisted us while we were in the Malay Peninsula; Maijol Kakut, our guide while at Mount Kinabalu, Borneo; James Enjah, guide from the Iban tribe, Miri, Borneo; Laurence Lye of Kuching, Borneo; and Masi, our guide in Fiji.

Thanks to Margaret Hodgson's and Roland Paine's son Naradarn Hodgson Paine for the many hours he put into typing the manuscript. Last but not least thank you to Margaret Hodgson's mother, Thelma Hodgson, for keeping the home fires burning.

CLIMATE KEY

Hot—Minimum 15 degrees Celsius (59°F)
Warm—Minimum 10 degrees Celsius (50°F)
Intermediate—Minimum 5 degrees Celsius (41°F)
Cool—Minimum 1 degree Celsius (33.8°F)

This key is for tropical to sub-tropical climates where daytime temperatures rise some 15 to 20 degrees Celsius above the night-time minimum. In cold climates this factor should be taken into consideration and minimums set higher.

ABBREVIATIONS

aff.—Akin to, close to forma form: a taxonomic level below subspecies.

Gk—Greek.

Lat.—Latin (including Neo-Latin and botanical Latin).

sp.—Species.

ssp.—Subspecies: a taxonomic level below species and above variety.

syn.—Synonym: indicates an older name that applies to the same species.

var.—Variety: a taxonomic level below subspecies, but often in almost the same way as subspecies.

X—Natural native hybrid cross; indicates the name given to the resultant plant, or is used to link the names of the two parents.

INTRODUCTION

Orchidaceae is the largest family of the flowering plant kingdom, comprising some 35 000 species, and possibly there are the same number of hybrids produced both by natural cross and artificial pollination.

The flowers of the world are divided into two basic groups:
• The *regular flowers* are symmetrical—when viewed face on they can be cut through the centre along any plane to produce identical halves.
• The *irregular flowers* have segments of different shape and size, and when viewed face on cannot be cut along any plane to produce identical halves.

The orchid is an irregular flower, but it is special—view it face on, and in one plane only can it be cut to produce identical halves. A line drawn from the apex of the dorsal sepal through the centre of the column to the apex of the labellum will produce halves, one a mirror image of the other. This type of flower is said to be *zygomorphic*, from the Gk *zygot* (occurring in pairs) and *morph* (shape or form) with reference to the one form but with identical halves.

The Orchidaceae family has to be the most diverse in the world for colour, size, shape, habitat and perfume. Orchids vary in height from the minute Australian species *Bulbophyllum minutissimum*, approximately 3mm (1/16″) high, to the tallest (also an Australian species) *Galeola foliata*, which climbs to heights of 30m (100′) or more.

Orchid flowers are beautiful and, at times, bizarre. Many of the exquisite species belong to the *Dendrobium* (epiphytes) and *Paphiopedilum* (terrestrials) genera, such as *Dendrobium nobile* from Asia and *Paphiopedilum insigne* from India. One of the more bizarre is the Australian terrestrial, *Arthrochilus irritabilis*. While the pollinating wasp attempts to pseudocopulate with the flower, the irritable claw which attaches the labellum to the column is activated by the weight of the insect, causing the hammer-shaped lamina of the labellum, to which the wasp clings, to hammer the pollinator against the column, thus transferring any pollinium the wasp may be carrying on to the stigma. The result is the fertilisation of the flower.

Perfumes of the orchid flowers may be sweetly fragrant or may have the foul smell of something dead. Many species of *Dendrobiums*, *Cymbidiums*, *Phaius* and *Zygopetalums* produce exquisite, almost intoxicating, perfumes. In contrast, many species of *Bulbophyllums*, *Oncidiums* and *Coelogynes* carry overpowering offensive smells.

The structure of the flowers varies greatly, from simple *Cymbidiums* and *Cattleyas* to complex *Gongoras*, *Catasetums* and *Coryanthes*. By design, the shape of the flowers is determined by the way they are pollinated; often the labellum resembles a moth, bee, fly, wasp or spider, such as in the following genera: *Phalaenopsis* from the Philippines, *Ophrys* from Europe, *Cryptostylis* and *Caladenia* from Australia and *Oncidium* from South America.

In spite of their diverse shapes, all orchids have the same basic structure. Six basic floral segments make up the arrangement of an orchid flower; three sepals and three petals, alternating around the column which holds the reproductive parts of the plant. The sepal at the top of the flower is called the dorsal sepal and is usually different from the lateral sepals and may vary in shape and size.

The petal opposite the dorsal sepal is known as the labellum, from the Latin *labium*, meaning 'a lip'; it is different from the other petals and is generally trilobed. The labellum is often the most beautiful segment of the orchid flower. In some genera the flowers are inverted, with the labellum superior and the dorsal sepal at the bottom. The *Prasophyllums* are typical. With this species the lateral sepals are connate, or joined (refer to botanical illustrations).

Like most other flowers, orchids are bisexual, having both female and male parts. But orchids are special because the female and male parts—the stamens, the style and stigma—are united in one structure, called the column. This feature separates the orchid from other flowers, although in some species the flowers are unisexual e.g. *Catasetums*.

Orchid hunting will take the enthusiast through a diverse range of habitats in most parts of the world, except arid and frozen regions. Orchids also grow from sea level to an altitude of 4200m (14 000′).

Life-forms of orchids are usually divided into two main groups: epiphytes and terrestrials. Epiphytes (Lat. *epi*—upon, and *phyt*—plant, meaning on another plant or tree-dweller) use trees as their host. The majority of epiphytic orchids are confined to rainforest regions, wet sclerophyll forests, coastal tree belts, Paper Bark (*Melaleuca*) swamps and mangroves. Their long aerial roots not only hold them to their hosts but draw nutriments from leaf mould collected around their root systems and moisture from the air.

Terrestrials (Lat. *terrestris*—growing on the ground) are earth dwellers growing in the ground. They have fleshy rhizomes, fibrous roots or small tubers. Terrestrials range from rainforest, grasslands, savannah and open woodlands to coastal wetlands, but the habitat for most terrestrials is forests and woodlands of both northern and southern hemispheres. Many terrestrials have a five- or seven-year flowering cycle.

There are also orchids which are lithophytes (Gk *litho*— a stone). These orchids grow on moist rocks or cliff faces. From time to time epiphytes and terrestrials become lithophytic if growing conditions are right.

Saprophytes (Gk *sapros*—rotten, putrid) are plants that grow and derive most of their nourishment from decaying organic matter, often apparently lacking chlorophyll, and are mostly leafless. These plants live on the by-products of fungi which break down leaf mould and other vegetative matter. Saprophytes include *Corallorrhiza maculata* from Canada, U.S.A., Mexico and Guatemala. *Dipodium punctatum* is a representative Australian saprophyte.

SYMPODIAL AND MONOPODIAL GROUPS

Orchid growth can be classified into two main groups: sympodial and monopodial.

Sympodial (from Gk *sym*—united, and *podo*—a foot) refers to the pseudobulbs or stems being joined by a rhizome which is not always visible between them. The rhizome is the woody part of the root stock which varies in length and which joins one pseudobulb to the next.

The majority of orchids have a sympodial growth pattern. Sympodial orchids have pseudobulbs, so called because they are not true bulbs but thickened bulb-like stems. These stems are a storehouse of moisture and food, enabling the plant to survive dry periods. The main stem growth stops at the end of each season, and the new growth is produced at the base of the previous season's growth, similar to most perennial herbaceous plants. There is enormous diversity in the shapes of pseudobulbs; they range from minute to large in size and from round to egg-shape, and have club to thick cane stems. Some examples of genera belonging to this group are: *Cattleya, Dendrobium, Lycaste, Oncidium, Cymbidium, Odontoglossum, Encyclia, Epidendrum, Coelogyne* and *Phaius.*

Some sympodial orchids, within the terrestrial group, are without pseudobulbs. However their natural habitat maintains a constant seasonal supply of moisture to keep their root system or rhizome alive, so they are ready to produce new growth from the base of the last season's growth (for example, *Paphiopedilum* and its close relative *Phragmipedium*).

Monopodial (from the Gk *mono*—one, and *podo*—a foot) with reference to the plant having a single shoot which continues to grow from its terminal bud. The monopodial orchid's growth pattern is principally an upward direction extending the growth of previous years. The main stem produces alternating leaves on each side. Pseudobulbs are not present with monopodial growth. Monopodials may be described as climbing orchids; *Arachnis* is a good example, climbing to heights up to 20m (66'). Other examples in the monopodial group are *Vanda, Angraecum* and *Aerides*. Less vigorous growing monopodials are *Doritis* and *Phalaenopsis*; their growth is slow and compact.

SYMPODIAL

MONOPODIAL

 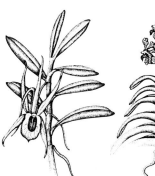

Cattleya labiata   *Dendrobium*   *Coelogyne speciosa*
                            canaliculatum

Phalaenopsis   *Angraecum*   *Vanda tricolor*
amabilis   *infundibulare*

Parts of an Orchid

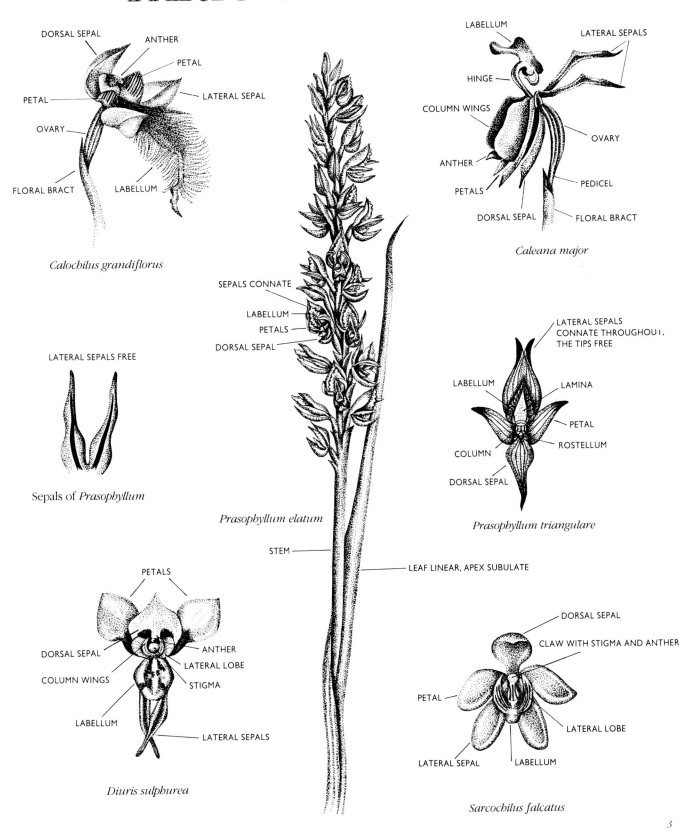

DORSAL SEPAL — **ANTHER** — **PETAL** — **LATERAL SEPAL** — **PETAL** — **OVARY** — **FLORAL BRACT** — **LABELLUM**

Calochilus grandiflorus

LABELLUM — **LATERAL SEPALS** — **HINGE** — **COLUMN WINGS** — **OVARY** — **ANTHER** — **PETALS** — **PEDICEL** — **DORSAL SEPAL** — **FLORAL BRACT**

Caleana major

LATERAL SEPALS FREE

Sepals of *Prasophyllum*

SEPALS CONNATE — **LABELLUM** — **PETALS** — **DORSAL SEPAL**

Prasophyllum elatum

STEM — **LEAF LINEAR, APEX SUBULATE**

LATERAL SEPALS CONNATE THROUGHOUT, THE TIPS FREE — **LABELLUM** — **LAMINA** — **PETAL** — **ROSTELLUM** — **COLUMN** — **DORSAL SEPAL**

Prasophyllum triangulare

PETALS — **DORSAL SEPAL** — **ANTHER** — **LATERAL LOBE** — **COLUMN WINGS** — **STIGMA** — **LABELLUM** — **LATERAL SEPALS**

Diuris sulphurea

DORSAL SEPAL — **CLAW WITH STIGMA AND ANTHER** — **PETAL** — **LATERAL LOBE** — **LATERAL SEPAL** — **LABELLUM**

Sarcochilus falcatus

3

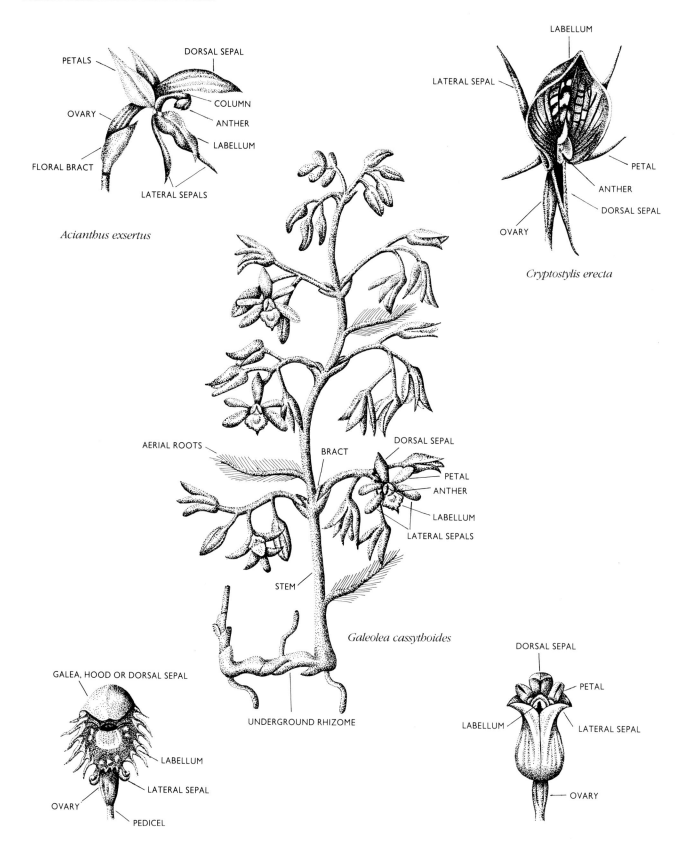

PETALS

DORSAL SEPAL

OVARY

COLUMN

ANTHER

LABELLUM

FLORAL BRACT

LATERAL SEPALS

Acianthus exsertus

LABELLUM

LATERAL SEPAL

PETAL

ANTHER

DORSAL SEPAL

OVARY

Cryptostylis erecta

AERIAL ROOTS

BRACT

DORSAL SEPAL

PETAL

ANTHER

LABELLUM

LATERAL SEPALS

STEM

Galeolea cassythoides

UNDERGROUND RHIZOME

GALEA, HOOD OR DORSAL SEPAL

LABELLUM

LATERAL SEPAL

OVARY

PEDICEL

Corybas undulatus

DORSAL SEPAL

PETAL

LABELLUM

LATERAL SEPAL

OVARY

Gastrodia sesamoides

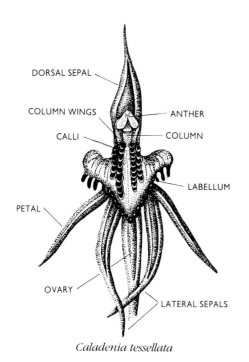

DORSAL SEPAL

COLUMN WINGS — ANTHER

CALLI — COLUMN

LABELLUM

PETAL

OVARY

LATERAL SEPALS

Caladenia tessellata

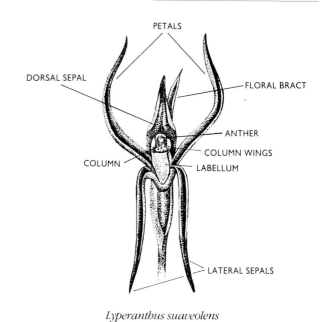

PETALS

DORSAL SEPAL — FLORAL BRACT

ANTHER

COLUMN — COLUMN WINGS

LABELLUM

LATERAL SEPALS

Lyperanthus suaveolens

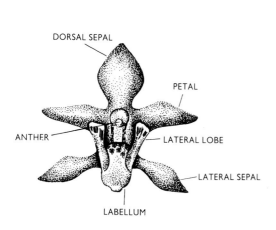

DORSAL SEPAL

PETAL

ANTHER — LATERAL LOBE

LATERAL SEPAL

LABELLUM

Pterocaras spathulatus

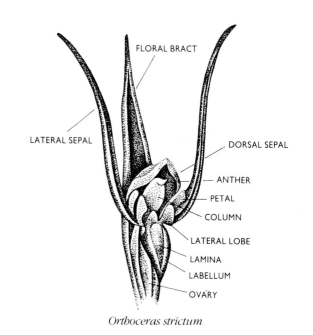

FLORAL BRACT

LATERAL SEPAL

DORSAL SEPAL

ANTHER

PETAL

COLUMN

LATERAL LOBE

LAMINA

LABELLUM

OVARY

Orthoceras strictum

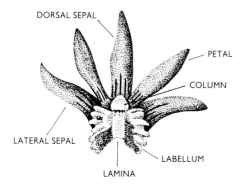

DORSAL SEPAL

PETAL

COLUMN

LATERAL SEPAL

LABELLUM

LAMINA

Dendrobium pugioniforme

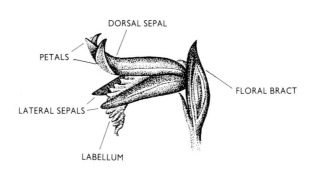

DORSAL SEPAL

PETALS

FLORAL BRACT

LATERAL SEPALS

LABELLUM

Spiranthes sinensis

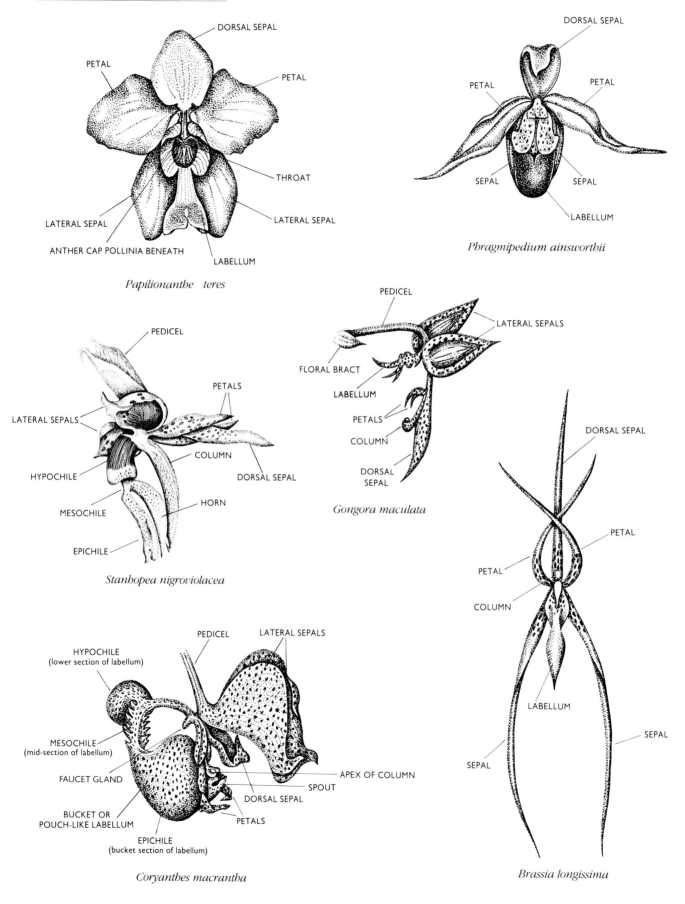

DORSAL SEPAL

PETAL

PETAL

THROAT

LATERAL SEPAL

LATERAL SEPAL

ANTHER CAP POLLINIA BENEATH

LABELLUM

Papilionanthe teres

DORSAL SEPAL

PETAL

PETAL

SEPAL

SEPAL

LABELLUM

Phragmipedium ainsworthii

PEDICEL

PETALS

LATERAL SEPALS

COLUMN

HYPOCHILE

DORSAL SEPAL

MESOCHILE

HORN

EPICHILE

Stanhopea nigroviolacea

PEDICEL

LATERAL SEPALS

FLORAL BRACT

LABELLUM

PETALS

COLUMN

DORSAL SEPAL

Gongora maculata

DORSAL SEPAL

PETAL

PETAL

COLUMN

LABELLUM

SEPAL

SEPAL

Brassia longissima

HYPOCHILE
(lower section of labellum)

PEDICEL

LATERAL SEPALS

MESOCHILE
(mid-section of labellum)

FAUCET GLAND

APEX OF COLUMN

SPOUT

DORSAL SEPAL

BUCKET OR
POUCH-LIKE LABELLUM

PETALS

EPICHILE
(bucket section of labellum)

Coryanthes macrantha

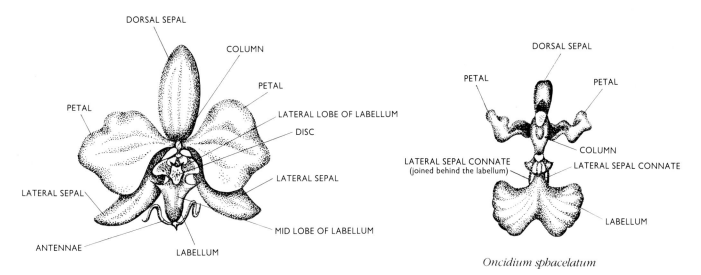

DORSAL SEPAL
COLUMN
PETAL
LATERAL LOBE OF LABELLUM
DISC
PETAL
LATERAL SEPAL
LATERAL SEPAL
MID LOBE OF LABELLUM
ANTENNAE
LABELLUM

Phalaenopsis sanderiana

DORSAL SEPAL
PETAL
PETAL
COLUMN
LATERAL SEPAL CONNATE
(joined behind the labellum)
LATERAL SEPAL CONNATE
LABELLUM

Oncidium sphacelatum

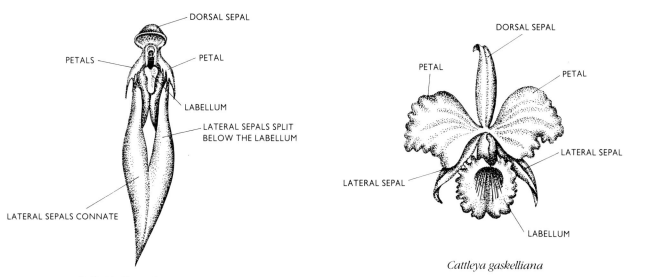

DORSAL SEPAL
PETALS
PETAL
LABELLUM
LATERAL SEPALS SPLIT
BELOW THE LABELLUM
LATERAL SEPALS CONNATE

Bulbophyllum picturatum

DORSAL SEPAL
PETAL
PETAL
LATERAL SEPAL
LATERAL SEPAL
LABELLUM

Cattleya gaskelliana

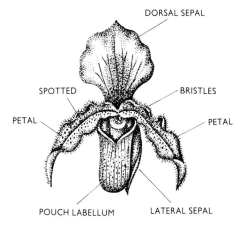

DORSAL SEPAL
SPOTTED
BRISTLES
PETAL
PETAL
POUCH LABELLUM
LATERAL SEPAL

Paphiopedilum hirsutissimum

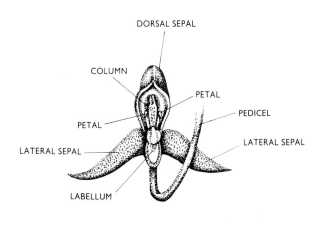

DORSAL SEPAL
COLUMN
PETAL
PETAL
PEDICEL
LATERAL SEPAL
LATERAL SEPAL
LABELLUM

Gongora galeata

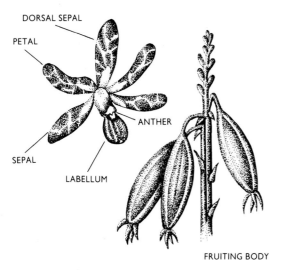

DORSAL SEPAL
PETAL
ANTHER
SEPAL
LABELLUM
FRUITING BODY

Dipodium punctatum

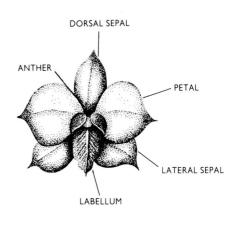

DORSAL SEPAL
ANTHER
PETAL
LATERAL SEPAL
LABELLUM

Dendrobium bigibbum

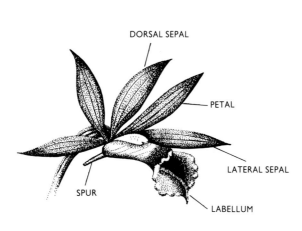

DORSAL SEPAL
PETAL
LATERAL SEPAL
SPUR
LABELLUM

Phaius australis

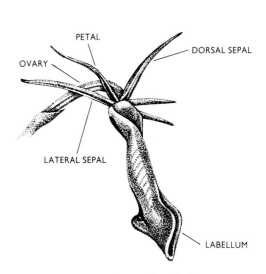

PETAL
OVARY
DORSAL SEPAL
LATERAL SEPAL
LABELLUM

Cryptostylis subulata

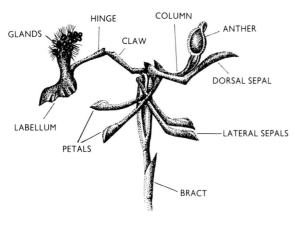

GLANDS
HINGE
COLUMN
CLAW
ANTHER
DORSAL SEPAL
LABELLUM
PETALS
LATERAL SEPALS
BRACT

Drakea elastica

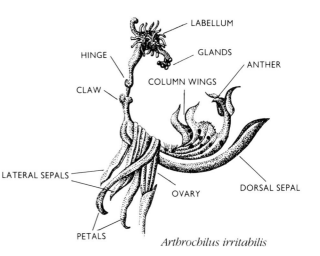

LABELLUM
HINGE
GLANDS
ANTHER
CLAW
COLUMN WINGS
LATERAL SEPALS
OVARY
DORSAL SEPAL
PETALS

Arthrochilus irritabilis

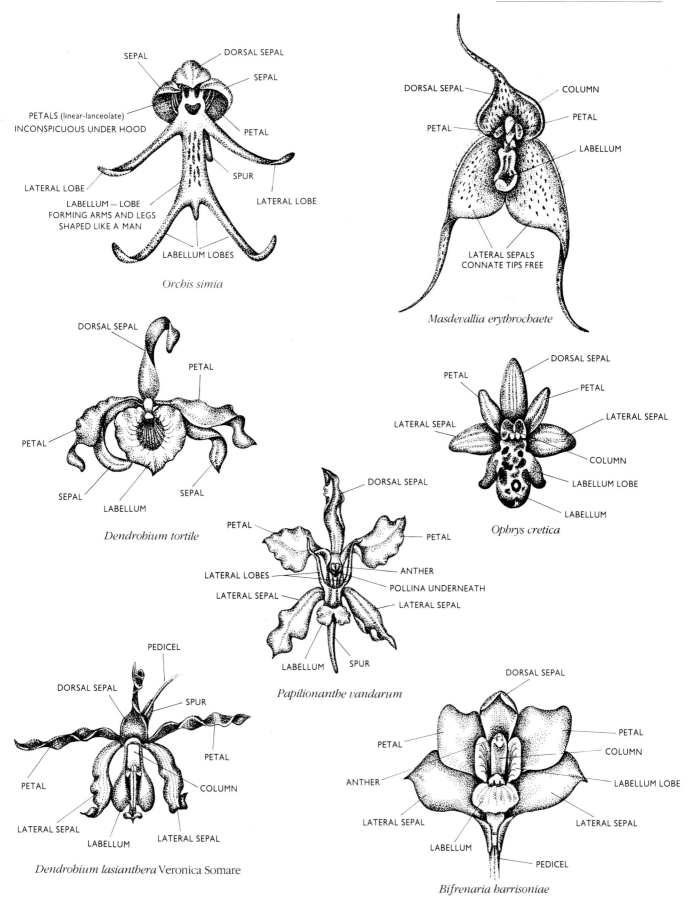

SEPAL
DORSAL SEPAL
SEPAL
PETALS (linear-lanceolate)
INCONSPICUOUS UNDER HOOD
PETAL
LATERAL LOBE
SPUR
LABELLUM — LOBE
FORMING ARMS AND LEGS
SHAPED LIKE A MAN
LATERAL LOBE
LABELLUM LOBES

Orchis simia

DORSAL SEPAL
COLUMN
PETAL
PETAL
LABELLUM
LATERAL SEPALS
CONNATE TIPS FREE

Masdevallia erythrochaete

DORSAL SEPAL
PETAL
PETAL
SEPAL
LABELLUM
SEPAL

Dendrobium tortile

PETAL
DORSAL SEPAL
PETAL
LATERAL SEPAL
LATERAL SEPAL
COLUMN
LABELLUM LOBE
LABELLUM

Ophrys cretica

DORSAL SEPAL
PETAL
PETAL
LATERAL LOBES
ANTHER
LATERAL SEPAL
POLLINA UNDERNEATH
LATERAL SEPAL
LABELLUM
SPUR

Papilionanthe vandarum

PEDICEL
DORSAL SEPAL
SPUR
PETAL
PETAL
COLUMN
LATERAL SEPAL
LATERAL SEPAL
LABELLUM

Dendrobium lasianthera Veronica Somare

DORSAL SEPAL
PETAL
PETAL
COLUMN
ANTHER
LABELLUM LOBE
LATERAL SEPAL
LATERAL SEPAL
LABELLUM
PEDICEL

Bifrenaria harrisoniae

LEAF AND PSEUDOBULBS ILLUSTRATED

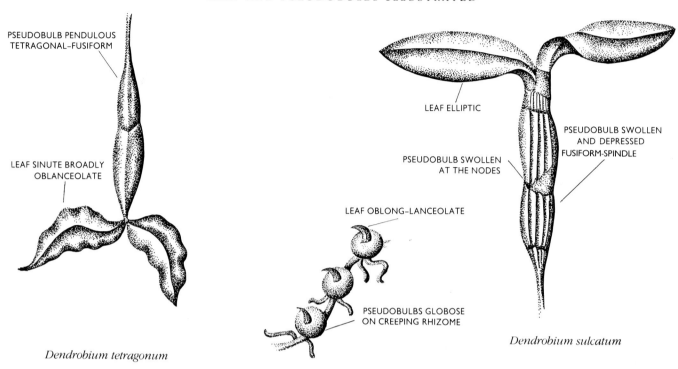

PSEUDOBULB PENDULOUS
TETRAGONAL–FUSIFORM

LEAF SINUTE BROADLY
OBLANCEOLATE

Dendrobium tetragonum

LEAF ELLIPTIC

PSEUDOBULB SWOLLEN
AT THE NODES

PSEUDOBULB SWOLLEN
AND DEPRESSED
FUSIFORM-SPINDLE

LEAF OBLONG-LANCEOLATE

PSEUDOBULBS GLOBOSE
ON CREEPING RHIZOME

Dendrobium sulcatum

Bulbophyllum minutissimum

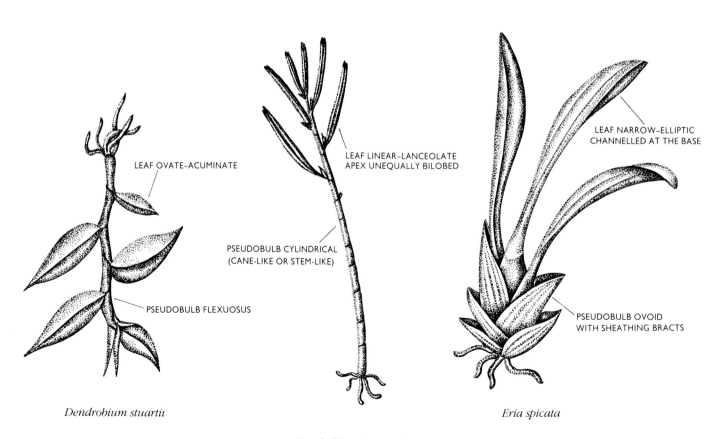

LEAF OVATE–ACUMINATE

PSEUDOBULB FLEXUOSUS

LEAF LINEAR–LANCEOLATE
APEX UNEQUALLY BILOBED

PSEUDOBULB CYLINDRICAL
(CANE-LIKE OR STEM-LIKE)

LEAF NARROW-ELLIPTIC
CHANNELLED AT THE BASE

PSEUDOBULB OVOID
WITH SHEATHING BRACTS

Dendrobium stuartii

Eria spicata

Dendrobium tozerensis

LEAF AND PSEUDOBULBS ILLUSTRATED

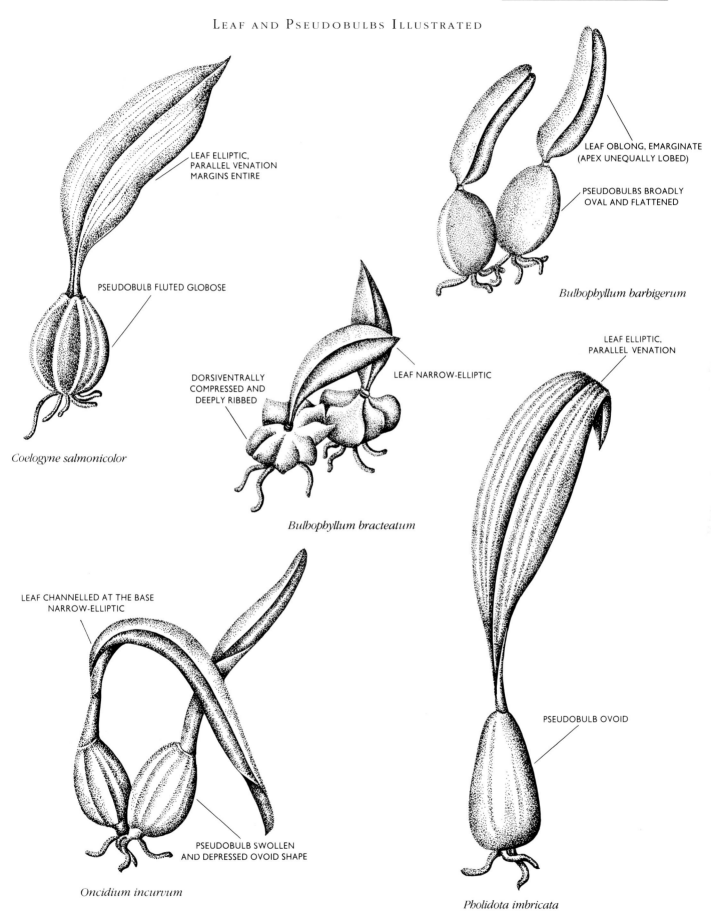

LEAF ELLIPTIC,
PARALLEL VENATION
MARGINS ENTIRE

PSEUDOBULB FLUTED GLOBOSE

Coelogyne salmonicolor

LEAF OBLONG, EMARGINATE
(APEX UNEQUALLY LOBED)

PSEUDOBULBS BROADLY
OVAL AND FLATTENED

Bulbophyllum barbigerum

DORSIVENTRALLY
COMPRESSED AND
DEEPLY RIBBED

LEAF NARROW-ELLIPTIC

Bulbophyllum bracteatum

LEAF ELLIPTIC,
PARALLEL VENATION

PSEUDOBULB OVOID

Pholidota imbricata

LEAF CHANNELLED AT THE BASE
NARROW-ELLIPTIC

PSEUDOBULB SWOLLEN
AND DEPRESSED OVOID SHAPE

Oncidium incurvum

Leaf and Pseudobulbs illustrated

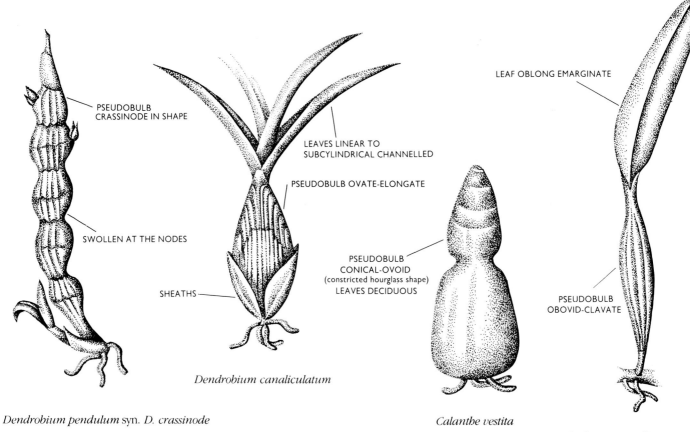

PSEUDOBULB
CRASSINODE IN SHAPE

SWOLLEN AT THE NODES

LEAVES LINEAR TO
SUBCYLINDRICAL CHANNELLED

PSEUDOBULB OVATE-ELONGATE

LEAF OBLONG EMARGINATE

PSEUDOBULB
CONICAL-OVOID
(constricted hourglass shape)
LEAVES DECIDUOUS

SHEATHS

PSEUDOBULB
OBOVID-CLAVATE

Dendrobium canaliculatum

Dendrobium pendulum syn. *D. crassinode*

Calanthe vestita

Cattleya percivaliana

Dendrobium Group Showing Variants Within a Genus

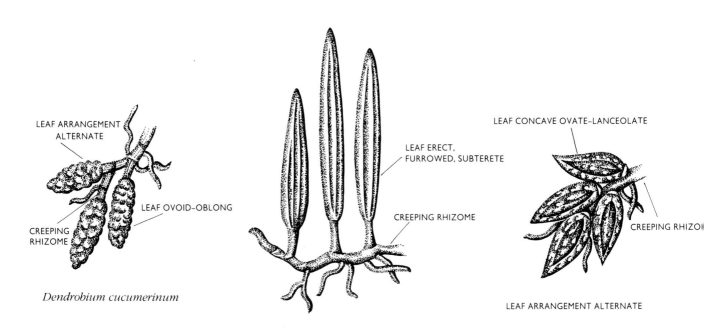

LEAF ARRANGEMENT
ALTERNATE

LEAF OVOID-OBLONG

CREEPING
RHIZOME

LEAF ERECT,
FURROWED, SUBTERETE

CREEPING RHIZOME

LEAF CONCAVE OVATE-LANCEOLATE

CREEPING RHIZOME

LEAF ARRANGEMENT ALTERNATE

Dendrobium cucumerinum

Dendrobium wassallii

Dendrobium toressae

DENDROBIUM GROUP SHOWING VARIANTS
WITHIN A GENUS

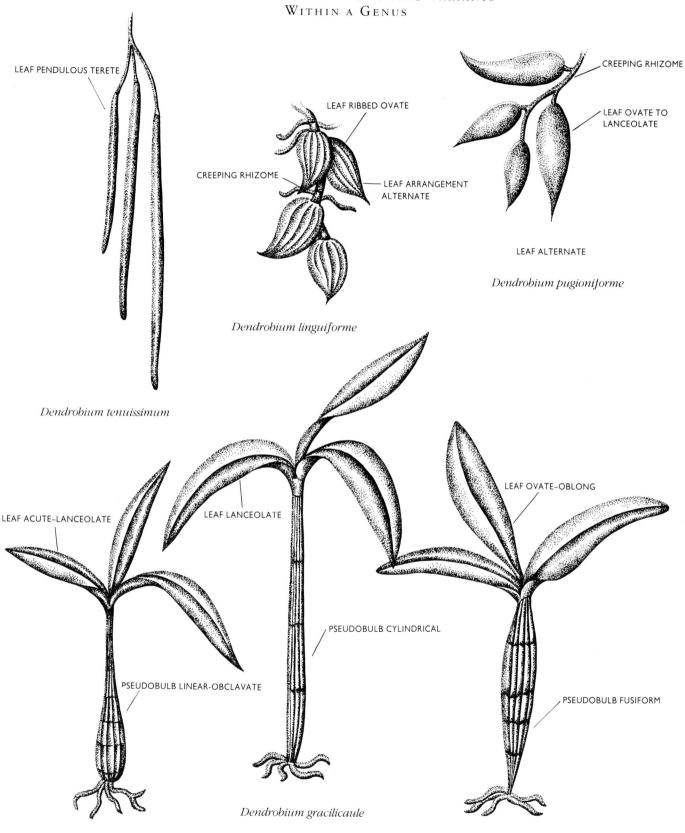

LEAF PENDULOUS TERETE

LEAF RIBBED OVATE

CREEPING RHIZOME

CREEPING RHIZOME

LEAF OVATE TO
LANCEOLATE

LEAF ARRANGEMENT
ALTERNATE

LEAF ALTERNATE

Dendrobium pugioniforme

Dendrobium linguiforme

Dendrobium tenuissimum

LEAF LANCEOLATE

LEAF OVATE–OBLONG

LEAF ACUTE–LANCEOLATE

PSEUDOBULB CYLINDRICAL

PSEUDOBULB LINEAR–OBCLAVATE

PSEUDOBULB FUSIFORM

Dendrobium gracilicaule

Dendrobium kingianum

Dendrobium ruppianum

L E A F   A N D   P E T A L   S H A P E S

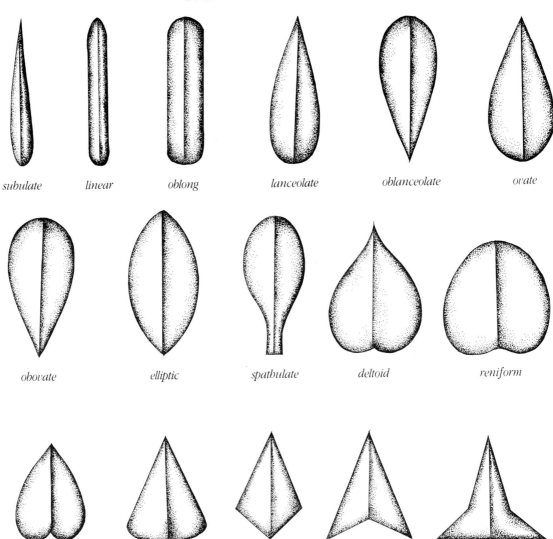

subulate   linear   oblong   lanceolate   oblanceolate   ovate

obovate   elliptic   spathulate   deltoid   reniform

cordate   triangular   trullate   sagittate   hastate

L E A F   A N D   P E T A L   T I P S

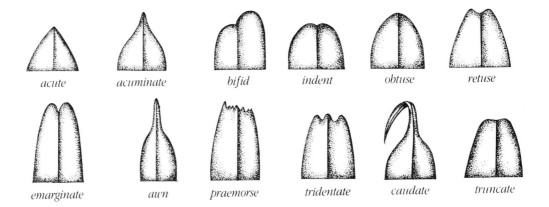

acute   acuminate   bifid   indent   obtuse   retuse

emarginate   awn   praemorse   tridentate   caudate   truncate

CLASSIFICATION OF ORCHIDS

Orchidaceae is one of the largest of the flowering plant families. It is an exceedingly rich and diverse group of more than 35 000 species, and this number increases with the discovery of new specimens by both amateur and professional collectors.

One of the first botanists to attempt to classify orchids into genera was the botanist L. Fuchs in 1542. In 1583 Dosloneus set about a further reclassification of the expanding orchid family. Orchid collections were growing in size as well, with more and more collections appearing throughout Europe as the rich indulged in a new found hobby.

Caspar Bauhin published his work on the classification of orchids in 1620. In 1753, Carl Von Linne' (Linnaeus), the father of modern taxonomy, published a detailed description of 69 species of 8 genera.

In America between 1788 and 1800, O. Swartz recognised the difference between species with one anther and those with two anthers.

A further development occurred in 1810 when R. Brown recognised the importance of the anther and pollinia character and habit of the species.

By 1825 the famous taxonomist John Lindley started the first major classification of orchids, and for the next forty years he worked continuously on revising his classification. Lindley's work was revised with the advent of a number of younger research taxonomists—Ames, Pfitzer, Rolfe and others.

In the early 1900s Rudolf Schlecter began to be known as 'a splitter'. He based his research on the works of Pfitzer, but first increased the number of subtribes in Pfitzer's classification. Where most taxonomists were content to recognise variations of a species, Schlecter split the variations off into new species, thus expanding the number of species in a genus. Often he placed them into a new genus, thus expanding the number of genera. This process became known as the Schlecter System and remained unchanged until about 1930. Since then the system has been under continual review and modification. Today taxonomists fall into one of two schools and are classified as either a 'splitter' or 'lumper'.

The Orchidaceae family is growing day by day as field workers, amateurs and professionals alike find new specimens. When describing these new arrivals, taxonomists often need to create a new genus; sometimes in doing so, they find a new home for a well known, but problematic species, hence a new name is bestowed on an old favourite and another synonym is born.

Even with all this splitting, lumping and reclassification, the Orchidaceae family remains in the sub-division of Angiospermae of the Spermataphyta division of the plant kingdom, in the Monocotyledonae class under the Microspermae order. The Orchidaceae family is divided into subfamilies, then into tribes and subtribes, these again into genera and species before our beloved orchid is finally given a name. From time to time an orchid may be found to be a subspecies or variety of the species.

When describing and naming orchids, taxonomists use Greek and Latin names. Usually, Greek is used for the genus and Latin for the species part of the name; for example, the *Ascoglossum* genus name comes from the Greek *asos* meaning a bag and *glossa* meaning a tongue, with reference to the shape of the labellum; and *leucanthus* the species name is from the Latin *leuco* meaning white and *anthus* meaning a flower. So the full name meaning is: a white flower with baggy labellum.

The taxonomist must follow the International Rules of Nomenclature when naming the orchid.
- All family names end with 'aceae,' e.g. Orchidaceae.
- Subfamily names end with 'oideae,' e.g. Orchidioideae.
- Tribe names end with 'eae,' e.g. Vandeae.
- Subtribe names end with 'inae,' e.g. Vandinae.
- Only genera and species names are printed in italics.
- Genera names end with 'a, e, as, is, um, us' e.g. *Vanda*.
- The species name ending should agree with the generic ending, e.g. *Vanda denisoniana*.
- Likewise subspecies and variety name endings should agree with the species and generic ending, e.g. var. *herbarica*.

Hence the taxonomic relationship of *Vanda denisoniana* var. *herbarica*:

Family:	Orchidaceae.
Subfamily:	Orchidioideae.
Tribe:	Vandeae.
Subtribe:	Vandinae.
Genus:	*Vanda*
Species:	*denisoniana* var. *herbarica*.

In the condensed classification chart overleaf, the Orchidaceae family is divided into 3 subfamilies, 12 tribes, 45 subtribes and 186 genera. While an expanded classification could contain up to 6 or more subfamilies with a tribal and subtribal increase of up to 800 genera, you should be able to find the place of your favourite orchid on the chart overleaf.

CLASSIFICATION CHART

Family: Orchidaceae

  I. Subfamily: Apostasioideae
      Tribe: Apostasieae
         Genera: *Apostasia, Adactylus, Neuwiedia*

  II. Subfamily: Cypripedioideae
      Tribe: Cypripedieae
         Genera: *Cypripedium, Paphiopedilum,*
                 Phragmipedium, Selenipedium

  III. Subfamily: Orchidioideae (Neottioideae)

    A. Tribe: Neottieae
      1. Subtribe: Limodorinae
         Genera: *Cephalanthera, Epipactis,*
              Limodorum
      2. Subtribe: Rhizanthellinae
         Genera: *Cryptanthemis, Rhizanthella*
      3. Subtribe: Pterostylidinae
         Genera: *Caleana, Pterostylis*
      4. Subtribe: Listerinae
         Genera: *Listera, Neottia*

    B. Tribe: Diurideae
      1. Subtribe: Chloraeinae
         Genera: *Bipinnula, Caladenia,*
              Chloraea, Codonorchis,
              Gavilea, Geoblasta
      2. Subtribe: Diuridinae
         Genera: *Diuris, Orthoceras*
      3. Subtribe: Cryptostylidinae
         Genera: *Coilochilus, Cryptostylis*
      4. Subtribe: Prasophyllinae
         Genera: *Microtis, Prasophyllum*

    C. Tribe: Cranichideae
      1. Subtribe: Tropidiinae
         Genera: *Corymborchis, Tropidia*
      2. Subtribe: Spiranthinae
         Genera: *Centrogenium, Lankesterella,*
              Pelexia, Sarcoglottis, Spiranthes
      3. Subtribe: Pachyplectrinae
         Genera: *Erythrodes, Goodyera*
      4. Subtribe: Cranichidinae
         Genera: *Altenstenia, Cranichis,*
              Pontheiva, Prescottia,
              Pseudocentrum, Stenoptera

    D. Tribe: Orchideae
      1. Subtribe: Epipogiinae
         Genera: *Epipogium, Stereosandra*
      2. Subtribe: Orchidinae
         Genera: *Bonatea, Dactylorchis,*
              Galeorchis, Habenaria,
              Ophrys, Orchis, Platanthera,
              Stenoglottis

      3. Subtribe: Disinae
         Genera: *Disa, Satyrium*
      4. Subtribe: Coryciinae
         Genera: *Ceratandra, Corycium*

    E. Tribe: Gastrodieae
      1. Subtribe: Vanillinae
         Genera: *Duckeella, Epistephium,*
              Eriaxis, Galeola, Vanilla
      2. Subtribe: Gastrodiinae
         Genera: *Didymoplexis, Gastrodia*
      3. Subtribe: Pogoniinae
         Genera: *Cleistes, Isotria,*
              Monophyllorchis, Nervilia,
              Pogonia, Triophora

    F. Tribe: Arethuseae
      1. Subtribe: Arethusinae
         Genera: *Arethusa, Calopogon, Bletilla*
      2. Subtribe: Bletiinae
         Genera: *Acanthephippium, Bletia,*
              Calanthe, Chysis, Coelia,
              Hexalectus, Phaius,
              Spathoglottis
      3. Subtribe: Sobraliinae
         Genera: *Arpophyllum, Elleanthus,*
              Isochilus, Palmorchis,
              Sertifera, Sobralia
      4. Subtribe: Thuniinae
         Genera: *Arundina, Thunia*
      5. Subtribe: Collabiinae
         Genera: *Chrysoglossum, Collabium,*
              Nephelaphyllum, Tainia
      6. Subtribe: Coelogyninae
         Genera: *Coelogyne, Dendrochilum,*
              Panisea, Pholidota, Pleione

    G. Tribe: Epidendreae
      1. Subtribe: Laeliinae
         Genera: *Alamania, Barkeria,*
              Brassavola, Broughtonia,
              Cattleya, Epidendrum,
              Hexisia, Laelia,
              Schomburgkia, Sophronitis,
              Tetramicra
      2. Subtribe: Eriinae
         Genera: *Appendicula, Eria, Glomera,*
              Neobenthamia, Podochilus,
              Polystachya
      3. Subtribe: Meiracylliinae
         Genus: *Meiracyllium*
      4. Subtribe: Pleurothallidinae
         Genus: *Lepanthes, Masdevallia,*
              Pleurothallis, Restrepia, Stelis

    5. Subtribe: Adrorhizinae
        Genera: *Adrorhizon, Josephia*
    6. Subtribe: Thelasiinae
        Genera: *Phreatia, Thelasis*
    7. Subtribe: Ridleyellinae
        Genera: *Ridleyella*

H. Tribe: Dendrobieae
    1. Subtribe: Bulbophyllinae
        Genera: *Bulbophyllum, Dendrobium*

I. Tribe: Malaxideae
    1. Subtribe: Liparidinae
        Genera: *Liparis, Malaxis, Oberonia*
    2. Subtribe: Genyorchidinae
        Genera: *Drymoda, Genyorchis, Ione*
    3. Subtribe: Thecostelinae
        Genera: *Thecostele*

J. Tribe: Vandeae
    1. Subtribe: Cymbidiinae
        Genera: *Ansellia, Aplectrum,*
                Corallorhiza, Cymbidiella,
                Cymbidium, Cyrtopodium,
                Eulophia, Galeandra,
                Grammatophyllum, Tipularia
    2. Subtribe: Catasetinae
        Genera: *Catasetum, Cycnoches,*
                Mormodes

    3. Subtribe: Vandinae
        Genera: *Aerangis, Aerides,*
                Angraecum, Phalaenopsis,
                Renanthera, Trichoglottis,
                Vanda
    4. Subtribe: Maxillariinae
        Genera: *Maxillaria, Trigonidium,*
                Xylobium
    5. Subtribe: Lycastinae
        Genera: *Anguloa, Bifrenaria, Lycaste*
    6. Subtribe: Zygopetalinae
        Genera: *Chondrorhyncha, Huntleya,*
                Pescatorea, Zygopetalum
    7. Subtribe: Stanhopeinae
        Genera: *Acineta, Coryanthes,*
                Gongora, Peristeria,
                Stanhopea
    8. Subtribe: Ornithocephalinae
        Genera: *Dichea, Ornithocephalus,*
                Telipogon, Trichoceros
    9. Subtribe: Oncidiinae
        Genera: *Aspasia, Brassia,*
                Comparettia, Gomesa,
                Ionopsis, Lockhartia,
                Miltonia, Odontoglossum,
                Oncidium, Rodriguezia,
                Trichocentrum, Trichopilia

Classification is ongoing. Research botanists consider that always 'there is room for improvement and modification of the present classification'. In 1981, Dressler and Dodson published a taxonomic key that they use in updating and revising their research. A copy of that key is available from the American Orchid Society.

HABITATS

Orchid habitats are diverse, ranging from the arctic regions to the tropics, from sea level to elevations as high as 3800m (12 500'); but the most preferred regions are the warmer areas of the globe. Orchid species in tropical, sub-tropical, warm and cool temperate rainforest conditions are largely epiphytic or lithophytic, growing on trees or rocks. Of the numerous epiphytic orchids, none is parasitic. In the arctic and temperate regions the orchids are by and large terrestrials.

In the early days of orchid collection, it was generally believed that orchids in the wild grew in the steamy impenetrable tropical jungles where the most extraordinary and mysterious plants thrive—the myth still lingers. It is partly true, for 'jungle' is applied in a general way to all rainforests and the larger concentration of orchid species do occur in the equatorial girdle of tropical rainforests.

But orchids are found in all of the following habitats: rainforests, monsoon forests, cloud forests, wet sclerophyll forests, dry sclerophyll forests, savannah, woodlands, mangrove swamps. These tree habitats are vital for the existence of orchids. Other essential orchid habitats include: coastal lowlands, littoral forests, *Melaleuca* (Paper Bark) forests, water meadows, bogs, swamps, sand dunes, grasslands, moist rocks, sheltered cliff faces, creeks and mountain streams, and edges of waterfalls.

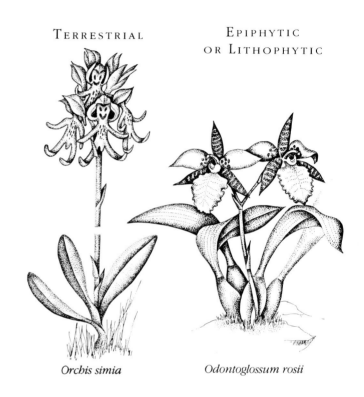

TERRESTRIAL

EPIPHYTIC OR LITHOPHYTIC

Orchis simia

Odontoglossum rosii

LEAFLESS EPIPHYTIC

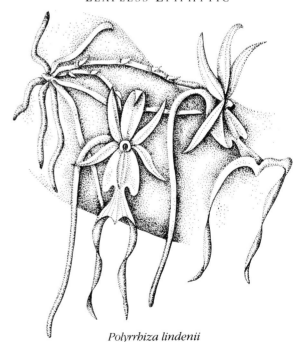

Polyrrhiza lindenii

Paper Barks (Melaleuca)

Heathlands

Tropical lowlands (Papua New Guinea)

Swamp and rocks in woodlands

Rock garden of Dendrobium kingianum

RAINFOREST HABITATS

More than half of the world's rainforests is in the neo-tropic group: central America, Amazon and Orinoco Rivers and Brazil, and more than one quarter is in India, Malaysia, Borneo, Indonesia and Papua New Guinea. A little less than one fifth of the world's rainforest is in eastern Africa, central Africa, western Africa and Madagascar. Embedded in the tropical rainforests are monsoon forests. Unlike tropical rainforests which receive rain all year round, monsoon rainforests receive their rain during the monsoonal season which is then followed by a dry period. The sub-tropical rainforests are above and below the tropics to latitudes of 35° north and south, while the temperate and cool temperate zones with their rainforests extend to latitudes 45° north and south.

Orchids growing in tropical rainforests tend to festoon the higher branches of tall, lofty trees together with ferns, bromeliads, mosses, and other epiphytic plants, where sufficient light and air movement penetrates the thick canopy for their growth. Their roots are exposed to the air or lie in leaf litter in the grooves of rough bark. So numerous does the concentration of plants become as these plants reach for light and air flow that the branches often break under the weight. The genera *Phalaenopsis*, *Robiquetias*, *Epidendrums* and *Stanhopeas* are among the orchids found at this altitude.

In the monsoon rainforests the base of the stems of the epiphytic orchids are swollen and bulb-like in formation. These pseudobulbs hold a supply of moisture to save the plant from dehydration and death during the dry season between the monsoonal rains. These epiphytic orchids include: *Coelogyne*, *Bulbophyllum* and *Dendrobium*.

In the sub-tropics, rain is seasonal. In these rainforests

the trees are not so tall, nor is the vegetation so close; there is an understorey of shorter trees with tree-ferns and on the forest floor lamandras grow. The canopy above is more open and the vines are not so thick. Epiphytes such as *Catasetum* and *Gongoras* grow in the upper limbs, while *Sarcochilus* grow on the tree trunks and lower branches.

In the cool, temperate rainforest the trees are not tall, their branches are adorned with hanging moss, the understorey is thicker and the lianas fewer. As in the wet sclerophyll forests, the terrestrial orchids are plentiful— orchids such as *Vandas, Oncidiums, Epidendrums, Encyclias, Maxillarias* and *Paphiopedilum.*

In all these forests along creeks, by waterfalls, and on rock faces where there are moderate amounts of shade, orchids such as *Calanthe, Phaius, Dendrobiums* and *Sarcochilus ceciliae* grow in abundance.

Above 750m (2500'), the lowland rainforests give way to montane forests. Here the trees are much shorter than in other rainforests and are of different species. The understorey is thicker. Orchids grow along the moss covered branches and on the forest floor are a great number of terrestrials in large groups. Often matting large areas are orchids such as *Bulbophyllum, Coelogyne, Lycaste, Maxillaria* and *Phragmipedium.*

At 1500m (5000') the growth ceiling of many plants is reached. There are no lofty trees and the trees diminish in height the higher one climbs. *Oncidium* and *Odontoglossum* grow here.

A complete change of vegetation seems to occur close to 2100m (7000'). Different species thrive in the damp, humid cloud forest. Every tree is covered with epiphytic growth, among which are orchids, such as *Bulbophyllums* and *Dendrobiums. Coelogyne* grow among the ferns, vines and plants that carpet the ground and which are almost impenetrable. At this altitude the canopy is more open allowing light to penetrate the forest, and here orchids grow and flourish.

Above 3300m (11 000'), on the edge of the tree line, the vegetation is stunted and sparse. At 3800m (12 500') the eye-catching pure white Mountain Necklace Orchid (*Coelogyne papillosa*) on Mount Kinabalu, in Sabah, grows in the rock crevices like cascading snow drifts.

Rainforest

Rainforest

Rainforest

Rainforest

Waterfalls

Cloud forest (Mt Kinabalu, Borneo)

NON-RAINFOREST HABITATS

In the coastal lowlands, terrestrials grow in open grasslands, forest areas or are partly buried underneath leaf mould on the forest floor at the base of trees and in rock crevices. Genera such as *Corybas, Orchis, Sobralia, Spiranthes* and *Thelymitra* grow here.

A small group of terrestrial orchids are leafless and are known as saprophytes. They grow in association with fungi and depend entirely on absorbing organic compounds produced from decaying matter. In the lowland forests in the south-eastern region of Western Australia there grows a subterranean saprophytic species. This amazing orchid, *Rhizanthella gardneri*, grows and flowers underground. The inflorescence rises to just below the surface. When the flower is ready to open, the floral bracts force open the soil allowing the rosette of flowers to open at ground level ready for

UNDERGROUND ORCHID (SUBTERRANEAN)

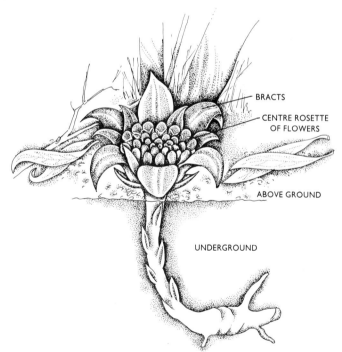

BRACTS

CENTRE ROSETTE OF FLOWERS

ABOVE GROUND

UNDERGROUND

Rhizanthella gardneri

pollination. This plant is rare. In the eastern parts of Australia, *Cryptanthemis slarateri* is the only known allied species and it is even more rare. First recorded in 1931 and again in 1975, rewards are now being offered to finders as government botanists are eager to conduct research work on these rare species.

Swamplands

Orchids grow at a lower level and usually in great numbers along the edges of rainforests, and near logging roads or tracks where sunlight and air can penetrate. Interestingly, beyond about 7.5m (25′) in from the edge of the rainforest or the forest logging roads the orchids become less numerous.

In the coastal lowland many orchid-growing habitats are found, including sand dunes, heathlands, bog or water meadows, mangrove swamps and grasslands. Open grasslands or grassy meadows together with heathlands, swamps and rock areas occur on the tablelands.

Among the various plants used to stabilise sand dunes are species of the *Epipactic* genus (such as *E. helleborine* in Europe and *E. gigantea* in South America) and *Geodorum densiflorum* in Australia and Papua New Guinea. These orchids have deep-seated root systems which penetrate the dunes.

Many species of orchids grow specifically in mangrove swamps, orchids such as *Epidendrum boothianum* in the Florida Keys and *Dendrobium mirbelianum* in the Pacific region.

Open grasslands are the home of thousands of species of terrestrial orchids. *Pterostylis* and *Diuris* in Australia, *Spiranthes* in southern Asia, *Neobenthamia* in Africa and *Orchis* in European regions.

Water meadows and wetlands are characterised by swamps and bogs and are the habitats for thousands of species, such as *Spathoglottis, Cypripediums, Habenaria, Calopogon, Prasophyllum, Orthoceras, Calochilus* and *Thelymitra.*

In rock habitats lithophytes abound. Some of the world's

Coastal

most beautiful orchids, such as *Rupicolia, Laelias, Cattleya* and *Dendrobium*, are lithophytic.

Of all orchid-growing areas of the world, Mount Kinabalu in Sabah, Borneo, must be the richest, with over 1500 known species. Mount Kinabalu is 4101m (13 455′) high, and comprises granite rock with sandstone surrounds. Orchids grow from sea level to 4000m (13 000′). At the higher altitude *Coelogyne papillosa* grows and is believed to be the highest growing orchid in the world.

Orchid habitats are extremely diverse so to grow any orchid species successfully it is most important to emulate as far as possible the growing conditions of that species' natural habitat.

POLLINATION

Cross-pollination is an important factor in the orchid flower's development. Cross-pollination results in cross-fertilisation which ensures the recycling of numerous genes throughout the entire species population. This redistribution of genes gives variety and strength to the species.

Self-pollination, or 'selfing', occurs towards the end of the life of the flower if cross-pollination by a pollinator does not take place. The rostellum is important in this selfing process. The rostellum is the beak-like cell which separates the pollinia at the top of the column beneath the anther cap from the stigma lower down the column. As the flower ages and begins to fade, the rostellum withers completely and the pollinia reaches the stigma, thus fertilising the ovaries. If selfing continues over many generations, the colony becomes weak, losing vigour.

Those features which attract us to the fascinating family of orchids—the tremendous variety of colour, shape, size and perfume—are designed by nature for one purpose: to attract a suitable pollinator. Insects, such as bees, wasps, butterflies, moths and flies, are the largest group of pollinators. Birds, such as honeyeaters and humming birds, together with small possums, fruit bats, and the like also play their part in the pollination process.

In their search for food (pollen or nectar) insects become agents in pollinating. A great number of orchids store nectar in the hollow of the spur. The spur is an extension at the back of the labellum. When the insect, bird or animal uses its long proboscis or tongue to reach down for the liquid it pushes up the anther cap, allowing the pollinia to be deposited on the head or body. When the nectar is exhausted the insect flies off in search of another orchid where the process is repeated, but this time the insect deposits pollinia on the stigma of the orchid as it reaches for the nectar.

POLLINATION BY
HONEYEATER BIRDS

CRIMSON TOPAZ HUMMING BIRD
TOPAZA PELLA

CATTLEYA

TRAP METHOD OF POLLINATION

Many orchids employ what is termed the trap mechanism for pollination. *Pterostylis*, an Australian genus, attracts mosquitoes and gnats to nectar at the base of the labellum. The sensitive labellum is attached by a moveable irritable claw to the foot of the column which acts like a trapdoor. Once the insect lands on the labellum, the claw prompts the labellum to snap shut. The insect can escape only by tunnelling its way between the labellum and the column, unwittingly collecting pollinia in the process. Once free, the insect carries the pollinia to the next flower it visits. (Refer to illustration of *Pterostylis nutans* on page 24.)

Orchids such as *Arthrochilus*, *Drakaea*, and *Spiculaea* in Australia, use what may be termed the *hammering process*.

The labellum is anvil- or hammer-like in shape, and is attached to the base of the column by a long, irritable, hinged claw. The male insect is attracted to the orchid by the deceptive scent of a female of its species. When it lands on the sensitive labellum with intent to copulate, the moveable claw swings, hammering the insect against the column, and pollinia is released onto the insect's back.

Another interesting orchid, the *Gongora* genus, presents its pollinator with the waxy surface of the labellum as a landing pad. On landing, the insect loses its grip, slides on its back, passing the column, dislodging the anther cap, and so gathering pollinia on its abdomen.

Trap Method of Pollination

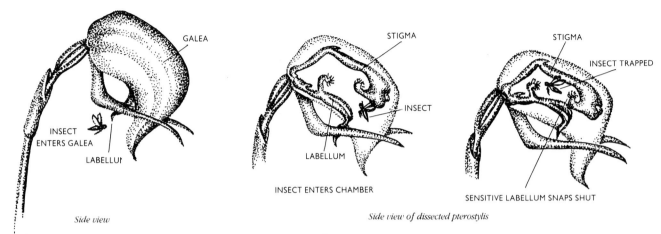

GALEA

INSECT
ENTERS GALEA

LABELLUM

Side view

STIGMA

INSECT

LABELLUM

INSECT ENTERS CHAMBER

Side view of dissected pterostylis

STIGMA

INSECT TRAPPED

SENSITIVE LABELLUM SNAPS SHUT

Pterostylis nutans

One of the most interesting traps is used by the *Coryanthes* genus (see illustration top of page 25). The trap utilises the complex organ of the pouch or bucket-like labellum. Bees are attracted by the large, brightly coloured flower and by the strong fragrant secretion on the inner margins of the epichile. Above this waxy cup-like labellum two fleshy 'faucet glands' secrete a clear liquid drop-by-drop, filling the cup to the level of an apical spout-like channel. On the inner margin or rim of this waxy cup the bees gather to gnaw on the secretion. Inevitably, a bee falls into the liquid. Its only exit is through the narrow channel just below the anther and the stigma of the column. Thus the bee leaves with the pollinia firmly attached to its back and ready to be transferred to the stigma of the next flower the bee visits. This is a perfect example of a plant in complete harmony with its pollinator. This cross-pollination by bees through the trap method is used by numerous other orchids, such as the *Stanhopea, Paphiopedilum* and *Cypripedium* genera groups.

The use of fragrance and colour to attract insects, such as moths, is common (see illustration at right). For example, the African genus *Angraecum* has perfected the selection of moths. The perfume is all but absent during the day; insects, birds and other moths pass the flowers by. With the onset of evening the night air is almost intoxicating with their scent. At night, a particular moth, attracted by the unusual perfume, locates the gleaming white flower which yields its nectar in return for fertilisation.

There are also orchids that attract flies as pollinators, such as *Bulbophyllums*, a large genera widespread throughout the world. Many species of *Bulbophyllums* give off a foul-smelling and most offensive odour, like something putrid or dead. Carrion flies are attracted to these orchids. Some *Oncidiums, Coelogyne* and *Himantoglossums* possess and give off such foul smelling odours.

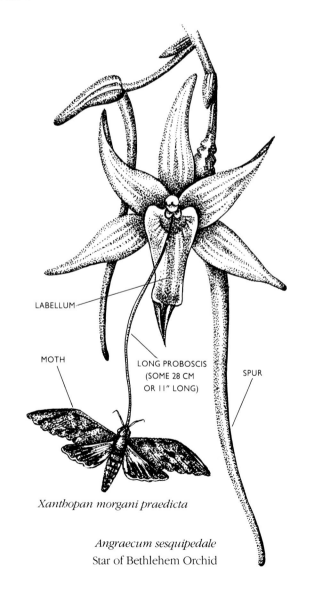

LABELLUM

MOTH

LONG PROBOSCIS
(SOME 28 CM
OR 11" LONG)

SPUR

Xanthopan morgani praedicta

Angraecum sesquipedale
Star of Bethlehem Orchid

THE BUCKET ORCHID TRAP

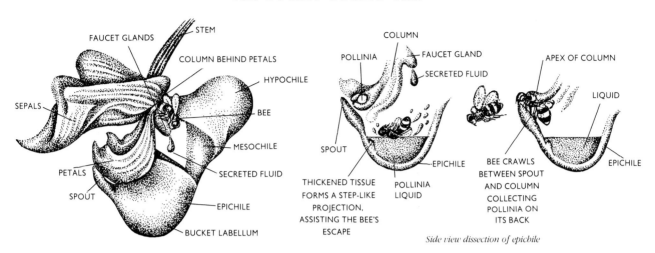

Side view dissection of epichile

Pollination of Coryanthes *by bees*

Pseudocopulation is another fascinating means of pollination. The *Ophrys* from Europe, northern Africa and the Middle East, *Cryptostylis* from Australia, *Trichoceros parviflorus* from Ecuador and *Oncidium henekenii* from the West Indies are examples.

These orchids practise a sexual deception on the males of many species of insects. Rather than produce a sweet nectar, the orchid produces a volatile secretion, the aroma of which is similar to that of a particular female wasp or insect. The flowering time of these orchids coincides with the emergence of the male of the species. By nature the female is a week or two later emerging from pupation, so leaving the male without a mate. The males are attracted to the source of the sexual aroma. Often the shape of an orchid's labellum resembles that of the body of a female wasp or insect. This similarity, together with the sexual aroma, prompts the male to approach the orchid, head first or injecting its tail under the base of the labellum, to try to copulate.

In Australia along the east coast and nearby mountains, late November and early December witness the common male Ichneumon Wasp *Lissopimpla semipunctata* frustratingly trying to copulate with the various species of the genus *Cryptostylis*. Not so noticeable is its cousin *L. excelsa*. During this period the male frantically seeks his mate and is deceived into believing that the flowers are the female of his species. During this pseudocopulation the pollinia is firmly attached to the wasp and carried to the next flower.

POLLINATION BY PSEUDOCOPULATION

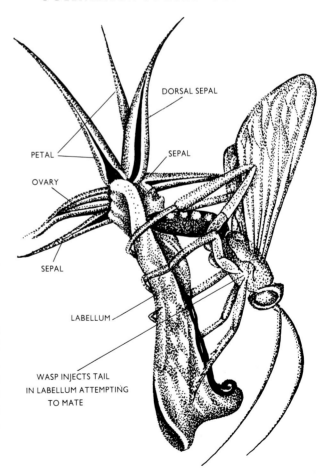

Cryptostylis subulata
LISSOPIMPLA SEMIPUNCTATA ICHNEUMON WASP (MALE)

ARTIFICIAL POLLINATION

Although there are some 35 000 species and hybrids occurring naturally around the world, orchidists are always looking for something new. To satisfy this appetite, breeders are continually producing more hybrids by artificially cross-pollinating species, not only within a genus but inter-genetically. The results of such propagation experiments have produced some extraordinarily beautiful flowers.

Most orchids produce bisexual flowers, and can be either self-pollinated or cross-pollinated using another plant that is genetically compatible. In the wild, a pollinating agent, usually an insect, collects the pollinia from a flower and deposits it on the stigma of another flower, thus pollinating the second flower. Should the second flower be a species different from the first flower from which the pollinia has been removed, and be compatible, the result is a natural hybrid. Fortunately, compatible species do not always occur in close proximity in the wild.

The artificial pollination of an orchid flower is a relatively simple procedure. With artificial propagation the orchidist carries out the same procedure as the insect. Taking a tooth-pick or sharpened matchstick the pollinia is removed from under the anther cap on the column of the flower chosen to be the female parent plant, and is discarded. Then, with another matchstick, the pollinia is removed from the flower chosen to be the male parent and is introduced to the stigma of the first flower, the female parent. (See diagram.) It is important to check the pollinia to see that no fungus is present.

On contact, the pollinia will adhere to the stigma. The pollen grains will grow, extending down the column tubes to the ovary, fertilising the ovules and forming the seed. On a typical orchid flower the ovary is below the flower segments with the sexual parts enclosed on the column. Once the ovary is fully swollen, after pollination, the seeds can be germinated using the 'green seed method'; the 'dry seed method' takes a little longer because the capsule must be mature. The resultant plant is a hybrid and there seems to be no end to the number of hybrids that can be propagated this way.

Possibly the world's best known hybrid is the *Vanda* X *Miss Joaquim* (*Vanda hookerana* X *Vanda teres*). This hybrid was the beginning of almost a century of *Vanda* hybridisation. First developed for the Singapore cut-flower market, *Vanda* X *Miss Joaquim* is possibly now the hybrid orchid of Hawaiian trade.

POLLINATION BY MAN

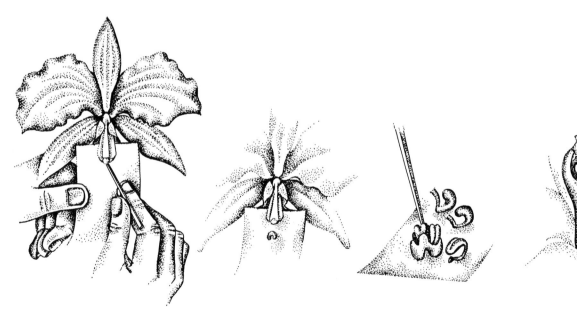

1 *Using a toothpick, remove anther from the flower selected as the parent. Shake anther onto clean paper.*

2 *Separate anther from column.*

3 *Separate the pollinia from the anther.*

4 *Pick up a pollinium. Bring its tip in contact with the sticky fluid of the stigma and touch the caudicle of a pollinium. Place pollinium on the stigma. Now pollination is complete.*

PROPAGATION

DIVISION AND TOP CUTTING

Mention propagation to most orchid fanciers and they will almost invariably think of laboratories with flasks, lamina-flow cabinets and culture mediums. But the most common form of propagation is by simple division. Most growers have split a plant of *Cymbidiums*, *Cattleyas* or *Dendrobiums* into two or more plants for repotting, and thus propagating more plants.

For many years this division was the only way to increase the number of plants of a particular clone: a clone is a group of individuals, each a ramet, produced asexually from a single parent, whether it is produced vegetatively (for example by division or a cutting or by apomixis) or is derived from a single seed, no matter how often it has been divided or multiplied. In fact, with *Paphiopedilums* division is still the main method of propagation because they are not

Having cut the rhizome, break apart.

Rootbound pot plant in need of division and repotting.

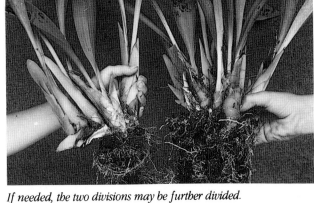

If needed, the two divisions may be further divided.

Select suitable position for separation.

Or the divisions can be repotted.

amenable to tissue culture. Propagation by division is suitable for all sympodial orchids, that is orchids whose main stem grows horizontally with new growth rising from and along the rhizome.

However, monopodial orchids cannot be divided in this way. Monopodial orchids have one foot; the plants grow perpendicular and their branches are lateral. Examples include *Ascocentrum*, *Vandas* and *Phalaenopsis*. Monopodial orchids are propagated by 'top cutting'. When the plants grow to a considerable length roots will emerge well up the stem. Once the roots have attained a reasonable length, cut off the top of the orchid below one or more roots and plant the top section. The stump will quickly send up one or more suckers and these will develop into flowering plants.

Cutting the top section of the monopodial. Cut below the aerial root second from the top and pot.

KEIKIS

Some orchids reproduce by means of keikis. The term *keiki* comes from the Hawaiian language and means 'baby'. It refers to the plantlets that grow from the nodes of pseudobulbs above the level of the potting material, sometimes on flower spikes, and rarely from the roots. Keikis develop in quite a number of genera including *Catasetum*, *Epidendrum*, *Lycaste*, *Zygopetalum* and especially *Dendrobiums*. It seems that all species of *Dendrobiums* are capable of reproduction in this manner, in particular the *Euganantbe* section and notably the species *nobile*. Some nurseries rely on this method for most of their plant reproduction.

Often if old back pseudobulbs are cut and placed in a plastic bag with a small amount of moist sphagnum moss, some of the unflowered nodes will start to grow and produce plantlets. Often each node at the bottom of a flower spike can be the source of a keiki if correctly treated. After flowering cut the spike into short sections with a node in the middle of each piece. Submerge vertically in sphagnum moss and enclose in a clear plastic bag. Once the keikis are of sufficient size, plant them out. Rare and endangered species, such as *Phaius tancarvilliae*, can be increased more rapidly using this method, than by the division of backbulbs. Keikis from time to time do develop along the roots of various *Phalaenopsis* species, such as *schilleriana* and *leuchorroda*. Keikis also develop along the flowering spikes of these species.

A keiki growing on a Dendrobium *cane.*

Cut the cane two nodes below the keiki.

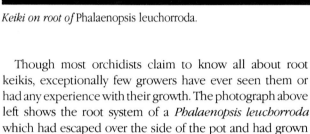

Keiki on root of Phalaenopsis leuchorroda.

Keiki on root of Phalaenopsis schilleriana.

Though most orchidists claim to know all about root keikis, exceptionally few growers have ever seen them or had any experience with their growth. The photograph above left shows the root system of a *Phalaenopsis leuchorroda* which had escaped over the side of the pot and had grown along the bench. At the time of repotting, the roots were torn from the plant. Within weeks the roots developed several eyes, from which keikis grew and which quickly resulted in several healthy plants. The photograph above shows a keiki growing from an eye on the root of a *Phalaenopsis schilleriana.* Naturally, the results are perfect clones of the parent plant.

SEED CULTURE

Orchid plants can be propagated in many different ways. Every orchid in cultivation today started life from a tiny seed. So small are they that as many as 72 000 seeds may be in a single seed pod. In the wild the naked seed (so called because it has no endosperm, that is stored carbohydrates needed for growth) is incapable of germination and depends upon the aid of a fungus. Should a plantlet emerge directly from the seed, it would not survive. The plantlet must first grow into a protocorm, many times the size of the seed, before developing a root or shoot. To do this it is dependent on a special association with several species of fungi growing within the vicinity of the parent orchid species.

Particular orchid species have associations with particular species of fungi. This fact accounts to some extent for the isolated distribution of many orchid species. It is very simple: if a fungus species does not grow or occur in an area, then the associated orchid species seed cannot germinate.

Early workers propagating with orchid seed used this knowledge to germinate not only species seed but also the seed of their attempted hybrids. To simplify somewhat, the method involved the following procedures: seed was sown onto a culture kept moist with distilled water, and a few cut-up pieces of the parent orchid's roots were scattered amongst the seed. In the moist conditions, the fungus on the roots grew and spread rapidly and allowed the seeds to germinate and develop into protocorms—then, in a short time into small plantlets.

Today, these crude but reasonably successful methods are no longer used. In the 1920s, Lewis Knudson, a plant physiologist, developed the asymbiotic method of germinating orchid seed.

First a sterilised agar-agar culture gel is prepared in a sterilised vessel or flask. This gel contains all the nutriments the seed will need to develop into a strong plantlet once germinated.

Growers today use one of two methods of seed preparation:

(a) The dry mature seed is taken from the seed pod and treated with a chlorine bleach solution to kill any fungi spores attached to the seed. The dry seed is then introduced onto the surface of the culture gel and the vessel or flask is immediately sealed.

(b) In the green seed method, the chlorine bleach is applied to the green fruiting body or pod containing the seed. On opening the pod the green seed (which because of its enclosure in the green pod is in a naturally sterilised condition) is introduced onto the surface of the culture gel, and the vessel or flask is immediately sealed.

This entire procedure—the sterilisation of vessels or flasks, the preparation of the gel-culture, and the chlorine treatment of the seed—is conducted in a sterile, clean-air chamber, known as a Lamina-Flow Cabinet, to reduce the risk of contamination by airborne fungi spores.

The green seed culture is the more popular method. The risk of damage to the seed by the harsh chlorine bleach is avoided using this method because only the capsule comes in contact with the bleach and the pod is harvested before the seed is mature. Once the pod is open and the seed sprinkled on the culture surface, the seed continues to mature.

Once the seed germinates and swells into a protocorm it takes approximately six weeks, depending on species, for the shoots (roots and leaf) to appear. The plantlets continue to grow in the flask until ready to be potted.

For those interested in germinating orchid seed the Knudson formula (C) is included below. It is simple to prepare.

KC – MEDIUM			KNUDSON C MEDIUM (1946)		
COMPOUND	ml STOCK PER LITRE OF MEDIUM	AMOUNT PER LITRE OF MEDIUM	COMPOUND	AMOUNT PER LITRE	
				MASS	MOLE
(a) KH_2PO_4	20	2.0 mmol	(a) KH_2PO_4	250 mg	1.84 mmol
$Ca(NO_3)_2$	40	4.0 "	$Ca(NO_3)_2 4H_2O$	1000 "	4.23 "
$(NH_4)_2SO_4$	40	4.0 "	$(NH_4)_2SO_4$	500 "	3.78 "
$MgSO_4$	10	1.0 "	$MgSO_4.7H_2O$	250 "	1.01 "
(b) $MnSO_4$	3.5	35 μmol	(b) $MnSO_4 4H_2O$	7.5 "	33.6 μmol
(c) $FeSO_4$	} 9	90 "	(c) $FeSO_4.7H_2O$	25 "	89.9 "
Na_2EDTA		90 "	———	———	
(d) SUCROSE	20.5386 g	60 mmol	(d) SUCROSE	20 g	58.4 "
(i) * AGAR	17.5 g	17.5 g	(i) * AGAR	17.5 g	17.5 g

* 17.5g AGAR is a relatively high concentration; it is possible that a less highly purified agar, such as *Difco Bacto–Agar*, might be used.

TISSUE CULTURE (Mericloning)

The term *mericlone* was coined by orchid growers, from *meristem* and *clone*, and refers to plants that have been propagated in the laboratory by the tissue culture technique. The first workers in this field believed they were producing plants from the *meristematic* tissue (particularly tips of roots and/or apex of vegetative or floral shoots), but later it was revealed that a much larger piece of tissue was used to form a protocorm, the tissue used contained one or more leaf axils and should have been termed *shoot-tip*. However *mericlone* has stuck.

The tissue culture technique involves taking a new growing shoot from the orchid plant; excise the tip together with any axillary shoots and introduce them onto a previously prepared sterile nutrient medium in laboratory glass culture dishes. (Refer to illustrations 1 to 10 on following pages.) On excision, the tissue or shoot is thoroughly cleansed and sterilised, as explained in the diagrams and instructions. Place the culture dishes into a lamina-flow, or a clean-air cabinet. With the aid of a microscope and using a sterilised scalpel, cut from the tiny growing tip 0.5cm squares and sow them onto a pre-prepared solid agar gel medium or place into a solution of the same nutriments.

This completed, place covers over the glass dishes and put them on a slowly revolving wheel (like a potter's wheel) or a shaker. Whether you use the wheel or shaker depends on the genus of the mericlone. It is only from experience that tissue culturists learn which genus is best suited to either the wheel or the shaker, and which genus does best on agar gel or in the nutrient solution. The principle is the same in both media forms.

The tiny tissue squares enlarge, forming protocorm-like bodies known as PLBs. The nutriments used in the medium are designed to produce PLBs—plantlets *do not* form at this stage. From these PLBs the excision process can be repeated as many times as is required. While the PLBs remain in the nutriment they continue to grow. The larger the PLBs grow, the more excisions can be made to produce more tiny PLBs to thus repeat the process. At any stage during this process PLBs can be transferred onto a culture medium, the ingredients of which will encourage shoots and roots to develop, and so new plantlets to form.

This method enables the nursery workers to produce particularly good, if not perfect, clones quite quickly. Thousands, if not millions, of plants can be propagated quite cheaply, hence accelerating the distribution of plants that will flower exactly the same as the original. Unfortunately, some genera cannot be propagated by this method, notably *Paphiopedilum*. Undoubtedly researchers are continuing to work on the problem.

1 *Select a new growing shoot, preferably before the young terminal leaf has split and opened.*

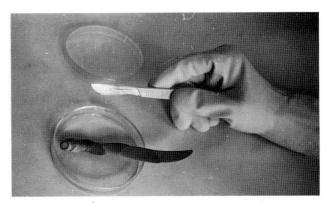

2 *Wash in clean running water for twenty minutes, then place in glass dish.*

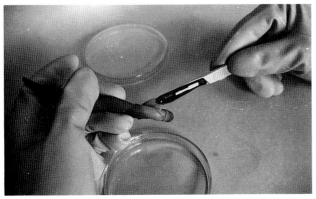

3 *Remove the node bud bracts and discard.*

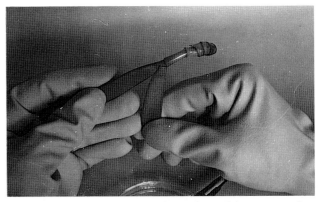

4 *Remove the terminal exposing the sterile tip of the new growth.*

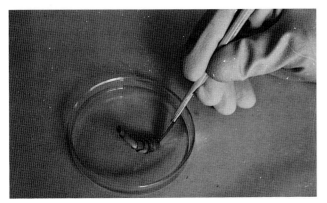

5 *Wash again for five minutes. Now let soak fully submerged in a solution of sugar and cold boiled water (a teaspoon of sugar to a cup of water) for up to four hours. The solution encourages any fungi spores to germinate. The shoot or tissue is sterilised in chlorine bleach for five minutes as compared with half an hour or more without the sugar solution treatment. The chlorine bleach is very hard on the tender tissue, so the less time the tissue is bleached the better. Wash the shoot in distilled water.*

6 *In a lamina-flow sterile cabinet excise the tip of the shoot, about a quarter of a square centimetre, and place in a sterile glass dish.*

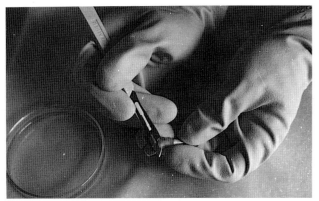

7 *Now excise the node buds which were under the node bracts and place in the sterile glass dish. Discard the rest of the shoot.*

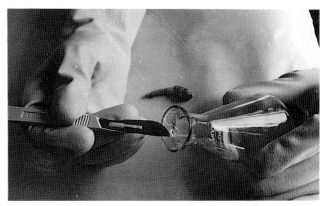

8 *With the tip of the scalpel, place the excised tissues in the pre-prepared nutrient solution or on nutrient agar-agar gel. Agitate slowly for an hour before placing on the 'light' shelf.*

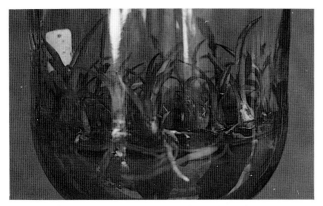

9 *The tissues develop into protocorm-like bodies. When large enough they may be divided again and again until you have the required number. These are then transferred on to a growing gel, and within weeks plantlets develop.*

10 *When the plantlets are large enough and at a healthy growing stage they are transferred to communal pots and can be placed in a nursery.*

POTTING

Orchidists today pot most if not all their plants. At first, all orchids were potted in the same way as terrestrials. Although the plants flourished at first they soon died. Botanists quickly realised that orchids were not all the same. Those that grew in the ground (terrestrials) could be potted, while those that grew in trees (epiphytes) must be treated differently.

With the advent of different potting mediums, horticulturists were soon achieving better results. Potting mediums vary considerably from country to country and in differing climates. In the tropics, volcanic and igneous rock are very popular ingredients in potting mix. In cooler climates, rock is often too cold for the plant's root system, and bark is used instead.

Consider the individual plant's needs when determining potting mixes and procedures. Epiphytic plants in the forest do not require composted organic material as their roots are aerial feeders, but they do require support. The modern day horticulturist adopts a regular fertilising program to supply the plant's nutrients so the potting mix doesn't need to include compost humus for epiphytes.

The size of the potting ingredients is very important. Epiphytic orchids require adequate ventilation and drainage around their roots. The primary purpose of the potting mix is to support the epiphyte. Newly potted epiphytes must be staked to give support until the root system can grow to give sufficient self support. For mature plants of the *Cattleya, Dendrobium, Phalenopsis* and *Vanda* species, use chunks of material approximately 2.5cm (1″) thick and 10 to 15cm (4 to 6″) pots. The mixture should include five parts sterilised pine bark, one part rock and one part charcoal. For smaller pots the chunks of potting medium need to be smaller. Likewise for larger plants, the pots should be larger and the chunks relatively larger: 3 to 4cm (1½ to

2″) thick. A mixture of rock and fibre chunks allows air movement and the retention of sufficient moisture. As the plant grows, roots will escape and surround the pot.

Terrestrial species require much more moisture around the roots. Here the potting media is much heavier. A mixture of sterilised conifer bark or artificial coarse composite medium, sphagnum and rice hulls or fine grade bark gives excellent results.

Epiphytic and or lithophytic species comprise the majority of cultivated orchids. With these species great care should be taken to ensure that the base, or rhizome, of the plant is not buried in the potting mixture or medium. The new growth rising from an eye at the base of the pseudobulb needs to elongate the rhizome along the surface of the potting medium before rising up to form a new pseudobulb.

When potting terrestrial species of orchids, the pseudobulbs need to be potted to a depth sufficient to cover the base or the crown of the roots. Species such as *Phaius*, *Calanthe* and *Spathoglottis* normally grow around the edges of swamps, along creeks or in the litter of the rainforests. Their roots are surface feeders, spreading out just beneath the surface of the soil or, in forests, beneath the leaf litter and debris on the forest floor. Support is needed for these newly potted plants until the root system develops through the mix to give the plant stability and support.

A firmly staked plant will establish itself more quickly and growth will be much faster than an unstaked or loosely potted plant, for the root system is easily damaged and new root tips will break off if allowed to move in the pots.

METHOD OF POTTING EPIPHYTES

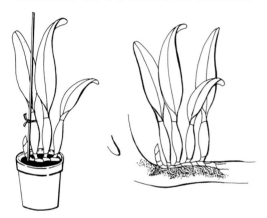

METHOD OF POTTING TERRESTRIALS

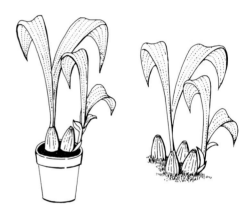

FERTILISING

There is an increasing move away from using composted organic mixtures, and towards using an inert or partly inert medium. Fertiliser should be viewed as a complete nutrient source similar to that used in hydroponic situations, rather than as an additive to a compost. For this reason many orchid fertilisers marketed as 'complete' were developed as additives and have insufficient quantities of some elements, such as calcium, whereas these are found in generous quantities in hydroponic formulations.

Possibly adding extra phosphorus before flowering on more floriferous species would be an advantage, as phosphorus levels in flowers are approximately six times that in the vegetative plant, and hydroponic formulations are generally based on plant growth rather than flower production. Therefore a recommended formula would consist of a 10:10:10 N.P.K. ratio with added calcium and trace elements.

AIR MOVEMENT

The majority of cultivated orchid species are either epiphytic or lithophytic, and these plants in the wild are often exposed to the extremes of climatic conditions. Many are exposed to typhoons, cyclones or tropical storms. Almost all orchid species receive constant air movement in their natural environment. One need only watch the wind in the trees in the areas where epiphytes are plentiful to be reminded

of the movement of air required; wind tends to gust rather than be of a constant velocity.

When orchidists house plants under artificial conditions, the addition of increased air movement is crucial to the well-being of the plants. Therefore, in glasshouse growing conditions, oscillating fans could be beneficial.

ORCHID GENERA

ACAMPE

(ah-kam-pee)

*A*campe from the Gk *akampes* (rigid) possibly refers to the brittle flowers. This genus has about a dozen species, several previously known as *Vanda* or *Saccolobium*, spread across South-east Asia, China, India and the African tropics. The plants are monopodial, robust *Vanda*-like in appearance; the leaves are fleshy and coriaceous. Inflorescence may be few or many-flowered in dense cylindrical racemes or tight heads. Flowers are small to medium-sized, fleshy, fragile and fragrant. Sepals and petals are free, spreading and subsimilar; the lateral sepals are adnate to labellum spur. The labellum is spurred or saccate. This is an interesting plant, but rare in collections. Hybridisation with the various allied genera is possible. *Acampe* crossed with *Vanda* produces *Vancampe.*

Culture: Compost, in large well-drained pots or baskets. Requirements are similar to those of the *Vanda.* Grow in baskets or on cork or tree-fern fibre to allow ample aeration of the fleshy roots.

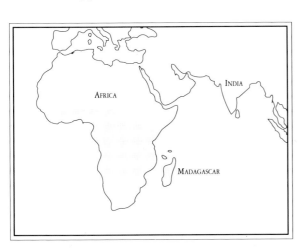

Acampe longifolia

Acampe longifolia

Acampe longifolia

COMMON NAME: None.
COLOUR: Flowers yellow with orange-brown markings. Labellum mostly cream with some purple spots at the base.
SIZE: Growing up to 1.2m (4') high.
CLIMATE: Intermediate.
DISTRIBUTION: Native to Himalayas, Peninsula Malaysia and Langkawi Island.
FLOWERING TIME: Summer.
DESCRIPTION: Leaves fleshy, sheathing, lanceolate. Inflorescence short. Flowers 2cm (¾") across. Some botanists consider *A. longifolia* as syn. with *A. rigida* which occurs from tropical to eastern Africa, but we consider it as sufficiently different to remain under *A. longifolia.*

ACANTHEPHIPPIUM
(ah-kan-the-fip-ee-um)

Acanthephippium from the Gk *akantha* (thorn) *ephippion* (saddle) with reference to the shape of the labellum blade which somewhat resembles a saddle. This genus of about fifteen species of terrestrial orchids is found in the tropics from southern China through Java, Papua New Guinea to Fiji. It is a large terrestrial herb with epiphytic-type roots. Pseudobulbs are long and furrowed with epiphytic-type roots. The leaves are large and plicate. Inflorescence is a stout erect raceme. There are few flowers; they are large, cup- to bottle-shaped, fleshy, showy and very fragrant. Sepals enclose the petals and labellum in a swollen fleshy tube. The petals are narrow and the labellum is tri-lobed and saddle-shaped.

Culture: Coarse compost in perfectly drained pots as for *Phaius.* Place in a shady, humid situation with plenty of water and frequent application of fertiliser. Do not allow roots to become too wet. Once pseudobulbs are fully grown, keep plants almost dry in a cooler place.

Acanthephippium unguiculatum

Acanthephippium vitiense

COMMON NAME: None.
COLOUR: Flowers yellow to pale pink, with maroon veining.
SIZE: Grows up to 45cm (18″) high.
CLIMATE: Warm to hot.
DISTRIBUTION: Native to Fiji. Grows in moist hot jungles in well-shaded areas.
FLOWERING TIME: Summer.
DESCRIPTION: Terrestrial herb. Pseudobulbs elongate, conical 15cm (6″) high. Leaves apical, plicate, broad-elliptic, 30cm (12″) long, petiole. It has few flowers, about 5cm (2″) long.

Acanthephippium vitiense

AERANTHES
(ah-er-an-theez)

*A*eranthes from the Gk *aer* (air, mist) *anthos* (flower) with reference to the epiphytic habit or the delicate flower (air-flower), or misty habitat (mist flower).This genus of some thirty species originates from Madagascar and the adjacent islands and has one genus in Africa. This is a most unusual epiphytic or lithophytic herb. It is typically stemless, the leaves are fleshy-coriaceous and distichous when a stem is present. Inflorescence is wire-like or branching, racemose and pendulous. The flowers are mostly large, green or white and fragrant. The sepals are long, attenuate and adnate to the column foot; the petals are similar, but smaller. The labellum is articulate, broad and the apex long-attenuate.

Culture: Compost as for *Angraecum* or *Vanda*; preferably mount it on a tree-fern fibre slab or in a basket with shredded tree-fern fibre or sphagnum moss; remember the inflorescence is pendulous. *Aeranthes* requires plenty of water and heat at all times. If grown in pots, the compost must have perfect drainage. The plants are rare in collections.

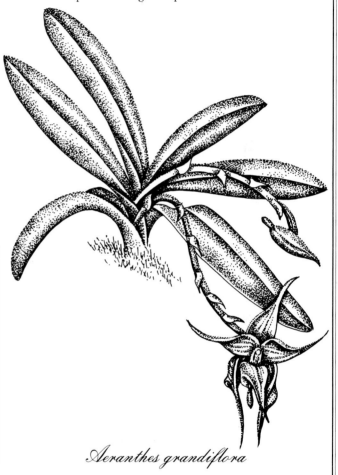

Aeranthes grandiflora

AFRICA

INDIA

MADAGASCAR

Aeranthes arachnitis

COMMON NAME: None.
COLOUR: Flowers green to lemon.
SIZE: Grows up to 20cm (8").
CLIMATE: Intermediate to warm.
DISTRIBUTION: Native to Madagascar.
FLOWERING TIME: Summer to autumn.
DESCRIPTION: Leaves long and leathery, up to 20cm (8") long. Flower spikes bear a few flowers which are fragrant and 5cm (2") across. The labellum is complex.

Aeranthes arachnitis

AERIDES
(ah-er-i-dee)

Aerides comes from the Gk *aer* (air) *eides* (resembling). The implied meaning is 'children of the air' which refers to the epiphytic habit. A genus of some seventy species, *Aerides* occurs in the tropics in the Himalayas, Burma, China, Japan, the Philippines, Borneo, Indonesia and Papua New Guinea. It is often known as the Fox-Tail Orchid. The epiphytic herbs fall into two groups: *Planifoliae* and *Teretifolia*. In the former, the leaves are flat, leathery and spreading, and in the latter the leaves are cylindrical and fleshy. Stems are leafy. The plant lacks pseudobulbs. The leaves are coriaceous. Inflorescence is long, dense, decurved with pendulous racemes. The flowers are waxen, fragrant and all open at the same time. Sepals and petals are broad and spreading; lateral sepals are adnate at base to column foot. The labellum is tri-lobed, complex with basal spur; lateral lobes range from obscure to large; the mid-lobe is variable in size, incurved, with margins beautifully fringed. It has variable colour shades of magenta and green in various combinations with white.

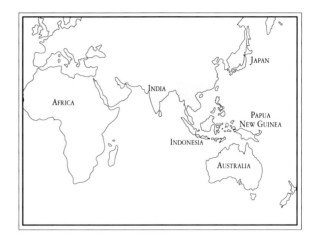

Culture: Plant in loose, chunky compost in hanging baskets, allowing the numerous long rampant roots to grow and hang outside; disturb as little as possible. It needs a humid, shady situation. *Aerides* is a willing parent when crossing with allied groups.

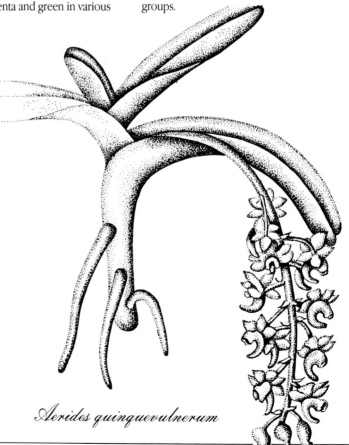

Aerides quinquevulnerum

Aerides fieldingii

COMMON NAME: Fox Brush Orchid.

COLOUR: Flowers pink or mauve, and may be white on the margins.

SIZE: A robust epiphytic species growing up to 25cm (10″) high.

CLIMATE: Intermediate.

DISTRIBUTION: Native to Thailand, and Assam and Sikkim in India.

FLOWERING TIME: Spring and summer.

DESCRIPTION: Flower scape about 45cm (18″) in length, resembles a fox tail, numerous blooms, about a hundred flowers to a stem, 2.5cm (1″) across.

Aerides fieldingii

Aerides krabiensis

Aerides krabiensis

COMMON NAME: None.

COLOUR: Flowers white to pink and marked with dark pink.

SIZE: Growing up to 15cm (6″) high.

CLIMATE: Warm.

DISTRIBUTION: Native to Thailand (Isthmus of Kra—Gulf of Krabi).

FLOWERING TIME: Spring to summer.

DESCRIPTION: A small epiphytic plant. Leaves linear-oblong, up to 10cm (4″) long. Inflorescence arching and pendulous, up to 15cm (6″) long. Flowers up to 1cm (½″) across.

Aerides multiflorum

COMMON NAME: Fox-Tail Orchid

COLOUR: Flowers white or rose-purple and may be spotted.

SIZE: A large epiphyte species growing erect or pendulous, up to 25cm (10″) long.

CLIMATE: Intermediate.

DISTRIBUTION: Native to Indo-China, Tenasserim (Burma), India and south to Thailand, and tropical Himalayas.

FLOWERING TIME: Summer

DESCRIPTION: Leaves strap-like, channelled and keeled, 35 cm (14″) long. Inflorescence up to 30cm (12″) long. Flowers numerous, up to 3.2 cm (1¼″) across.

Aerides multiflorum

Aerides odoratum

COMMON NAME: None.
COLOUR: Flowers purple or mauve, may be spotted and tipped with purple. Apex of spur is green-yellow.
SIZE: A variable epiphytic species, up to 90cm (3') high.
CLIMATE: Intermediate.
DISTRIBUTION: Native to tropical Himalayas of India and Nepal, South-east Asia, southern China, Java and the Philippines.
FLOWERING TIME: Late summer and autumn.
DESCRIPTION: Leaves incurved, oblong strap-like apex lobed up to 30cm (12") long. Inflorescence pendulous, flowers numerous, fragrant, and about 4cm (1½") across.

Aerides odoratum

Aerides odoratum var. *alba*

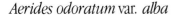

COMMON NAME: None.
COLOUR: Alba flower is white.
SIZE: Same as the type.
CLIMATE: Intermediate.
DISTRIBUTION: Native to Philippines, and from India to Thailand.
FLOWERING TIME: Same as the type.
DESCRIPTION: Same as the type, except for colour.

Aerides odoratum var. *alba*

Aerides quinquevulnerum

Aerides quinquevulnerum

COMMON NAME: None.
COLOUR: Flowers white, tipped and spotted with amethyst purple.
SIZE: Growing up to 40cm (16") high.
CLIMATE: Warm.
DISTRIBUTION: Native to the Philippines (Luzon).
FLOWERING TIME: Late summer to autumn.
DESCRIPTION: A robust plant, often branching stems up to 40cm (16") long. Leaves oblong-lanceolate, up to 30cm (12") long. Inflorescence up to 40cm (16") long; blooms densely numerous. Flowers fragrant, up to 2.5cm (1") long. Labellum trilobed.

ANGRAECUM
(an-gry-kum)

Angraecum comes from the Malayan word *angurek*, given to a group of epiphytic orchids resembling the appearance of the *Vandas*. This genus has over two hundred species and is widely distributed throughout tropical Africa and Madagascar, with several species in Sri Lanka. Because of differing and complex descriptions by various botanists in the past, recent work restricts the once very large genus to those species in which the labellum is deeply concave with the base enveloping the column, the apex of which is deeply divided in front. These small to large epiphytic or lithophytic herbs have monopodial stems, not pseudobulbous, and are usually leafy along the full length. The leaves are fleshy and distichous. Inflorescence has short to elongated racemes. Flowers are small to large, fleshy, star-shaped, white, yellow or green and often very beautiful. The sepals and petals are very similar. The labellum is larger than the sepals and petals; it is concave with the base enveloping the column. The spur has a wide mouth, often exceedingly long, as with *A. sesquipedale*, the spur of which is up to 30cm (12″) long. The column is short with the apex deeply cleft in front.

Culture: Compost in pot or basket for the lithophytic species and for the epiphytic, mount on a tree-fern slab or other suitable support. Smaller species, such as *A. distichum*, are best in small pots packed in shredded tree-fern fibre or sphagnum moss. Water well during the growing period. Place the plant in shady positions.

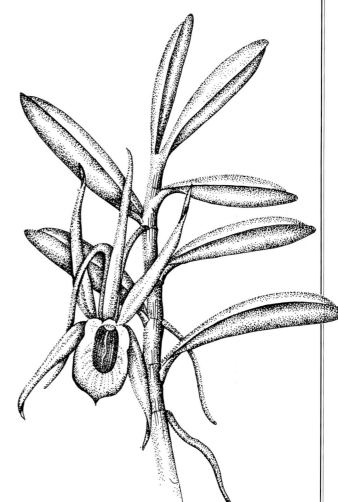

Angraecum infundibulare

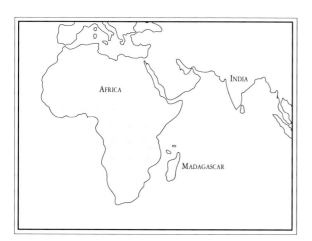

Angraecum compactum

COMMON NAME: None.
COLOUR: Flowers white. Spur greenish.
SIZE: Growing up to 20cm (8″) high.
CLIMATE: Intermediate.
DISTRIBUTION: Native to Madagascar. Growing at altitudes of 800 to 2000m (2500 to 6000′).
FLOWERING TIME: Spring to summer.
DESCRIPTION: Leaves green, thick, succulent, oblong, up to 12.5cm (5″) long. Flowers up to 7.5cm (3″) across.

Angraecum didieri

COMMON NAME: None.
COLOUR: Flower white.
SIZE: Growing up to 10cm (4″) high.
CLIMATE: Intermediate.
DISTRIBUTION: Native to Madagascar, grows at elevations of 1000m (3300′).
FLOWERING TIME: Spring to summer.
DESCRIPTION: A small angraecoid plant, epiphytic. Leaves alternate linear-oblong, up to 5cm (2″) long. Inflorescence short, flowers solitary, large, showy, 7.5cm (3″) across. Spur up to 17.5cm (7″) long.

Angraecum compactum

Angraecum didieri

Angraecum eburneum

COMMON NAME: None.
COLOUR: Flowers white and green, and yellow.
SIZE: A large epiphytic, terrestrial or lithophytic species up to 90cm (3′) high.
CLIMATE: Intermediate.
DISTRIBUTION: Native to Madagascar, eastern Africa, Mascarene Islands, Comoro Island.
FLOWERING TIME: Autumn to early winter.
DESCRIPTION: Leaves strap-like, unequally emarginate, 30cm (12″) long. Flowers inverted, showy, up to 8cm (3½″) across. Spur long and elegant up to 10cm (4″) long.

Angraecum eburneum

Angraecum sesquipedale

COMMON NAME: Star of Bethlehem or Comet Orchid.
COLOUR: Flowers white, spur greenish.
SIZE: Generally solitary stem, about 90cm (3′) high.
CLIMATE: Intermediate.
DISTRIBUTION: Native to Madagascar. Growing at sea level to 100m (330′) altitude.
FLOWERING TIME: Summer.
DESCRIPTION: Leaves oblong, strap-like, sheathing at the base, about 30cm (12″) long. Inflorescence horizontal to arching. Flowers few, fragrant, star-shaped, long-lived, up to 17.5cm (7″) across. Spur long, about 30cm (12″) long.

Angraecum sesquipedale

ANSELLIA
(an-sel-ee-ah)

Ansellia is named after John Ansell, who collected the first species on Fernando Poo Island (Macias Nguema), West Coast Africa. This genus has highly variable species. This is a large epiphytic, often terrestrial, herb. The pseudobulbs are tall, 30 to 50cm (12 to 20″) long, cane-like, tufted, with many aerial roots. It has 6 to 7 plicate leaves. Inflorescences are erect, paniculate, up to 50cm (20″) long, with many flowers. These flowers are variable in shape, are showy, yellow, and the sepals and petals are deeply blotched with brown or maroon; they are sub-similar, free and spreading. The labellum is tri-lobed, with side lobes erect and mid-lobe subacute. The column is slender and about 1cm (⅓″) long.

Culture: Easy to grow; use compost in a large well-drained pot as the roots grow vigorously. Water carefully until the roots are well established, then use plenty of water. Once fully grown, the plants require less water. The plant requires light, shady conditions.

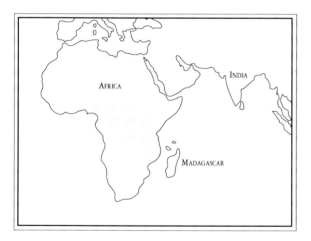

Ansellia gigantea var. *azanica*

Ansellia africana

COMMON NAME: African Leopard Orchid.
COLOUR: Flowers yellow, blotched with chocolate brown.
SIZE: Grows up to 60cm (24″) high.
CLIMATE: Cool to intermediate.
DISTRIBUTION: Native to Madagascar and eastern Africa.
FLOWERING TIME: Spring.
DESCRIPTION: Pseudobulbs cylindrical, joined, up to 60cm (24″) high. Leaves lanceolate, ribbed. Inflorescence spreading, branching. Flowers numerous, 6.3cm (2½″) across.

Ansellia africana

ARMODORUM
(ar-mo-doe-rum)

*A*rmodorum is a diminutive of Lat. *armata* (to be armed) and *ornare* (ornament) which refers to the pronounced horn-like spur at the base of the labellum. This genus of at least three epiphytic species is widespread from Assam, through Burma, to Sumatra and Java. It is classified as a 'very rare orchid'. It is a robust plant with climbing vine-like stems, at times up to about a metre (3′) in length. Leaves are distichous or at distinct intervals, coriaceous, dark green, and are 16 to 25cm (7 to 10″) long. Inflorescence is horizontal or ascending, to 20cm (8″) long. The three to eight flowers are fleshy or waxen, long-lasting and fragrant. Sepals and petals are sub-similar, free, spreading, blotched yellow or greenish with red-brown margins. The labellum is tri-lobed, erect, fleshy, convex, white or yellowish or streaked with brown, with a cylindrical spur, curved forward.

Culture: As for *Vanda*. Compost. Use large well-drained pots or baskets. Plants have strong aerial root growth, so pots and benches soon become overgrown. *Armodorum* will do well on large tree-fern slabs or on trees in the open garden.

Armodorum stavachilus

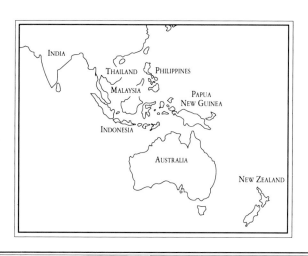

Armodorum stavachilus

Armodorum stavachilus

COMMON NAME: None.
COLOUR: Flowers cream to white, marked brown. Labellum white, blotched purple.
SIZE: Climbing up to 60cm (24″) high.
CLIMATE: Warm.
DISTRIBUTION: Native to Java and Sumatra.
FLOWERING TIME: Autumn.
DESCRIPTION: A climbing, branching epiphyte. Leaves fleshy, linear-oblong, acute, up to 20cm (8″) long. Inflorescence pendulous. Flowers numerous, small, 5mm (¼″) across.

ARPOPHYLLUM
(ar-poe-fil-um)

Arpophyllum from the Gk *hape* (sickle) *phyllon* (leaf) with reference to the shape of the leaf of the type species *A. spicatum*. The genus is widespread from Mexico to Costa Rica, through Guatemala and Honduras. The genus has about five species of exceedingly spectacular, epiphytic or terrestrial herbs. The rhizomes are simple and branching. The stems are slender, pseudobulb-like, and grow to 75cm (30″) long. Leaves are fleshy with a leathery texture. The inflorescence is very showy, terminal, erect, densely flowered, with a cylindrical raceme. The flowers are purple. The sepals and petals are similar and spreading. Labellum is upper and is saccate at the base. The column is erect.

Culture: Compost in well-drained pots. Plants need plenty of water while growing, but once growth is complete water just sufficiently to avoid shrivelling. Plant requires shade, but also plenty of light and also humidity. Treat as for *Cattleya*.

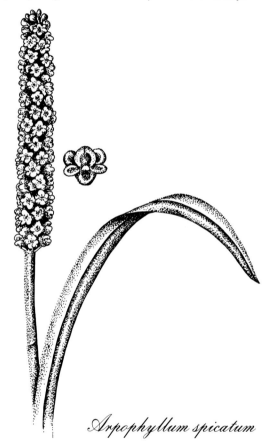

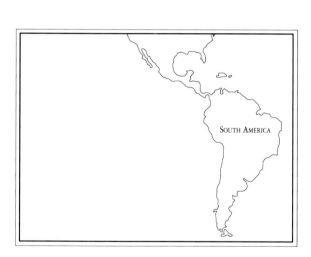

Arpophyllum spicatum

Arpophyllum spicatum

COMMON NAME: None.
COLOUR: Flowers pink to purple.
SIZE: Up to 1.2m (4′) high.
CLIMATE: Intermediate.
DISTRIBUTION: Native to Jamaica, Mexico, Guatemala, Honduras, Costa Rica and Colombia.
FLOWERING TIME: Spring.
DESCRIPTION: Pseudobulbs, stem-like, up to 1.2m (4′) high. Leaves long, narrow, channelled and leathery. Flower spike dense forming a cylindrical shape. Flowers 10mm (¼″) across.

Arpophyllum spicatum

ARTHROCHILUS
(ar-thro-ki-lus)

*A*rthrochilus from the Gk *arthros* (a joint) *chilus* (labellum) and referring to the irritable hinged labellum. This genus of four species extends through southern Papua New Guinea and the following parts of Australia: tropical Northern Territory, Queensland, and along the east coast of New South Wales and Victoria. *Arthrochilus* differs from *Spiculaea*, from which it was separated, in that the labellum is superior over the column. It is a glabrous terrestrial plant. The leaves form a prostrate rosette, unattached to the flowering stem and not present at time of flowering. Inflorescence is in the form of a terminal raceme up to 40cm (16″) high. Flowers are few or many. Sepals and petals are more or less similar, either spreading or deflexed. The dorsal sepal is erect. The labellum is superior to the column, and is articulate on a highly moveable claw; the blade or lamina is peltate, hammer-shaped or large insectiform callus.

Culture: Place in a pot or garden plot. Apply a liberal dressing of leaf compost and disturb as little as possible.

Arthrochilus huntiana

Arthrochilus irritabilis syn. *Spiculaea irritabilis*

Arthrochilus irritabilis syn. *Spiculaea irritabilis*

COMMON NAME: Leafy Elbow Orchid.
COLOUR: Flowers green with red markings.
SIZE: Growing up to 40cm (16″) high.
CLIMATE: Cool.
DISTRIBUTION: Native to coastal eastern Australia.
FLOWERING TIME: Summer to autumn.
DESCRIPTION: Slender terrestrial. Leaves basal, ovate-lanceolate, up to 10cm (4″) long. Flowers 15mm (¾″) long. Labellum hammer shaped.

ARUNDINA
(ah-run-dee-na)

Arundina from the Gk *arundo* (reed-like) referring to the reed-like stems. This is a small genus and possibly consists of only one highly variable species. It is widespread, extending from the Himalayas across Burma, to southern China down through Indonesia to the Pacific Islands. It is a tall terrestrial herb. Stems are 1.3 to 2.5m (4 to 8′) high. The distichous, grass-like leaves are 10 to 30cm (4 to 12″) long. Inflorescence is terminal, erect and produces a succession of blooms. The flowers are large, showy and resemble a *Cattleya.* Sepals and petals are free, spreading, acuminate, white, flesh-coloured, purple-red to pastel rose-mauve, and are up to 10cm (4″) long. The labellum is tubular at the base, the throat is pale-rose veined with purple, the tip is bright rose-purple, the disc is yellow with three lamellate nerves, margins are crisped, and the apex emarginate. The very rare *A.* sp. var. *alba* is white with a yellow throat.

Culture: As for *Sobralia.* Compost in well-drained pots. Plants require lots of careful watering and moderate shade. From northern Queensland, Fiji and the Hawaiian Islands come reports of plants naturalising and growing wild in domestic gardens.

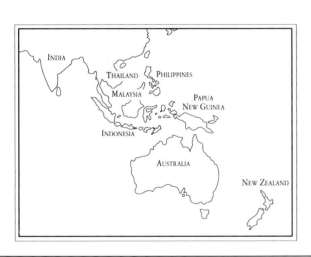

Arundina graminifolia

Arundina graminifolia syn. *A. bambusifolia*

Common Name: Bamboo Orchid.
Colour: Flowers are white to pale lilac. Labellum generally a deeper pink to purple.
Size: Growing up to 3.6m (12′) high.
Climate: Warm to hot.
Distribution: Native to southern China, the Himalayas, Malaysia, Indonesia and the Pacific Islands.
Flowering Time: Throughout the year.
Description: Leafy, erect stems growing up to 3.6m (12′) high. Leaves are grass-like and linear and grow up to 30cm (12″) long. Flowers are terminal, resembling small *Cattleya,* and measure up to 7.5cm (3″) across. Labellum is tubular with apex spreading.

Arundina graminifolia syn. *A. bambusifolia*

ASCOCENTRUM
(as-koe-sen-trum)

*A*scocentrum from the Gk *ascos* (bag) *kentron* (spur) with reference to the spur of the labellum. This genus of about nine or more species is allied to *Vanda* and *Ascoglossum*. It extends from the Himalayas, through Southeast Asia to Formosa, the Philippines, Borneo and Java. It is a small epiphytic monopodial plant. The stems are fleshy, densely leafy, less than 25cm (10″) high, with cord-like roots. Leaves are distichous, bifid or truncate, falling with age. Inflorescence is erect, densely flowered, showy, facing in all directions. The flowers are small, scarlet, rose-red, orange or yellow. Sepals and petals are similar. The labellum is trilobed, adnate at base to column, side-lobes erect, mid-lobe tongue-shaped porrect or recurved. The spur is cylindrical and shorter than the lamina.

Culture: As for *Vanda*. Being a small plant, it is best grown in pans or in a basket. Use loose compost. It needs humid conditions at all times, with plenty of light. Water often during the growing period and drain well.

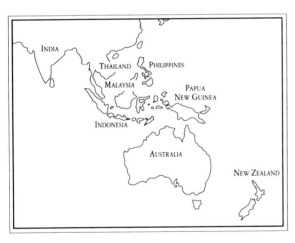

Ascocentrum ampullaceum

Ascocentrum miniatum (orange form)

Ascocentrum miniatum

COMMON NAME: None.
COLOUR: Flower colour is variable, from orange-yellow, orange to red.
SIZE: Growing up to 25cm (10″) high.
CLIMATE: Warm.
DISTRIBUTION: Native to Borneo, the Himalayas to the Peninsula Malaysia and Java.
FLOWERING TIME: Spring to early summer.
DESCRIPTION: An erect epiphytic herb. Stems are thick, woody and grow up to 20cm (8″) long. Leaves are fleshy, keeled underneath, linear, unequally emarginate, up to 20cm (8″) long. Inflorescence erect, up to 25cm (10″) high. Flowers are numerous, measuring up to 1.5cm (½″) across.

ASPASIA
(as-paz-ee-ah)

*A*spasia derives from either the Gk *aspasios* (glad, delightful) with reference to the delightful flower, or is named in honour of Aspasia, the delightful Athenian wife of Pericles. The genus is allied to *Brassia, Miltonia, Helcia* and *Trichopilia*, but differs in that the margins of the labellum are joined to the base of the column for half its length, the lamina then bends at right angles to the column. The genus has about nine species found in the tropics of Central America, from Guatemala, Nicaragua to Brazil, up to 1000m (3000′) altitude. This epiphytic herb is often found on the branches of trees overhanging streams or rivers, and is 40cm (16″) or more tall. Pseudobulbs are short, erect and are covered by leaf-like bracts. Leaves are coriaceous, spreading, up to 30cm (12″) long. Inflorescence is an erect raceme with one to a few flowers. Flowers are showy and faintly fragrant. Sepals and petals are sub-similar, free, spreading, up to 7cm (3″) long, and are variable in colour, being dull-white or pink, or greenish with spots or blotches. The labellum is adnate at base to column; lamina free, perpendicular to column, pandurate, spreading.

Culture: Grow in compost using shredded or very small chunks of tree-fern in pots. They thrive when mounted on slabs of tree-fern. They require warm, moist temperatures, and bright light.

SOUTH AMERICA

Aspasia epidendroides

Aspasia lunata

COMMON NAME: None.

COLOUR: Flowers cream and spotted green, barred with brown. Labellum white blotched with violet.

SIZE: Growing to 25cm (10″) high.

CLIMATE: Intermediate.

DISTRIBUTION: Native to Brazil.

FLOWERING TIME: Spring.

DESCRIPTION: Pseudobulbs oval, compressed, up to 5cm (2″) high. Leaves strap-like, acute, up to 20cm (8″) long. Flowers about 4cm (1½″) long.

Aspasia lunata

BAPTISTONIA
(bap-tis-ton-ee-ah)

Baptistonia is named after Jean Baptiste Antoine Guillemin. Originally it was known as *Oncidium brunleesianum*. It comes from Rio de Janeiro and Sao Paulo, Brazil. For a time, botanists moved the plant between both old and new genera until renamed *Baptistonia* by Dr Joao Barrbosa-Rodrigues, author of *Orchidearum Novarum, Brazil* (1877–82). This genus of a single species was little known until about 1970 when it began to appear more frequently in collections. Pseudobulbs are compressed, oblong, and narrowing upwards. Leaves are coriaceous. Inflorescence is erect or arching and is densely flowered. Flowers are 2cm (¾″) across. Sepals and petals curve forward. Petals have markings on the apical half. The labellum is tri-lobed; lateral lobes incurved to column; mid-lobe smaller, reflexed, almost black in colour; disc or crest shallow, dark purple with two erect white teeth. The column is terete with broad round wings and the anther is hooded.

Culture: As for *Oncidium.* Compost in well-drained pots. The plant requires humid conditions. Water frequently. Care must be taken with fragile new growth; don't let water lie around the new growing tips as rotting may occur. The plant cannot tolerate stale conditions.

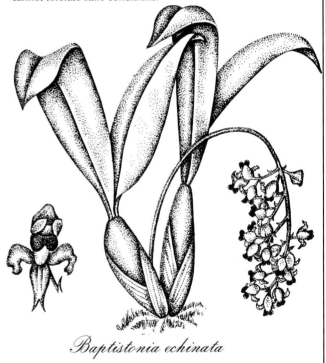

Baptistonia echinata

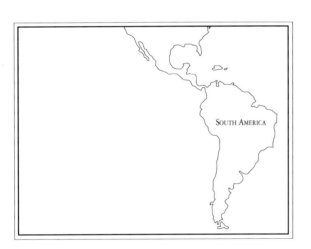

SOUTH AMERICA

Baptistonia echinata syn. *Oncidium brunleesianum*

Baptistonia echinata syn. *Oncidium brunleesianum*

COMMON NAME: None.
COLOUR: Flowers yellow. Labellum maroon.
SIZE: Growing up to 20cm (8″) high.
CLIMATE: Intermediate to warm.
DISTRIBUTION: Native to Brazil.
FLOWERING TIME: Early spring.
DESCRIPTION: Pseudobulbs elongate, covered in papery bracts, up to 7.5cm (3″) high. Leaf is solitary, apical, lanceolate and grows up to 12.5cm (5″) long. Inflorescence up to 30cm (12″) long, paniculate. Flowers numerous, shy openers, cup-shaped, nodding, about 1.5cm (½″) across.

BIFRENARIA
(bi-fre-nah-ree-ah)

*B*ifrenaria comes from the Lat. *bi* (two) *frenum* (strap, rein) with reference to the two strap-like stalks between the viscidium and the pollinia. This feature distinguishes the genus from *Maxillaria. Bifrenaria* is a genus of about thirty species and spreads from Panama to Brazil. The genus *Stenocoryne* is considered a synonym. This is a small epiphytic, often terrestrial herb. Pseudobulbs are four-cornered, 5 to 7cm (2 to 3″) tall. Leaves are erect coriaceous or papyraceous, plicate, glossy, and are up to 30cm (12″) long. Inflorescence is basal, erect and racemose with one to five flowers. These flowers are showy, often fragrant, large, up to 7.5cm (3″) across, and come in various combinations or shades of purple, yellow and white. Sepals and petals are sub-similar coriaceous, free, spreading, up to 5cm (2″) long; lateral sepals are adnate to column base, dorsal sepal is concave. Labellum is clawed, articulate to column-base, tri-lobed, with side-lobes erect, mid-lobe reflexed, fleshy, crisp, margin undulate, pubescent; the spur is sub-cylindrical.

Culture: The plant is easily grown, even by the novice hobbyist. Compost, in well-drained pots. It requires intermediate warmth and shade, as much humidity as possible, and plenty of water while growing.

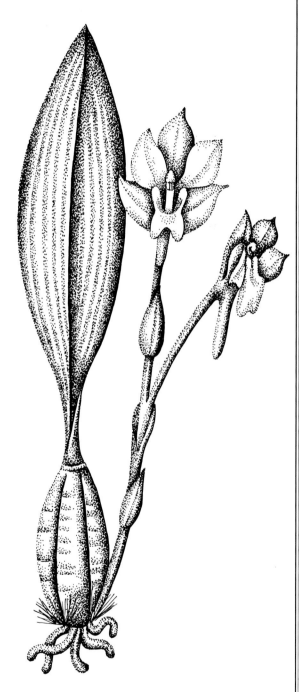

Bifrenaria tyrianthina

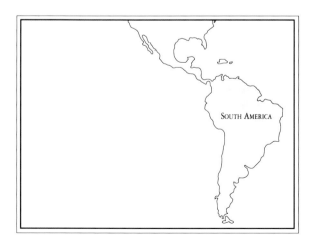

SOUTH AMERICA

Bifrenaria harrisoniae

COMMON NAME: None.
COLOUR: Variable, white or yellow-green with purple labellum.
SIZE: Up to 37.5cm (15") high.
CLIMATE: Cool to intermediate.
DISTRIBUTION: Native from Panama to Brazil.
FLOWERING TIME: Spring to early summer.
DESCRIPTION: Pseudobulbs angular ovoid, clustered, up to 7.5cm (3") high. Leaf solitary, broad, oblong-elliptic, acute, rigid, up to 30cm (12") long. Flowers are large, growing singly or in pairs, fragrant, with a waxy labellum.

Bifrenaria harrisoniae

Bifrenaria tyrianthina

COMMON NAME: None.
COLOUR: Flowers purple, darker at the base. Labellum darker purple.
SIZE: Grows up to 37cm (15") high.
CLIMATE: Intermediate.
DISTRIBUTION: Native to Brazil.
FLOWERING TIME: Spring to early summer.
DESCRIPTION: Pseudobulbs, ovoid, angled, up to 12.5cm (5") high. Leaves solitary, elliptic-oblong, acute, up to 30cm (12") long. Flowers up to 7.5cm (3") across. Labellum tri-lobed; throat white, mid-lobed and hairy.

Bifrenaria tetragona

COMMON NAME: None.
COLOUR: Flowers olive-green streaked maroon. Labellum white, blotched purple underneath. Dark maroon purple throat.
SIZE: Growing up to 45cm (18") high.
CLIMATE: Intermediate.
DISTRIBUTION: Native to Brazil.
FLOWERING TIME: Spring to early summer.
DESCRIPTION: Pseudobulbs tetragonal, tapering to the apex, up to 12.5cm (5") high. Leaf broad-lanceolate, up to 35cm (14") long. Inflorescence short, produced from base of pseudobulbs, bearing three to four blooms. Flowers up to 5cm (2") across. Lateral sepals fused to foot of the column.

Bifrenaria tyrianthina

Bifrenaria tetragona

BRASSAVOLA
(bra-sah-voe-la)

*B*rassavola is named after Sr Antonio Musa Brassavola, botanist and Professor of Logic, Physics and Medicine at Ferrara, Italy. *Brassavola* is a genus of about fifteen species extending from Mexico, Central America, Jamaica to Bolivia, Argentina and Peru. This polymorphic genus of epiphytic or terrestrial orchids is allied to *Laelia*, differing in that the lamina of the labellum of *Brassavola* widens abruptly. It has primary stems or rhizomes. Stems are erect or pendulous, up to 50cm (20″) long with secondary stems developing into pseudobulbs. Leaves at summit, plicate to flat, fleshy or coriaceous. Inflorescence is erect with a one- to many-flowered raceme. Flowers are small to large, showy, and are green, yellow or white in colour. Sepals and petals are sub-equal, spreading, linear up to 12.5cm (5″) long; lateral sepals are adnate to column-foot. The labellum is clawed and joined to the column, is tubular at base, and margins are entire, lacerate, retuse or bifid.

Culture: Compost. *Brassavola* are very easily grown. They are best in a hanging basket. They require high humidity and plenty of light. Do not allow leaves to shrivel during the resting period.

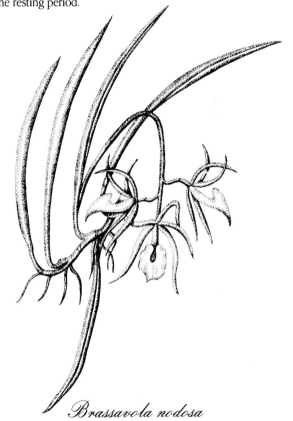

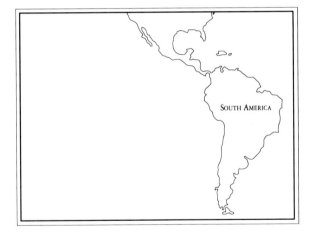
SOUTH AMERICA

Brassavola nodosa

Brassavola nodosa

COMMON NAME: None.
COLOUR: Flowers green. Labellum white, spotted purple.
SIZE: Epiphytic or lithophytic species up to 45cm (18″) high.
CLIMATE: Warm.
DISTRIBUTION: Native to Mexico, Panama and Venezuela. Altitude: sea level to 500m (1640′). Often found growing in xerophytic conditions on cacti and roots of mangroves.
FLOWERING TIME: Throughout the year.
DESCRIPTION: Leaves linear to almost terete, up to 20cm (8″) long. Inflorescence terminal. Flowers large and showy, up to 10cm (4″) across.

Brassavola nodosa

BRASSIA
(bras-ee-ah)

Brassia is named after William Brass, botanical illustrator and plant collector for Sir Joseph Banks in western and southern Africa. This is a confusing genus of about twenty-five species of small to large plants. They are found throughout tropical America from southern Florida and Mexico to Peru and Brazil. Rhizomes are creeping and stout. Pseudobulbs are rather flat with sheathing leaf-like bracts. Leaves are large, coriaceous, usually three at apex of pseudobulb. Inflorescence is a spike from base of pseudo-bulb, a raceme with few to many flowers. Flowers are small to large and are showy. Sepals and petals are sub-equal, free-spreading, narrow-linear, up to 20cm (8″) long. The labellum is sessile, shorter and wider than other segments, spreading and pandurate. The column is very short, footless and wingless.

Culture: Compost in well-drained pots as for *Cattleya*. Water often up to flowering or during the growing period. Do not disturb for several years. Roots will leave the pot; this is usually a good sign of a healthy plant. Avoid shrivelling during the rest period.

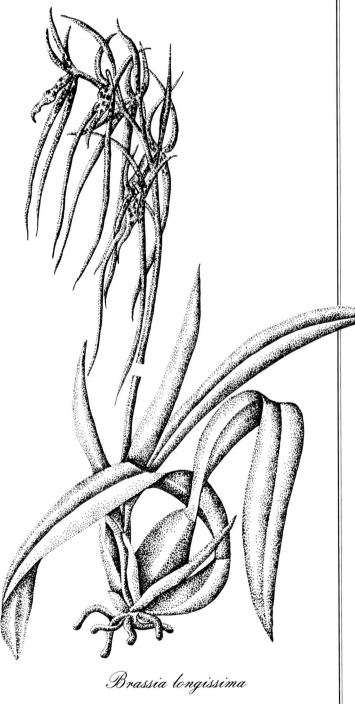

SOUTH AMERICA

Brassia longissima

Brassia gireoudiana

COMMON NAME: None.

COLOUR: Flowers green to yellow and spotted and blotched red-brown at the base.

SIZE: Up to 50cm (20″) high.

CLIMATE: Intermediate to warm.

DISTRIBUTION: Native to Panama and Costa Rica.

FLOWERING TIME: Late spring to summer.

DESCRIPTION: Pseudobulbs, compressed, ovate-oblong, up to 10cm (4″) high. Leaves oblong-oblanceolate, up to 40cm (16″) long. Inflorescence spreading. Flowers about 30cm (12″) long.

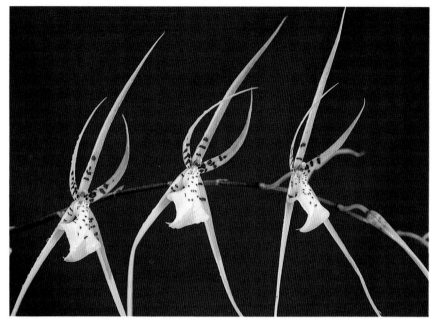

Brassia gireoudiana

Brassia verrucosa

COMMON NAME: Spider Orchid.

COLOUR: Flowers yellow to green. Labellum white spotted, with green at the centre margin.

SIZE: Up to 47.5cm (19″) high.

CLIMATE: Intermediate.

DISTRIBUTION: Native to central America and Mexico.

FLOWERING TIME: Spring and summer.

DESCRIPTION: Pseudobulbs compressed, ovoid, up to 10cm (4″) high. Leaves in pairs oblong-elliptic, up to 37.5cm (15″) long. Flower scape bears eight to ten flowers on an arching inflorescence. Flower long and elegant. Entire length of flower is 17 to 20cm (7 to 8″). Petals and sepals long and linear. Labellum broad.

Brassia longissima

Brassia longissima

COMMON NAME: None.

COLOUR: Flowers orange or yellow-green with maroon blotches. Labellum cream, spotted purple.

SIZE: Up to 60cm (2′) high.

CLIMATE: Intermediate to warm.

DISTRIBUTION: Native to Peru, Panama, Ecuador and Costa Rica.

FLOWERING TIME: Spring.

DESCRIPTION: A large, variable species with a creeping rhizome. Pseudobulbs compressed, ovoid, up to 18cm (7″) high. Leaves oblong-elliptic, 55cm (22″) long. Flowers numerous, large, up to 25cm (10″).

Brassia verrucosa

BULBOPHYLLUM
(bul-bow-fil-um)

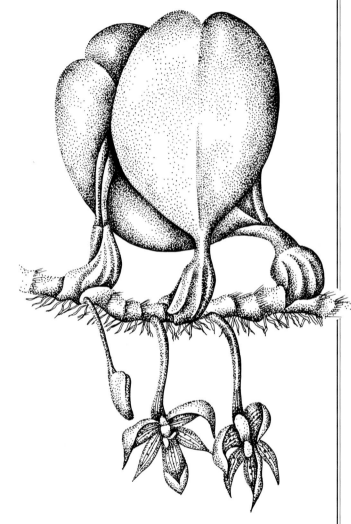

Bulbophyllum baileyi

Bulbophyllum from the Gk *bulbos* (bulb) *phyllum* (leaf) with reference to the leafy pseudobulbs. This is the largest collection of species in one genus of Orchidaceae. The genus spreads throughout tropical and sub-tropical areas of the world. Recent estimates suggest about 2000 species with Papua New Guinea the possible dissemination centre, having more than 600 species. The genus has from very tiny to large epiphytic herbs. Rhizomes are creeping. Pseudobulbs are very small to medium, spherical to conical, spreading or clustered along the rhizomes. It has one or two leaves terminal on pseudobulb, fleshy, coriaceous, erect or pendulous. Inflorescence rising from rhizome at base of pseudobulb, one to many-flowered. Flowers are tiny to medium, with colours ranging from white, green, yellow to near black with various shades and hues in-between. The dorsal sepal is free. Lateral sepals are connate at base, with petals free, often complicated, and smaller than sepals; the labellum is tri-lobed, fleshy and often pubescent. The flower often has a foul smell.

Culture: Compost. Mount the plant on tree-fern or platyserium slabs. It requires high humidity and shade. Species from mist forests must be kept moist. Leave the plant undisturbed for as long as possible.

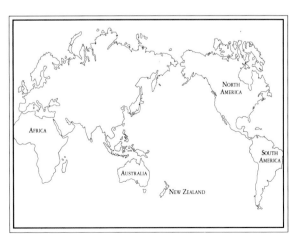

Bulbophyllum affine

COMMON NAME: None.
COLOUR: Flower yellow to green, veined red to purple. Labellum yellow to orange.
SIZE: Growing up to 15cm (6″) high.
CLIMATE: Intermediate to warm.
DISTRIBUTION: Native to Thailand, North Vietnam and India, growing at altitudes of 800 to 1300m (2600 to 4250′).
FLOWERING TIME: Summer.
DESCRIPTION: Pseudobulbs elongate on a creeping rhizome, up to 4cm (1½″) or higher. Leaves apical from pseudobulb, linear-lanceolate, up to 15cm (6″) long. Inflorescence basal from pseudobulb. Flower solitary and measures up to 2.5cm (1″) across.

Bulbophyllum affine

Bulbophyllum baileyi

COMMON NAME: Spotted Bulbophyllum.
COLOUR: Flowers lemon and spotted purple.
SIZE: Up to 20cm (8″) high.
CLIMATE: Warm to hot.
DISTRIBUTION: Native to north-eastern Australian and Papua New Guinean rainforests. Altitude up to 900m (3000′).
FLOWERING TIME: Summer.
DESCRIPTION: An epiphytic or lithophytic plant on creeping rhizome. Pseudobulbs short and angular. Leaves single channelled, emarginate up to 20cm (8″) long. Flowers 4cm (1½″) across.

Bulbophyllum baileyi

Bulbophyllum aurantiacum

COMMON NAME: None.
COLOUR: Flowers pale to dark apricot.
SIZE: Pendulous to 45cm (18″) long.
CLIMATE: Cool.
DISTRIBUTION: Native to eastern Australia.
FLOWERING TIME: Mainly summer.
DESCRIPTION: Pseudobulbs small and ovoid on creeping pendulous rhizomes. Leaves thick, oblong-linear, up to 10cm (4″) long. Numerous flowers 6mm (¼″) long.

Bulbophyllum aurantiacum

Bulbophyllum careyanum

COMMON NAME: Carrion Orchid.
COLOUR: Flowers orange-yellow or green, spotted and suffused red-brown. Labellum purple or orange-yellow.
SIZE: Growing up to 30cm (12″) high.
CLIMATE: Intermediate.
DISTRIBUTION: Native to Nepal, India, Kasia Hills, Burma and China.
FLOWERING TIME: Autumn.
DESCRIPTION: An epiphytic plant on a creeping rhizome. Pseudobulbs globose-ovoid, up to 5cm (2″) high. Leaves linear-oblong, up to 25cm (10″) long. Flowers small, densely-imbricate. Has an unpleasant odour of rotting meat, hence its common name.

Bulbophyllum concinnum

Bulbophyllum concinnum

COMMON NAME: None.
COLOUR: Flowers yellow, with tip of sepals orange. Labellum orange.
SIZE: Growing up to 10cm (4″) high.
CLIMATE: Intermediate to warm.
DISTRIBUTION: Native to Singapore, Johore, Thailand and Sumatra, growing along rivers and estuaries, and using mangroves as its host.
FLOWERING TIME: Summer to autumn.
DESCRIPTION: Pseudobulbs borne on elongated creeping rhizome, cylindrical, up to 2.5cm (1″) high. Leaves solitary, broad-lanceolate, up to 4cm (1½″) long. Inflorescence basal, up to 10cm (4″) long. Flowers produced in a terminal cluster, up to 4cm (1½″) long. Flowers are small, up to 5mm (¼″) long.

Bulbophyllum careyanum

Bulbophyllum elisae

COMMON NAME: None.
COLOUR: Flowers green. Labellum red to purple.
SIZE: Growing up to 12.5cm (5″) high.
CLIMATE: Cool.
DISTRIBUTION: Native to Australia, central east coast and mountain ranges, up to an altitude of 1100m (3500′).
FLOWERING TIME: Winter to late spring.
DESCRIPTION: Lithophytic on granite boulders or occasionally epiphytic. Pseudobulbs ovoid, knobbly, up to 3cm (1¼″) high. Leaf solitary, lanceolate, up to 10cm (4″) long. Flowers small, delicate, wing-like.

Bulbophyllum macranthum

Bulbophyllum elisae

Bulbophyllum macranthum

COMMON NAME: None.
COLOUR: Flower white-cream, densely spotted red-purple. Labellum yellow-cream.
SIZE: Up to 32.5cm (13″) long.
CLIMATE: Warm to hot.
DISTRIBUTION: Native to Papua New Guinea, Borneo, Java, Sumatra, Peninsula Malaysia, Celebes and Thailand. Altitude up to 1200m (4000′).
FLOWERING TIME: Spring.
DESCRIPTION: Pseudobulbs ovoid about 2.5cm (1″) high. Leaves lanceolate up to 30cm (12″) long. Flowers solitary.

Bulbophyllum scabratum

COMMON NAME: None.
COLOUR: Flower ochre to yellow.
SIZE: A dwarf epiphytic plant, 12.5cm (5″) high.
CLIMATE: Intermediate.
DISTRIBUTION: Native to Nepal, Sikkim, Meghalaya and east Bengal, growing at elevations of 1000 to 2000m (3280 to 6550′).
FLOWERING TIME: Spring.
DESCRIPTION: Pseudobulbs clustered, small, ovoid up to 1.5cm (½″) high. Leaves solitary, linear-lanceolate, up to 10cm (4″) long. Flower scape up to 4cm (1½″) high. Flower 1.5cm (½″) long. Lateral sepal connate, tips free.

Bulbophyllum scabratum

Bulbophyllum longiflorum

COMMON NAME: None.
COLOUR: Flowers white to cream. Dorsal sepal, petals and labellum marked golden crimson.
SIZE: Growing up to 25cm (10″) high.
CLIMATE: Warm.
DISTRIBUTION: Native to Australia and extending from Uganda to Fiji, Madagascar and Mascarene Islands. Growing in shady, humid areas, usually in rainforest.
FLOWERING TIME: Autumn to spring.
DESCRIPTION: Pseudobulbs borne along a creeping rhizome, ovoid, tetragonal, 4cm (1½″) high. Leaf solitary, erect, oblong, up to 20cm (8″) long. Inflorescences usually erect, 25cm (10″) long, up to twelve blooms in a hanging umbel. Flowers 5cm (2″) long.

Bulbophyllum longiflorum

CALADENIA
(kal-a-den-ee-ah)

Caladenia from the Gk *kalos* (beautiful) *aden* (a gland) and possibly referring to the calli or glands on the labellum. This genus, little known to orchidists, has about seventy species of terrestrial plants and is found mainly in Australia with many species in Indonesia, New Caledonia and New Zealand. It is a terrestrial herb growing up to 30cm (12″) high, and is often hairy. Tubers are small and globular; the leaf is basal, solitary, ranging from linear to linear-lanceolate, is hairy and is up to 20cm (8″) long. Flowers are solitary or in a loose raceme, and are erect, complex, very variable within species, and of various colours. The dorsal sepal is incurved over the column, the lateral sepals are flat, spreading and often reflexed. Petals are erect and spreading; sepals and petals grow up to 12cm (5″) long. The labellum is erect on a freely moveable claw, is tri-lobed or entire, with side-lobes erect; lamina calli arranged in longitudinal rows or scattered or crowded, in bright attractive hues.

Culture: *Caladenia* is not easy to grow. It requires rich, well-drained, free-moving compost. In pots, use broken crock, granulated or crushed brick, topped with equal parts of shredded tree-fern, leaf mould, crumbled loam, sharp gritty sand and sphagnum moss. Slightly bury the tubers, feed with liquid fertiliser as plants rapidly exhaust the compost. The plants are spectacular with large flowers; they make a very admirable addition to collections.

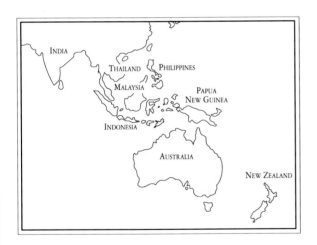

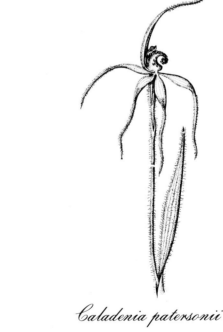

Caladenia patersonii

Caladenia recticulata

Common Name: Veined Spider Orchid.
Colour: Flowers dark red and green.
Size: Slender terrestrial up to 30cm (12″) high.
Climate: Cool.
Distribution: Native to eastern Australia (widespread).
Flowering Time: Late winter to spring.
Description: Leaf solitary, radical, linear-lanceolate. Flowers usually solitary.

Caladenia recticulata

CALANTHE
(ka-lan-thee)

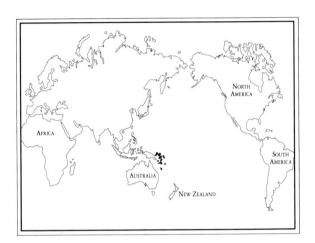

Calanthe from the Gk *kalos* (beautiful) *anthe* (flower), refers to the pretty flowers. This genus of about 150 species is distributed throughout tropical Asia, Indonesia, Papua New Guinea, Australia, extending across India to Madagascar and Africa. This medium to large terrestrial herb is divided into two groups, those with corm-like insignificant pseudobulbs, and those with short or long stems with several leaves. Leaves are large, petiolate, plicate and grow up to 60cm (2′) long. Inflorescence is terminal or grows from the side of the pseudobulb and is erect, racemose, densely-flowered, and up to 90cm (3′) long. Flowers are small to medium in size and are showy. Sepals are sub-equal and spreading; petals are similar to sepals. Labellum is adnate to base of column, tri-lobed, with the mid-lobe often bifid. The genus is allied to *Phaius*.

Culture: Compost. Deciduous species need moderate shade, warmth and moisture while growing. After leaf fall they need to be kept cool and dry. Flowering will occur from the base of the pseudobulbs. The evergreen species need more shade. Never let the roots become dry. Less water is required once flowering and growth are completed. This is a very popular plant with growers.

Calanthe veratrifolia

Calanthe rubens

COMMON NAME: None.
COLOUR: Flowers pink and rarely white.
Labellum pink, flushed with crimson.
SIZE: Up to 55cm (22″) high.
CLIMATE: Intermediate.
DISTRIBUTION: Native to Thailand and north
Malaysia. Limestone habitat.
FLOWERING TIME: Autumn.
DESCRIPTION: Pseudobulbs grooved, ovoid, up to
15cm (6″) high. Leaves elliptic petiolate, up to
40cm (16″) long. Inflorescence 50cm (20″)
long. Flowers 3cm (1¼″) across.

Calanthe rubens

Calanthe triplicata

Calanthe triplicata

COMMON NAME: Christmas Orchid or Scrub Lily.
COLOUR: Flower white.
SIZE: Tall perennial terrestrial up to 90cm (3′)
high.
CLIMATE: Cool, intermediate to warm.
DISTRIBUTION: Native to southern India, South-
east Asia, Japan, Thailand, Malaysia, Indonesia,
Papua New Guinea, Australia and Fiji. Growing
in leaf litter in shaded gullies.
FLOWERING TIME: Summer.
DESCRIPTION: Pseudobulbs are small ovoid.
Leaves large, broad 90cm (3′) long. Flower
scape up to 1.5m (5′) long. Basal inflorescence,
with the flower 3cm (1¼″) across. Plant
resembles *Phaius*.

Calanthe vestita

Calanthe vestita

COMMON NAME: None.
COLOUR: Flower colour is highly variable; may be white, yellow, or orange
to red. Labellum may be pink.
SIZE: Growing up to 45cm (18″) high.
CLIMATE: Intermediate.
DISTRIBUTION: Native to Burma, Thailand, Vietnam, Peninsula Malaysia,
Borneo and Celebes.
FLOWERING TIME: Winter.
DESCRIPTION: Pseudobulbs conical, ovoid, angled, up to 20cm (8″) high.
Leaves deciduous lanceolate, acute, folded, up to fifteen blooms. Flowers
up to 7.5cm (3″) long. The photograph shows the alba form.

CALEANA
(kal-ee-ah-na)

Caleana is named after George Caley, a collector of Australian plants in the nineteenth century. The genus comprises about five species found in Australia and New Zealand. They are terrestrial glabrous herbs. Two elongated tubers form the root system. The leaf is solitary. The raceme is a slender pedicel with one to eight flowers. The dorsal sepal is usually recurved, and lateral sepals spread with the petals erect and incurved. These plants are rare in collections.

Culture: As for *Caladenia*. When grouped in smaller beds or pots, they make a spectacular display.

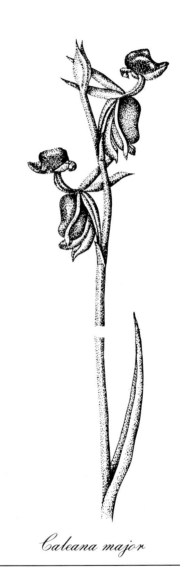

Caleana major

Caleana major

Caleana major

COMMON NAME: Flying Duck Orchid.
COLOUR: Flower perianth dark red-brown, and rarely green.
SIZE: Slender terrestrial up to 50cm (20″) high.
CLIMATE: Cool.
DISTRIBUTION: Native to eastern Australia. Occurs in swampy areas.
FLOWERING TIME: Summer.
DESCRIPTION: Leaves lanceolate to oblong and grow up to 10cm (4″) long. Up to four flowers, 25mm (1″) long. Flower resembles a flying duck, thus the common name.

CALOCHILUS
(kal-ok-i-lis)

Calochilus from the Gk *kolos* (beautiful) *chilos* (a lip) 'a beautiful lip' with reference to the labellum. It is commonly known as the Bearded Orchid. This genus of about twelve unusually beautiful terrestrial orchids is found in Australia, Papua New Guinea, New Caledonia and New Zealand. This is a tall terrestrial herb up to 60cm (2') high, rising from ovoid subterranean tubers. The leaf is basal, solitary and channelled. Inflorescence is terminal, with the raceme up to 60cm (2') long and having as many as sixteen blooms. The flowers are complex and beautiful. Sepals and petals are green, brown, rusty or yellow-green with coloured stripes. The labellum's upper surface is clothed with rather long hairs of copper-red, red-blue or purple hues of metallic lustre; its lip is up to 36mm (1½") long. The complex column gives the illusion of the nose and eyes of an old man with a beard.

Culture: As for *Caladenia.* This genus is common in collections.

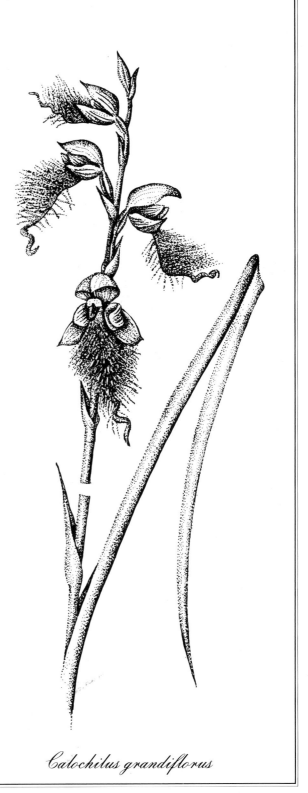

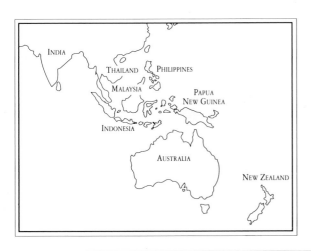

Calochilus grandiflorus

Calochilus campestris

COMMON NAME: Copper Bearded Orchid.
COLOUR: Flowers yellow-green with red-brown or purple markings.
SIZE: A glabrous terrestrial herb up to 60cm (24″) high.
CLIMATE: Cool.
DISTRIBUTION: Native to eastern Australia and New Zealand. Growing from high rainfall areas to montane areas and mallee sandhills.
FLOWERING TIME: Spring to summer.
DESCRIPTION: Solitary leaf up to 30cm (12″) long. Two to fifteen flowers.

Calochilus campestris

Calochilus grandiflorus

COMMON NAME: Bearded Orchid.
COLOUR: Flower golden-yellow and red-purple.
SIZE: Slender glabrous herb, up to 60cm (24″) high.
CLIMATE: Cool.
DISTRIBUTION: Native to eastern Australia.
FLOWERING TIME: Spring.
DESCRIPTION: Leaf erect, filiform, channelled, 20 to 50cm (8 to 20″) long. Flower can be solitary or up to ten. Labellum fringed. Flower resembles face of an old man with a beard.

Calochilus robertsonii

Calochilus robertsonii

COMMON NAME: Purple Bearded Orchid.
COLOUR: Flowers green. Labellum has violet-red hairs.
SIZE: Small terrestrial up to 45cm (18″) high.
CLIMATE: Cool.
DISTRIBUTION: Native to coast and nearby mountains of Australia except in the Northern Territory.
FLOWERING TIME: Spring.
DESCRIPTION: Leaf basal, channelled, linear-lanceolate, up to 40cm (16″) long. One to nine flowers. Labellum hairy, up to 3cm (1¼″) long.

Calochilus grandiflorus

CATASETUM

(kat-a-see-tum)

*C*atasetum from the Gk *kata* (down) Lat. *seta* (bristle) with reference to the two antenna-like appendages at the base of the column of the male flowers. This genus comprises about one hundred species found in tropical and central South America and the West Indies, from Mexico to Peru, with Brazil the centre of dissemination. *Catasetum* includes some of the most complex, unusual and interesting orchids. It is a truly epiphytic plant. Pseudobulbs are fleshy, ovoid, conical or fusiform, losing leaf-sheaths with age. Stems are short. Leaves are large, plicate and deciduous. Inflorescence from base of pseudobulb, erect, arching or pendulous.

The genus is divided into two groups. Group (a): (*Clowesia*) bearing perfect flowers (hermaphroditic). Group (b): (*Ortho-catasetum*) producing unisexual flowers or very rarely perfect flowers. The male (staminate) and female (pistillate) flowers of this group are not alike and may produce on separate inflorescences at the same time or at different times. In the male (staminate) flower, the labellum is concave, saccate or helmet shaped; margins are fimbriate, dentate, crenulate or entire. The column has two sensitive antennae at the base which explosively release the pollinia on touch. The female (pistillate) flowers are less numerous. The labellum is helmet-shaped or saccate, and the column is very short, anther-less and antennae-less.

Bees of the *Euglossa*, *Eulaema* and *Euplusia* genera are believed to be agents in the pollination of the *Catasetum* species. The male (staminate) flower emits a musty odour which attracts the bees. While attempting to reach the source of the odour at the base of the column, the bees touch the antennae, thus triggering the rostellum, releasing the viscidium which is thrown on to the back of the bee. The sticky secretion on the viscidium sets rapidly. The stipe hangs along the abdomen of the bee. The anther cap falls off exposing the large pollinia in the correct position to make contact with the stigmata surface of the female (pistillate) flower, resulting in the pollination of the ovary.

Culture: Grows well in a variety of composts in well-drained pots or baskets. Requires humidity and plenty of water while growing. Once new shoots appear water with caution to prevent rotting. Temperature control is vital—between 12 and 15 degrees Celsius (54-59°F) while resting, and between 15 and 18 degrees Celsius (59-64°F) during the growth period.

SOUTH AMERICA

Catasetum viridiflavum

Catasetum barbatum (male)

COMMON NAME: None.
COLOUR: Male flowers dark green, spotted brown. Labellum deep pink. Female flowers green.
SIZE: Growing up to 60cm (24″) high.
CLIMATE: Intermediate to warm.
DISTRIBUTION: Native to Guyana, Brazil and Peru.
FLOWERING TIME: Summer.
DESCRIPTION: This large epiphytic species has two sexual flower forms. Both male and female flowers may be produced on the one plant on different inflorescences, but they usually occur on different plants. The male flower is photographed here. Pseudobulbs fusiform, up to 15cm (6″) high. Leaves oblong-lanceolate, up to 45cm (18″) long. Inflorescence borne from the base, longer than the leaves. Flowers are numerous, up to 4cm (1½″) long. Female flowers are smaller than male flowers.

Catasetum barbatum (male)

Catasetum saccatum var. *incurvum* syn. *C. cruciatum, C. stupendum (male)*

Catasetum saccatum var. *incurvum* syn. *C. cruciatum, C. stupendum* (male)

COMMON NAME: None.
COLOUR: A blend of purple-black, green, red-brown, pink and white. Stem purplish. (Male flower illustrated.)
SIZE: Up to 60cm (24″) high.
CLIMATE: Intermediate to warm.
DISTRIBUTION: Native to Guyana, Peru and Brazil.
FLOWERING TIME: Summer.
DESCRIPTION: A large variable plant. Pseudobulbs somewhat compressed, sub-conical, up to 20cm (8″) long. Leaves lanceolate acuminate up to 40cm (16″) long. Male flower about 10cm (4″) long.

Catasetum expansum (male)

COMMON NAME: None.
COLOUR: Flowers green. Labellum cream-yellow.
SIZE: Growing up to 45cm (18″) high.
CLIMATE: Intermediate to warm.
DISTRIBUTION: Native to Venezuela and Brazil.
FLOWERING TIME: Summer.
DESCRIPTION: Pseudobulbs elongate, up to 15cm (6″) high. Leaves basal, sheathing, ribbed, broad-lanceolate, up to 35cm (14″) long. Inflorescence basal, up to 35cm (14″) long, erect or arching. Flowers 4cm (1½″) across. Both male and female flowers may be produced on the one plant, but occur more often on separate plants. The male flower is photographed here.

Catasetum expansum (male)

CATTLEYA
(kat-lee-ya)

Cattleya is named after William Cattley, the first horticulturist to grow epiphytic orchids successfully in England. This genus of over sixty species has untold varieties and forms together with a myriad of natural and artificial hybrids. It is found in tropical Central and northern South America from Mexico to Brazil. It is an epiphytic plant with pseudobulb-like stems. Leaves are thick, fleshy or coriaceous. Inflorescence is terminal, and has one or more racemes. Flowers are both solitary and several, are large and very showy. Sepals are free and wide. Petals are crisped or frilled, and spreading. The labellum is large, ornate, sessile, free, trilobed, with side-lobes folding and rather tube-shaped. The genus is divided into two groups: group (a) has pseudobulbs with a single apical leaf; and group (b) has pseudobulbs with two apical leaves. Flowers simulate *Laelia* and *Sobralia*.

Culture: This is one of the easiest orchids to grow. Compost in well-drained pots. It requires shade, but plenty of light, humidity, and plenty of water while growing. Once the new pseudobulbs form, reduce the water. This is possibly the most popular orchid in cultivated collections.

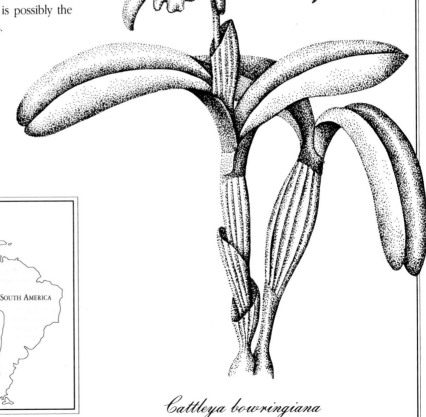

SOUTH AMERICA

Cattleya bowringiana

Cattleya amethystoglossa

COMMON NAME: None.
COLOUR: Flowers pale pink, spotted dark purple. Sepals pale pink. Labellum purple inside.
SIZE: Growing up to 60cm (24″) high.
CLIMATE: Intermediate.
DISTRIBUTION: Native to Brazil.
FLOWERING TIME: Autumn to winter.
DESCRIPTION: Pseudobulbs stem-like. Leaves in pairs, elliptic-oblong, up to 20cm (8″) long. Flowers clustered, up to 10cm (4″) across.

Cattleya amethystoglossa

Cattleya aurantiaca

COMMON NAME: None.
COLOUR: Flowers scarlet, orange or orange-yellow, may have brown or purple spots or streaks.
SIZE: Up to 55cm (22″) high.
CLIMATE: Intermediate.
DISTRIBUTION: Native to El Salvador, Mexico, Guatemala, Honduras and Nicaragua.
FLOWERING TIME: Summer to autumn.
DESCRIPTION: Pseudobulbs, cylindrical, spindly up to 37.5cm (15″) high. Leaves in pairs, broad-ovate, up to 18cm (7″) long. Flowers about 4cm (1½″) across.

Cattleya aurantiaca

Cattleya bicolor ssp. *minasgeriasensis* syn. *C. bicolor* var. *grossii*

Cattleya bicolor ssp. minasgeriasensis syn. *C. bicolor* var. *grossii*

COMMON NAME: None.
COLOUR: Flower red-brown. Labellum white and pinkish-lilac.
SIZE: Grows up to 30cm (12″) high.
CLIMATE: Intermediate.
DISTRIBUTION: Native to Brazil.
FLOWERING TIME: Summer.
DESCRIPTION: A tetraploid species and much more vigorous than the type species; pseudobulbs cylindrical up to 30cm (12″) tall. Leaves paired broad-lanceolate, apical, up to 20cm (8″) long. Inflorescence short with up to four blooms. Flowers are fragrant and grow up to 10cm (4″) across.

Cattleya bowringiana var. *coerulea*

Cattleya bowringiana

COMMON NAME: None.
COLOUR: Petals and sepals pink to purple with white throat.
SIZE: Growing up to 60cm (24″) high.
CLIMATE: Intermediate.
DISTRIBUTION: Native to British Honduras. Rare in Guatemala and Belize. Grows on rocks along streams.
FLOWERING TIME: Autumn.
DESCRIPTION: The canes have a flat bulbous swelling at the base. Leaves linear-oblong, up to 20cm (8″) long. Flower spike may produce up to fifteen blooms. Flowers 8cm (3″) across.

Cattleya bowringiana

Cattleya bowringiana var. coerulea

COMMON NAME: None.
COLOUR: Flowers blue-lilac. Labellum throat lemon, veined and edged with purple.
SIZE: Grows up to 60cm (24″) high.
CLIMATE: Intermediate.
DISTRIBUTION: Native to Guatemala and Honduras. Growing in exposed positions on rocks in ravines and along streams.
FLOWERING TIME: Autumn.
DESCRIPTION: A rare plant. Pseudobulbs clavate, up to 35cm (14″) high. Leaves linear-oblong, up to 20cm (8″) long. Inflorescence up to 25cm (10″) long, producing about three to ten blooms. Flowers showy, up to 7cm (2¾″) across. Similar to its type but blue-lilac in colour, and fewer flowers with a slender growth.

Cattleya chocoensis syn. *C. labiata* var. *quadricolor*

COMMON NAME: None.
COLOUR: Flowers white and may be tinted lilac. Labellum throat amethyst-purple, disc yellow-orange, with a purple blotch.
SIZE: Up to 50cm (20″) high.
CLIMATE: Intermediate.
DISTRIBUTION: Native to Colombia.
FLOWERING TIME: Summer.
DESCRIPTION: Pseudobulbs clavate, up to 25cm (10″) high. Leaf solitary, oblong, up to 25cm (10″) high. Flower doesn't open fully, giving it a bell-shaped appearance; fragrant.

Cattleya chocoensis syn. *C. labiata* var. *quadricolor*

Cattleya dormaniana

COMMON NAME: None.
COLOUR: Flowers dark olive-brown. Labellum bright pink.
SIZE: Grows up to 90cm (36″) high.
CLIMATE: Intermediate.
DISTRIBUTION: Native to Brazil.
FLOWERING TIME: Autumn.
DESCRIPTION: A closely allied species to *C. guttata* and *C. leopoldii.* Pseudobulbs elongate, cylindrical, up to 70cm (28″) high. Leaves borne in pairs at the apex of the pseudobulbs, oblong-elliptic, up to 20cm (8″) long. Inflorescence terminal up to 20cm (8″) long. Flowers up to 10cm (4″) across.

Cattleya dormaniana

Cattleya forbesii

Cattleya forbesii

COMMON NAME: None.
COLOUR: Flower colour variable, typical form olive-green. Labellum off-white, outside flushed with deep pink, inside yellow, throat veined red.
SIZE: Up to 45cm (18″) high.
CLIMATE: Intermediate.
DISTRIBUTION: Native to Brazil. An epiphyte growing near streams and the coast.
FLOWERING TIME: Summer to autumn.
DESCRIPTION: Pseudobulbs cylindrical; furrowing when mature, up to 30cm (12″) high. Leaves in pairs, narrow-elliptic up to 15cm (6″) long. Flowers fragrant, up to 10cm (4″) across.

Cattleya granulosa var. *schofieldiana*

Cattleya gaskelliana

COMMON NAME: None.
COLOUR: Flower colour variable, white to pale amethyst-purple. Labellum throat yellow, may be blushed pink.
SIZE: Up to 42.5cm (17″) high.
CLIMATE: Intermediate.
DISTRIBUTION: Native to Venezuela. Altitude 750 to 1000m (3500 to 3280′).
FLOWERING TIME: Summer.
DESCRIPTION: Pseudobulbs compressed, grooved, clavate, up to 20cm (8″) long. Leaf apical, elliptic-ovate, about 23cm (9″) long. Flowers large, showy, up to 17cm (6¾″) across.

Cattleya gaskelliana

Cattleya granulosa var. *schofieldiana*

COMMON NAME: None.
COLOUR: Flowers olive-green, speckled with maroon. Labellum white, marked with purple.
SIZE: Growing up to 60cm (24″) high.
CLIMATE: Intermediate.
DISTRIBUTION: Native to Brazil.
FLOWERING TIME: Autumn to early winter.
DESCRIPTION: Pseudobulbs compressed, elongate, up to 60cm (24″) high. Leaves oblong-lanceolate, up to 18cm (7″) long. Inflorescence short, terminal. Flower large, showy, fragrant, up to 15cm (6″) across. Labellum tri-lobed.

Cattleya intermedia var. *acquinii*

Cattleya labiata

Cattleya labiata

COMMON NAME: None.
COLOUR: Flowers pale to rose pink. Labellum purple-magenta, throat yellow.
SIZE: Growing up to 55cm (22″) high.
CLIMATE: Intermediate.
DISTRIBUTION: Native to eastern Brazil.
FLOWERING TIME: Spring to summer.
DESCRIPTION: Pseudobulbs club-shaped, up to 30cm (12″) high. Leaf solitary, up to 25cm (10″) long. Flowers up to 12.5cm (5″) across. A highly variable species, comprising of some seventeen variants; but horticulturally these varieties are treated as species: *C. dowiana, C. eldorado, C. gaskelliana, C. lueddemanniana, C. mendelii, C. mossiae, C. percivaliana, C. quadricolor, C. rex, C. trianaei, C. wageneri, C. warneri, C. warscewiczii.*

Cattleya intermedia var. acquinii

COMMON NAME: None.
COLOUR: Flowers pale mauve to white. Labellum and petal tips splashed purple.
SIZE: Growing up to 40cm (16″) high.
CLIMATE: Intermediate.
DISTRIBUTION: Native to Brazil, Paraguay and Uruguay. An epiphyte or lithophyte growing by streams or the sea.
FLOWERING TIME: Spring to summer.
DESCRIPTION: Pseudobulbs cylindrical up to 40cm (16″) high. Leaves ovate-oblong up to 15cm (6″) long. Inflorescence terminal up to 25cm (10″) long. Flowers up to 12.5cm (5″) across.

Cattleya loddigesii

Cattleya intermedia var. *alba*

Cattleya intermedia var. alba

COMMON NAME: None.
COLOUR: Flower is pure white.
SIZE: Growing up to 40cm (16″) high.
CLIMATE: Intermediate.
DISTRIBUTION: Native to Paraguay. Similar in habitat to the type form.
FLOWERING TIME: Spring to summer.
DESCRIPTION: Same as *C. intermedia* var. *acquinii* except for white colour.

Cattleya loddigesii

COMMON NAME: None.
COLOUR: Flowers lilac-pink. Labellum purple.
SIZE: Thickened stems up to 30cm (12″) high.
CLIMATE: Intermediate.
DISTRIBUTION: Native to southern Brazil and Paraguay.
FLOWERING TIME: Autumn to early spring.
DESCRIPTION: An epiphytic or lithophytic species. Pseudobulbs cylindrical, up to 30cm (11¾″) high. Leaves oblong-elliptic up to 12.5cm (5″) long. Flowers up to 10cm (4″) across.

Cattleya loddigesii var. harrisoniana

COMMON NAME: None.
COLOUR: Labellum disc yellow to yellow-orange.
SIZE: Growing up to 40cm (16").
CLIMATE: Intermediate.
DISTRIBUTION: Native to Brazil.
FLOWERING TIME: Autumn to early spring.
DESCRIPTION: The variety differs from the type by having longer, slender canes. Labellum disc corrugated, mid-lobe side margins are reflexed.

Cattleya luteola

Cattleya luteola

COMMON NAME: None.
COLOUR: Flowers yellow to yellow-green. Labellum marked and spotted dark red.
SIZE: Growing up to 30cm (12") high.
CLIMATE: Intermediate.
DISTRIBUTION: Native to Peru (Amazon Basin), Bolivia, Brazil and Ecuador.
FLOWERING TIME: Summer.
DESCRIPTION: A dwarf epiphyte. Pseudobulbs clavate, ellipsoid, up to 15cm (6") high. Leaves oblong-elliptic, emarginate, up to 17.5cm (7") long. Inflorescence terminal. Flowers small.

Cattleya loddigesii var. *harrisoniana*

Cattleya maxima

COMMON NAME: None.
COLOUR: Flowers rose-lilac. Labellum pink, purple veined.
SIZE: Growing up to 60cm (24") high.
CLIMATE: Intermediate.
DISTRIBUTION: Native to Peru, Ecuador and Colombia.
FLOWERING TIME: Autumn to winter.
DESCRIPTION: Pseudobulbs almost cylindrical, up to 40cm (16") high. Leaves solitary, oblong, strap-like, up to 25cm (10") long. Inflorescence terminal. Flowers large and showy.

Cattleya maxima

Cattleya skinneri

COMMON NAME: None.
COLOUR: Flowers rose-purple. Labellum throat cream.
SIZE: Growing up to 55cm (22") high.
CLIMATE: Intermediate.
DISTRIBUTION: Native to Costa Rica, Mexico, Belize, Guatemala, Honduras and Panama. An epiphyte or lithophyte, growing in forest and on granite slopes. Altitude 1250m (4100').
FLOWERING TIME: Early spring.
DESCRIPTION: The national flower of Costa Rica. Pseudobulbs compressed, clavate, up to 35cm (14") high. Leaves oblong-elliptic, up to 20cm (8") long. Flowers large and showy.

Cattleya skinneri

Cattleya skinneri var. alba

COMMON NAME: None.
COLOUR: Flowers white.
SIZE: As type form.
CLIMATE: Intermediate.
DISTRIBUTION: Native to Costa Rica. Habitat as type form.
FLOWERING TIME: As type form.
DESCRIPTION: As type form, except for flower colour.

Cattleya skinneri (alba form)

Cattleya trianaei

COMMON NAME: None.
COLOUR: Flower colour variable from white, pink-white to amethyst-purple. Mid-lobe of labellum unusually purple-crimson, but may be as pale as the rest of the floral segments. Disc orange-yellow, may be veined with white or lilac.
SIZE: Growing up to 50cm (20″) high.
CLIMATE: Intermediate.
DISTRIBUTION: Native to Colombia.
FLOWERING TIME: Summer.
DESCRIPTION: Pseudobulbs clavate, up to 25cm (10″) high. Leaf solitary, oblong, up to 25cm (10″) long. Flowers 20cm (8″) across.

Cattleya violacea

COMMON NAME: None.
COLOUR: Flowers red-purple, may be fused with white. Labellum red-purple, disc white, blotched and streaked white on both sides.
SIZE: Growing up to 40cm (16″) high.
CLIMATE: Intermediate.
DISTRIBUTION: Native to Colombia, Venezuela, Guyana, Peru and Brazil.
FLOWERING TIME: Winter.
DESCRIPTION: Pseudobulbs clavate, furrowed with age, up to 25cm (10″) long. Leaves oblong-ovate, sometimes flushed red, up to 15cm (6″) long. Fragrant flowers up to 12.5cm (5″) across.

Cattleya walkeriana

Cattleya walkeriana var. *alba*

COMMON NAME: None.
COLOUR: Flowers white.
SIZE: Growing up to 20cm (8″) high.
CLIMATE: Intermediate.
DISTRIBUTION: Native to Brazil. Habitat similar to the type form.
FLOWERING TIME: Spring.
DESCRIPTION: As for type form, except for flower colour.

Cattleya trianaei

Cattleya walkeriana

COMMON NAME: None.
COLOUR: Flowers rose-purple to pale hues.
SIZE: Growing up to 20cm (8″) high.
CLIMATE: Intermediate.
DISTRIBUTION: Native to Brazil. Growing on trees or rocks by streams.
FLOWERING TIME: Spring.
DESCRIPTION: Small creeping epiphyte or lithophyte. Pseudobulbs short, bulbous, 12.5cm (5″) high. Leaves elliptic or ovate up to 12.5cm (5″) long. Flowers up to 10cm (4″) across.

Cattleya violacea

Cattleya walkeriana (alba form)

CERATOSTYLIS
(se-rat-oh-sty-lis)

Ceratostylis from the Gk *keras* or *kerato* (horn) *stylis* (style) with reference to the fleshy horn-like appearance of the column. This is a genus of about sixty species distributed through India, South-east Asia, the Philippines, Indonesia and the Pacific Islands. A small epiphytic herb, many species resemble a small or large tuft of grass. The roots are fibrous. Leaves are fleshy or coriaceous or sub-terete. Flowers are small and solitary. Sepals are erect. Petals are narrower. The labellum is short, erect, fleshy, and is joined to the column by a long claw.

Culture: Compost in a shallow basket. It requires moderate shade, frequent watering and humid conditions. Plants must never be left dry for too long. Plants flower frequently.

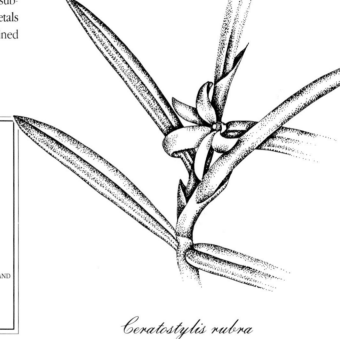

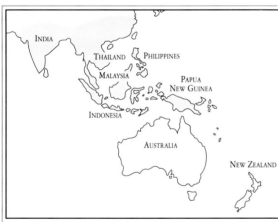

Ceratostylis rubra

Ceratostylis rubra

COMMON NAME: None.
COLOUR: Flowers red-brown. Labellum yellow-cream.
SIZE: Growing up to 12.5cm (5″) high.
CLIMATE: Warm.
DISTRIBUTION: Native to the Philippines.
FLOWERING TIME: Throughout the year.
DESCRIPTION: Stems are clustered and clothed by papery bracts. Leaves are grooved, semi-terete, up to 12.5cm (5″) long. Flowers measure approximately 2.5cm (1″) across.

Ceratostylis rubra

CHYSIS
(kye-sis)

Chysis from the Gk *chysis* (melting) with reference to the appearance of the pollinia after self-fertilisation. This small genus of about six species is spread throughout tropical America from Mexico, south to Venezuela and Peru. It is an epiphytic herb. Pseudobulbs are prominent, fleshy, club-shaped, pendulous and are covered by scarious sheaths. It has several leaves near apex, which are distichous, folded and eventually deciduous. Inflorescence has short raceme from nodes of old pseudobulbs produced with new growth. Flowers are showy, large, long-lived, and highly fragrant or aromatic. Sepals and petals are sub-equal, concave, large, free and spreading. The labellum is tri-lobed, erect and complexly excavated. Disc nervous with red-tipped calli. Column is erect and two winged; eight waxy pollinia.

Culture: Compost and grow in baskets. Plants require shade, humidity, warmth and water. When leaves fall at the end of growth, keep cooler and almost dry.

Chysis aurea

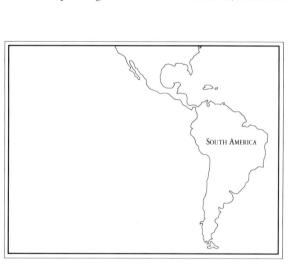

SOUTH AMERICA

Chysis aurea

Chysis aurea

COMMON NAME: None.

COLOUR: Flowers lemon, marked with brown-maroon.

SIZE: An arching to pendulous epiphyte 75cm (30″) long.

CLIMATE: Intermediate to warm.

DISTRIBUTION: Native to Venezuela, Colombia, Peru, Mexico to Panama. Up to 1700m (5777′) in altitude.

FLOWERING TIME: Mostly summer.

DESCRIPTION: Pseudobulbs are compressed, clavate, fusiform, up to 45cm (18″) long. Leaves are undulate, oblong-lanceolate, up to 45cm (18″) long. Flowers measure 7.5cm (3″) across.

CIRRHOPETALUM
(see-row-pet-a-lum)

Cirrhopetalum possibly from the Gk *kirrhos* (tawny-orange or pale yellow) *petalon* (petal) with reference to the flower colour; more likely it originates from the Latin *cirrus* (tendril or fringe) and refers to the curled sepals and petal fringe of some species. This genus of about thirty species spreads from India across tropical South-east Asia to Papua New Guinea and Pacific Islands, also to Africa and Madagascar. The genus is easily recognised by the articulate labellum on the column foot. The genus comprises creeping epiphytes of various sized plants. Pseudobulbs are spaced along creeping rhizomes. The leaf is apical and solitary. Inflorescence is erect and umbellate. Flowers one to many and are showy. The dorsal sepal is much shorter than the lateral sepals; the sepals converge. Petals are often fringed with hairs. The labellum is very small and mobile on stipe.

Culture: As for *Bulbophyllum*. Compost. Best grown in a basket or shallow pan. The plant has a creeping habit, so will spread while growing. It requires plenty of water, but less once the pseudobulbs have developed. The plant needs a shady, humid situation.

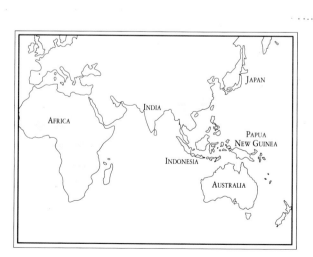

Cirrhopetalum picturatum

Cirrhopetalum fascinator

COMMON NAME: None.
COLOUR: Flower is a blend of green to red, spotted purple. Lateral sepal has numerous basal red warts.
SIZE: Growing up to 12.5cm (5″) high.
CLIMATE: Intermediate to warm.
DISTRIBUTION: Native to Vietnam and Laos.
FLOWERING TIME: Autumn.
DESCRIPTION: Pseudobulbs glabrous, shiny and 2.5cm (1″) high. Solitary leaf is narrow-elliptic, up to 10cm (4″) long. Solitary flower is 23cm (9″) long. Lateral sepals are connate.

Cirrhopetalum ornatissimum

Cirrhopetalum fascinator

Cirrhopetalum graveolens syn. Bulbophyllum graveolens

COMMON NAME: None.
COLOUR: Flowers are olive-green. Labellum scarlet.
SIZE: Growing up to 30cm (12″) high.
CLIMATE: Hot.
DISTRIBUTION: Native to Papua New Guinea.
FLOWERING TIME: Spring.
DESCRIPTION: Pseudobulbs borne on creeping rhizome, tetragonal, up to 10cm (4″) high. Leaves lanceolate-spathulate, up to 25cm (10″) long. Flower scape 17cm (7″) long. Flowers terminal in carousel arrangement, showy, up to 10cm (4″) long.

Cirrhopetalum ornatissimum

COMMON NAME: None.
COLOUR: Flowers and labellum are maroon.
SIZE: Growing up to 17.5cm (7″) high.
CLIMATE: Intermediate to warm.
DISTRIBUTION: Native to Borneo, Sumatra and Peninsula Malaysia.
FLOWERING TIME: Autumn to early winter.
DESCRIPTION: Pseudobulbs tetragonal, ovoid, 3.5cm (1½″) high on creeping rhizome, about 5cm (2″) apart. Leaf solitary, oblong, up to 15cm (6″) long. Inflorescence apical, fan-shape, umbel, with three to five blooms. Flowers are fragrant. Lateral sepals connate, tips free.

Cirrhopetalum graveolens syn. *Bulbophyllum graveolens*

Cirrhopetalum pulchrum

Cirrhopetalum pulchrum

COMMON NAME: None.
COLOUR: Flowers are white, veined with deep maroon.
SIZE: Growing up to 15cm (6″) high.
CLIMATE: Intermediate.
DISTRIBUTION: Native to India.
FLOWERING TIME: Autumn.
DESCRIPTION: Pseudobulbs are tetragonal, clustered on a creeping rhizome, 2.5cm (1″) high. Leaves apical, solitary, lanceolate to oblong, up to 15cm (6″) long. Inflorescence basal, up to 15cm (6″) long, flowers umbels. Flowers grow up to 5cm (2″) across.

COCHLEANTHES
(kok-lee-an-theez)

Cochleanthes from the Gk *kochlias* (spiral shell) *anthos* (flower) with reference to the appearance of the flower. This is a genus of about ten species widely spread throughout the tropical Americas. This genus is placed by many authors in the *Zygopetalum* genera. We feel it is readily distinguishable by the structure of the column foot and the semi-circular plate-like callus at the base of the column. It is a pseudobulbless epiphytic orchid with numerous distichous leaves. The inflorescence is short. Flowers are large, showy, fleshy, coloured white to blue, and are very aromatic. Sepals and petals are free, spreading, similar, with lateral sepals joined to base of column. The labellum is tri-lobed or entire, the claw is very short, with transverse semi-circular plate-like fleshy callus, lateral lobes surrounding column.

Culture: Compost. As for *Zygopetalum* and *Chondrorhyncha.* Treat as a terrestrial. Plant in large, well-drained pots. It requires humid conditions, shade, plenty of water while growing, but much less water required once bulbs are fully grown.

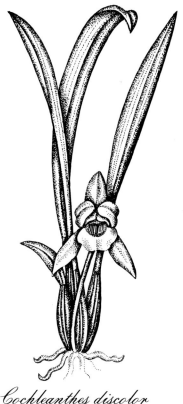

Cochleanthes discolor

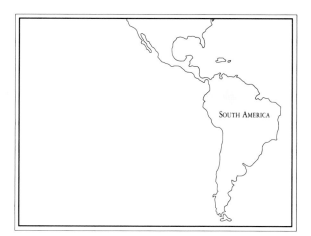

SOUTH AMERICA

Cochleanthes candida

COMMON NAME: None.
COLOUR: Flower white. Labellum veined purple.
SIZE: Growing up to 20cm (8″) long.
CLIMATE: Intermediate to warm.
DISTRIBUTION: Native to Cuba, Honduras, Panama and Venezuela.
FLOWERING TIME: Winter.
DESCRIPTION: A tufted epiphytic plant. Leaves are strap-shaped, up to 20cm (8″) long. Inflorescence short, 7.5cm (3″) long. Flowers solitary, 3.5cm (1½″) across.

Cochleanthes candida

COELEOPSIS
(see-lee-op-sis)

Coeleopsis from the Gk *koilos* (hollow) *opsis* (likened to) with reference to the flowers not opening fully. This single species genus from Costa Rica and Panama was first described by Reinhenbach in 1872, who placed it in the subtribe Gongorinae. Though closely allied to *Eriopsis*, *Coeliopsis* is easily distinguished by the noticeable difference in vegetation appearance.

Coeliopsis is rare in the field and very rare in collections. Very little is known of its genetic compatibility with allied genera as very few breeders have taken *Coeliopsis* in hand. It is very similar in vegetative habit to *Stanhopea*. It is epiphytic. Flower spike turns downward, inflorescences are pendulous, with a cluster of small white flowers.

Culture: Use a moisture-retaining compost in a hanging basket. As for *Stanhopea*. Water frequently. Use 1:1:1 ratio fertiliser monthly. It requires high humidity and shade.

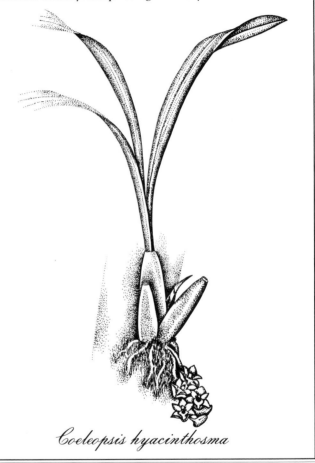

Coeleopsis hyacinthosma

SOUTH AMERICA

Coeleopsis hyacinthosma

COMMON NAME: None.
COLOUR: Flowers white. Labellum throat yellow.
SIZE: Growing up to 60cm (24″) high.
CLIMATE: Intermediate to warm.
DISTRIBUTION: Native to Panama and Costa Rica.
FLOWERING TIME: Spring.
DESCRIPTION: A rare epiphytic plant. Pseudobulbs elongate-ovoid, may be wrinkled, up to 10cm (4″) high. Leaves plicate, ribbed, narrow-lanceolate, up to 60cm (2′) long. Inflorescence 8cm (3″) long, basal, borne from the pseudobulbs, pushing through the compost, in habit of *Stanhopea*. Flowers are borne in a cluster, are fragrant, waxy, and grow up to 2.5cm (1″) across.

Coeleopsis hyacinthosma

COELOGYNE

(see-loj-in-ee)

Coelogyne from the Gk *koilos* (hollow) *gyne* (female) with reference to the deep stigmatic cavity. This genus of about 120 species extends from the Himalayas, through China, the Philippines, Indonesia, Papua New Guinea to the Pacific Islands. It is an epiphytic plant. Pseudobulbs are often angular on creeping rhizomes, clustered or at intervals, with one to four apical leaves. Leaves are erect, rigid, coriaceous, and often plicate. Inflorescence is erect, with an arching or pendulous raceme, and either one to two or multiflorous. Flowers are large, fragrant, in various colours, white-brown, yellow or green with blotching of yellow, brown and/or to almost black. Sepals are free, concave, larger than petals, spreading and joined to column foot. Petals are free, and either similar in shape to the sepals or much narrower. The labellum is tri-lobed, with lateral lobes erect, guarding the column; the mid-lobe is concave at base with lamina spreading. The disc has longitudinal veins.

Culture: Compost. Plant in basket or on tree-fern fibre slabs. Because of the great variance of temperature requirements of the various species, the genus can be divided in three groups of species: (a) Those that require warm conditions at all times. These grow continuously and do not need a rest period; (b) Those needing a more intermediate temperature, and requiring a short rest period, and; (c) Those from high altitudes which thrive in cooler climates require cool greenhouse conditions. Difficulties do arise with this group, but with attention to details of culture most problems can be overcome.

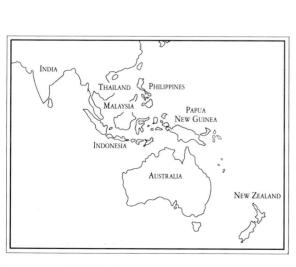

Coelogyne virescens

Coelogyne confusa

COMMON NAME: None.
COLOUR: Flowers yellowish-green. Labellum whitish-green with orange markings.
SIZE: Growing up to 25cm (10″) high.
CLIMATE: Intermediate to warm.
DISTRIBUTION: Native to the Himalayas, Java, the Philippines and found rarely on the Camigiun Island.
FLOWERING TIME: Spring.
DESCRIPTION: An epiphytic or lithophytic plant. Pseudobulbs conical, up to 7.5cm (3″) high. Leaves in pairs, elliptic-lanceolate, acuminate, up to 22cm (9″) long. Inflorescence up to 25cm (10″) long. Flowers about 4cm (1½″) across.

Coelogyne confusa

Coelogyne dayana

COMMON NAME: None.
COLOUR: Flowers pale yellow. Labellum marked with brown fringed ridges. Lateral lobes brown.
SIZE: Growing up to 1.2m (4′) high.
CLIMATE: Warm.
DISTRIBUTION: Native to Borneo.
FLOWERING TIME: Spring and summer.
DESCRIPTION: Pseudobulbs 12 to 25cm (5 to 10″) long. Leaves 60 to 108cm (24 to 43″) long. Flower scape pendulous, long with numerous blooms.

Coelogyne elata

COMMON NAME: None.
COLOUR: Flowers white. Labellum central band yellow.
SIZE: Growing up to 45cm (18″) high.
CLIMATE: Cool to intermediate.
DISTRIBUTION: Native to the Himalayas. Grows at high altitudes.
FLOWERING TIME: Spring.
DESCRIPTION: Pseudobulbs cylindrical, angular, up to 15cm (6″) high. Leaves narrow-lanceolate, up to 30cm (12″) long. Inflorescence terminal, arching 60cm (24″) high. Flowers fragrant, 3.5cm (1½″) across.

Coelogyne elata

Coelogyne cristata

COMMON NAME: None.
COLOUR: Flowers white. Labellum keel yellow.
SIZE: Growing up to 35cm (14″) high.
CLIMATE: Cool.
DISTRIBUTION: Native to the Himalayas. Altitude 1500 to 2100m (4921 to 7000′).
FLOWERING TIME: Winter to spring.
DESCRIPTION: Pseudobulbs oblong, up to 6.3cm (2½″) high. Leaves linear-lanceolate, undulate, up to 30cm (12″) long. Inflorescence arching or pendulous. Flowers fragrant, up to 10cm (4″) across.

Coelogyne cristata

Coelogyne lamellata

COMMON NAME: None.
COLOUR: Flowers green. Labellum white heavily marked orange to brown.
SIZE: Growing up to 30cm (12″) high.
CLIMATE: Warm.
DISTRIBUTION: Native to New Hebrides and Fiji.
FLOWERING TIME: Summer.
DESCRIPTION: Pseudobulbs elongate-conical, furrowed when mature. Leaves broad-lanceolate, plicate, up to 30cm (12″) long. Inflorescence short and produced from immature growth. Flowers are shy openers, up to 5cm (2″) across.

Coelogyne dayana

Coelogyne lamellata

Coelogyne marmorata syn. *C. zahlbructnerae*

Coelogyne merrillii

COMMON NAME: None.
COLOUR: Flowers white to cream. Labellum throat white, heavily marked red-brown.
SIZE: Growing up to 40cm (16") high.
CLIMATE: Intermediate.
DISTRIBUTION: Native to the Philippines.
FLOWERING TIME: Autumn.
DESCRIPTION: Pseudobulbs oblong-ovoid, up to 12.5cm (5") high, deeply furrowed with age. Leaves ribbed, lanceolate, up to 20cm (12") long. Inflorescence produced from immature growth, flattened arching to 30cm (12") long. Flowers spreading up to 10cm (4") across.

Coelogyne ovalis

Coelogyne marmorata syn. C. zahlbructnerae

COMMON NAME: None.
COLOUR: Flowers white and yellow. Labellum spotted brown.
SIZE: Grows up to 50cm (20") high.
CLIMATE: Intermediate.
DISTRIBUTION: Native to the Philippines, Himalayas; growing in mountain areas.
FLOWERING TIME: Spring.
DESCRIPTION: Pseudobulbs clustered elongate up to 10cm (4") high. Leaves lanceolate-oblong, up to 40cm (16") long. Inflorescence shorter than the leaves, bearing three to eight flowers. Flowers up to 6.5cm (2½") across.

Coelogyne merrillii

Coelogyne ochracea

COMMON NAME: None.
COLOUR: Flowers white with yellow, orange and brown markings.
SIZE: Growing up to 25cm (10") high.
CLIMATE: Cool to intermediate.
DISTRIBUTION: Native to the Himalayas. High elevations.
FLOWERING TIME: Autumn.
DESCRIPTION: Pseudobulbs small and cylindrical. Leaves in pairs, narrow-lanceolate, up to 20cm (8") long. Numerous flowers.

Coelogyne ovalis

COMMON NAME: None.
COLOUR: Flowers soft buff-brown. Labellum with darker brown markings.
SIZE: Growing up to 25cm (10") high.
CLIMATE: Cool.
DISTRIBUTION: Native to the Himalayas, Thailand, Tibet, China, Assam and Burma. Medium altitudes.
FLOWERING TIME: Summer.
DESCRIPTION: Pseudobulbs borne on a creeping elongated rhizome, ovoid-fusiform, up to 15cm (6") high. Leaves narrow-elliptic, up to 15cm (6") long. Flowers up to 5cm (2") across.

Coelogyne ochracea

Coelogyne pandurata

COMMON NAME: Black orchid.
COLOUR: Petals and sepals emerald green. Labellum veined with black markings on green background. Mid-lobe fringed with black warts.
SIZE: Growing up to 90cm (36") high.
CLIMATE: Warm to hot.
DISTRIBUTION: This tropical species is native to the Philippines, Sumatra, Burma, China, northern India, Malaysia, Borneo and Indonesia.
FLOWERING TIME: Summer.
DESCRIPTION: Pseudobulbs compressed, oblong or sub-orbicular, 7.5 to 12.5cm (3 to 5") long, well spaced on short rhizome. Leaves lanceolate, up to 20 to 45cm (8 to 18") long. Inflorescence few-flowered, 15 to 30cm (6 to 12") long. Flowers fragrant, bright green, 10 to 12.5cm (4 to 5") across. Labellum tri-lobed, side lobes small, mid-lobe panduriform, cordate at base, with two high ridges, margins crisp-undulate.

Coelogyne pandurata

Coelogyne rochussenii

COMMON NAME: None.
COLOUR: Flowers lemon-green. Labellum marked with yellow and brown.
SIZE: Growing up to 50cm (20″) high.
CLIMATE: Warm.
DISTRIBUTION: Native to Borneo, the Philippines, Thailand Peninsula, Peninsula Malaysia, Sumatra and Java.
FLOWERING TIME: Autumn.
DESCRIPTION: Pseudobulbs cylindrical ribbed, up to 20cm (8″) high. Leaves oval-elliptic, up to 30cm (12″) long. Numerous fragrant flowers, up to 3.7cm (1½″) across, borne on a pendulous inflorescence.

Coelogyne rochussenii

Coelogyne rossiana

COMMON NAME: None.
COLOUR: Flowers white. Labellum yellow with brown markings.
SIZE: Growing up to 30cm (12″) high.
CLIMATE: Intermediate.
DISTRIBUTION: Native to Burma.
FLOWERING TIME: Autumn.
DESCRIPTION: Pseudobulbs ovoid, about 10cm (4″) high. Leaves oval-elliptic, up to 30cm (12″) long. Flowers about 2.5cm (1″) across.

Coelogyne rossiana

Coelogyne speciosa

COMMON NAME: None.
COLOUR: Flowers yellowish brown. Labellum marked with dark brown-black.
SIZE: Growing up to 32.5cm (13″) high.
CLIMATE: Intermediate to warm.
DISTRIBUTION: Native to Borneo, Java, Malaysia, Sumatra and Lesser Sunda Islands.
FLOWERING TIME: Throughout the year.
DESCRIPTION: Pseudobulbs ovoid up to 7.5cm (3″) high. Leaves elliptic, 25cm (10″) long. Flowers have a musk fragrance, grow about 7.5cm (3″) across. Labellum mid-lobe margins fringed.

Coelogyne tomentosa

Coelogyne tomentosa

COMMON NAME: None.
COLOUR: Flowers light orange or salmon. Labellum yellow streaked with brown.
SIZE: Growing up to 30cm (12″) high.
CLIMATE: Intermediate to warm.
DISTRIBUTION: Native to Borneo, Malaysia, Thailand, Sumatra and Java.
FLOWERING TIME: Spring.
DESCRIPTION: Pseudobulbs ovoid-conical, up to 5cm (2″) high. Leaves lanceolate, up to 30cm (12″) long. Flowers have musk fragrance and are about 5cm (2″) across.

Coelogyne speciosa

Coelogyne virescens

COMMON NAME: None.
COLOUR: Flower colour variable from cream to light green. Labellum cream to light green with black-brown markings.
SIZE: Epiphytic plant, up to 25cm (10″) high.
CLIMATE: Cool.
DISTRIBUTION: Native to India, Burma, Northern Thailand and Indo-China; growing at elevations up to 1000m (3300′).
FLOWERING TIME: Spring.
DESCRIPTION: Pseudobulbs grooved, oblong-tetragonal, borne on a creeping stem, up to 10cm (4″) high. Leaves in pairs, linear-lanceolate, up to 20cm (8″) long. Inflorescence borne from the apex of the immature pseudobulbs, up to 15cm (6″) long. Flowers up to 4cm (1½″) across.

Coelogyne virescens

CORYANTHES

(ko-ree-an-theez)

Coryanthes from the Gk *cory(s)* (a helmet or cap), *anthos* (a flower) meaning helmet flower with reference to the labellum. It is often referred to as the Bucket Orchid. This small genus of about twenty species is an extraordinary and fascinating epiphytic orchid; it ranges from British Honduras and Guatemala to Peru and Brazil. The stems are truncate, thickened into fleshy deeply-grooved pseudobulbs. Leaves are apical, plicate, acuminate or acute, with the base narrowed into the petiole. Inflorescence is pendulous, rising from the base of the pseudobulb; it is loosely racemose. The fleshy flowers are medium to large, with segments spreading. They are unusual in their complexity of formation, and remarkable for their most unusual pollination mechanism. Sepals are free or adnate to column, and are fragile. The dorsal sepal is small, and lateral sepals are larger and oblique. Petals are narrower than the sepals. The labellum cannot be explained in a few words (refer to illustration on page 25 for detail). The whole flower is of a most complicated structure and design.

In 1916, Rudolf Schlechter attempted to subdivide *Coryanthes* into two groups (a) *Eu-coryanthes*: those with a smooth mesochile and (b) *Lamellunguis*: those with a corrugated mesochile. However, with the discovery of new species it was noted that variations occurred within species; for example, *Coryanthes boyi* from Rio Nanay in Peru has forms with both smooth and corrugated mesochiles.

Coryanthes are exceedingly rare in orchid collections; their amazing appearance makes them most desirable, but their ecology makes cultivation difficult.

Coryanthes usually occurs as a major partner in the myrmecophilous habitat, in the nests of ants of *Camponotus* and *Azteca* genera, and often in association with orange- or purple-coloured tufted *Epidendrum*. It is not uncommon to find in the wild as many as four or five species of *Coryanthes* in flower growing in different parts of the same large ant nest. Interbreeding does not occur since each species is exceedingly pollinator-specific. The pollinator of *Coryanthes macrantha* is the *Eulaema signulata*. *Coryanthes trifoliata's* pollinator is the bee *Englossa ignita*; *Coryanthes rodrigurezii* (*C. boyi*) is pollinated by the bee *Englossa superba*; *Coryanthes maculata* is pollinated by bees of *Englossa azureoviridis*. *Coryanthes leucocorys* attracts bees of *Englossa ignita* and bees of *Eulaema marianna*, but *Englossa ignita* is too small and passes under the anther without dislodging the pollen. Possibly the specific pollinators are attracted by the different odors of the various species of *Coryanthes.*

The *Coryanthes* genus is possibly the most complex of Orchidaceae. The flower is profoundly structured to attract insects and assure pollination. The flowers last but several days. *Hymenopterous* insects are attracted to the large brightly coloured flowers by a strong fragrant secretion on the inner margins of the epichile. The large sepals soon wither leaving an unobstructed path to the intricate and marvellous labellum, unique in Orchidaceae. The apex of the apical-lobe or epichile resembles a waxy cup or a helmet inverted, the front of which is prolonged into a spout-like channel just below the sharply reflexed apex of the column, with its anther and stigma exposed to any insect making its way out of the labellum before taking flight. Above the cup, at the base of the column are two fleshy glands, these secrete a clear liquid, drop-by-drop filling the cup to the level of the apical spout-like channel. On the fully open flower, bees gather to feed on the secretions of the inner margins of the cup. Any bee losing its footing plunges into the liquid. Because of wet wings, the bee's only exit is through the narrow channel just below the stigma and the anther; thus the first bee through, leaves with the pollinia firmly attached to its back and ready to be inserted in the stigma of another flower.

Coryanthes maculata of Panama is reported to grow in

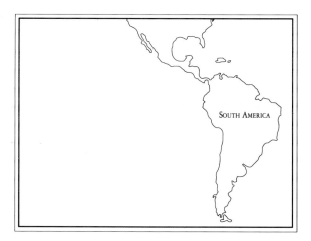

SOUTH AMERICA

ant nests at the top of trees in association with *Epidendrum imatophyllum*, protected by belligerent ants capable of inflicting burning painful bites, making collection and transportation a very painful project. *Coryanthes* do not thrive long in cultivation without the essential element supplied in their natural association with ants and *Epidendrum* sp. in the wild.

Dr J.A. Fowlic collected ant nests along the Rio Nanay in Peru on which *Coryanthes* grow and found that they were loaded with formic acid. He then soaked material from these ants' nests and found that the water squeezed from them had a pH of 3; therefore, an exceedingly acid medium is essential for successful cultivation of *Coryanthes*. He also found that *Coryanthes* thrive when potted in 'Palco' wool and kept exceedingly wet. 'Palco' wool is manufactured from the bark of Redwood trees and has a pH of 3.

On the Rio Nanay in Peru where the Amazon floods its banks regularly, the trees stand for part of the year in about a metre (a few feet) of water. In the 'dry' the Amazon falls by about 6 metres (20 feet) leaving the trees standing in mud with a constant humidity close to 100 per cent and a temperature above 32°C (90°F). Unfortunately, these conditions of high temperature, high humidity and excessive moisture do not necessarily guarantee success in private cultivation.

Culture: Compost, in baskets. The plants require humidity, shade, with special attention to the essential element, formic acid which is supplied by ants.

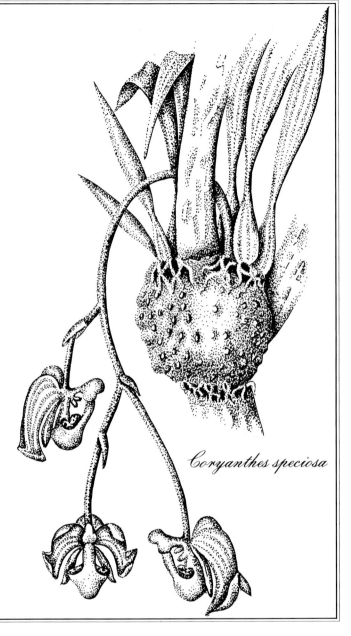

Coryanthes speciosa

Coryanthes leucocorys

Coryanthes leucocorys

COMMON NAME: Bucket Orchid.
COLOUR: Flower sepals yellow-green to cream, marked and spotted pink-brown. Petals cream. Labellum, the hypochile white, and the bucket-like epichile pink-brown.
SIZE: Growing up to 30cm (12″) high.
CLIMATE: Warm to hot.
DISTRIBUTION: Native to Peru. Growing at elevations of up to 900m (3000′) in conditions of high humidity usually near water.
FLOWERING TIME: Autumn.
DESCRIPTION: Pseudobulbs oblong or ovoid, furrowed, up to 7.5cm (3″) high. Leaves lanceolate-elliptic, 25cm (10″) long. Flowers large. The fluid released by the faucet glands has a smell similar to liniment.

CORYBAS
(ko-rye-bas)

Corybas is named after one of the dancing priests of Phrygia. This genus of over forty species spreads over an area bounded by the Himalayas in the west, the Philippines in the north, the Polynesian Islands and New Zealand in the east and by eight Australian species in the south. This is a small terrestrial plant of great interest and unusual beauty. It has one or more small subterranean globular tubers. The solitary cordate leaf lies flat on the ground, the underside having a frost-like appearance, and often with a coloured stripe. Flowers are solitary, proportionately large—about 25mm (1″) diameter—fleshy and almost sessile. The dorsal sepal forms a helmet-like hood over the large labellum and the minute sepals and petals; this appearance gives rise to the common genus name—Helmet Orchids. The labellum is large, complex with various degrees of fringing.

Culture: As for *Caladenia*. Use light dressings of a mixture of damp forest leaf litter and forest humus. The plant requires plenty of shade and normal watering. With care, these plants can be maintained well beyond three or four years and with an increase in the size of the colony.

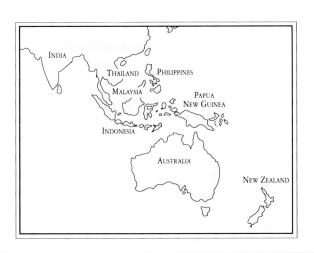

Corybas aconitiflorus

Corybas unguiculatus

Corybas unguiculatus

COMMON NAME: Small Helmet Orchid.
COLOUR: Flower red to purple to black.
SIZE: Small terrestrial plant up to 3cm (1¼″) high.
CLIMATE: Cool.
DISTRIBUTION: Native to the Australian southern coast and nearby mountains.
FLOWERING TIME: Autumn to spring.
DESCRIPTION: Leaf ovate-lanceolate, up to 4cm (1½″) long. Flower solitary about 2.5cm (1″) across. Lamina hooded. Flower resembles a helmet.

CRYPTOSTYLIS
(krip-toe-sty-lis)

Cryptostylis from the Gk *krypto* (covered, hidden), *stylo* (column) with reference to the inconspicuous style (filamentous connection) between stigma and ovary. This is a small genus of about twenty species of unusually attractive and seldom cultivated terrestrial orchids. It is distributed across the tropical lowlands of northern India, Sri Lanka, southern China, Taiwan, Indonesia, Papua New Guinea, the Pacific Islands, Fiji and Australia.

This is a terrestrial herb with a thick, fleshy, subterranean rhizome. Leaves are either absent, few or many, and may be spotted or darky veined. Flowers are many and terminal on a tall slender stem. Sepals and petals are spreading, with sepals longer than petals. The labellum is entire, broad, concave or convex. The column is short. The genus has a remarkable plant–insect relationship in which pseudo-copulation occurs between the male Ichneumon Wasp (*Lissopimpla semi-punctata*) and various species of the genus.

Culture: As for *Phaius*. Use a coarse compost in perfectly drained pots. Roots need to be kept moist, but not wet. It requires shade, cool conditions, and less water once growth is complete.

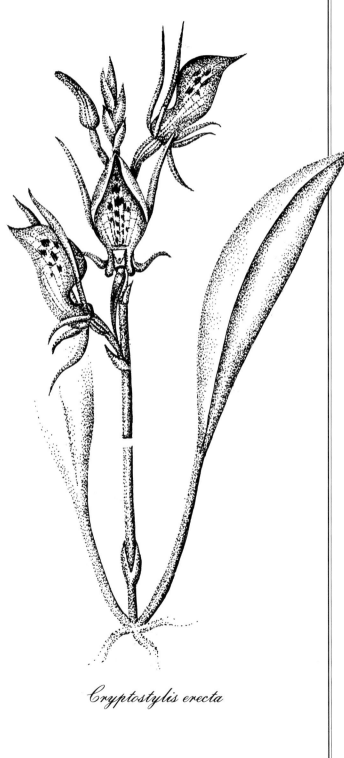

Cryptostylis erecta

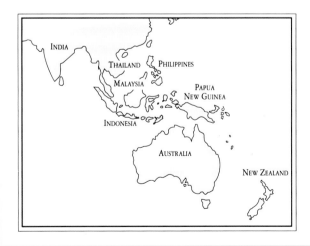

Cryptostylis erecta

COMMON NAME: Striped Hood Orchid.

COLOUR: Green petals and sepals. Labellum white, purple-veined.

SIZE: Small herbaceous terrestrial up to 45cm (18") high.

CLIMATE: Cool.

DISTRIBUTION: Native to the Australian eastern coast and nearby mountains; found in moist areas.

FLOWERING TIME: Summer.

DESCRIPTION: Leaves fleshy, broad to lanceolate, up to 15cm (6") long. Labellum forms a large striped hood.

Cryptostylis leptochila

Cryptostylis erecta

Cryptostylis leptochila

COMMON NAME: Small Tongue Orchid.

COLOUR: Sepals and petals green. Labellum red-pink with white and brown markings.

SIZE: An erect terrestrial, up to 40cm (16") high.

CLIMATE: Cool.

DISTRIBUTION: Native to Australian eastern highland forests.

FLOWERING TIME: Summer.

DESCRIPTION: Leaves few, radical, lanceolate, up to 10cm (4") long. Three to twelve flowers. Labellum red-pink, oblong, contracted at centre, covered with minute hairs, three rows of dome-shaped calli extend almost the full length.

Cryptostylis subulata

COMMON NAME: Slipper Orchid or Wasp Orchid.

COLOUR: Petals and sepals green. Labellum red with black stripe.

SIZE: Small terrestrial up to 45cm (18") high.

CLIMATE: Cool.

DISTRIBUTION: Native to eastern half of Australia; coastal mountains and swampy areas.

FLOWERING TIME: Spring to summer.

DESCRIPTION: Leaves broad-lanceolate. Labellum oblong, up to 3cm (1¼") long, margins rolled upwards.

Cryptostylis subulata

CYMBIDIUM

(sim-bid-ee-um)

Cymbidium from the Gk *kymbion* (boat-shaped) with reference to the boat-like shape of the labellum. This is a large genus of about three hundred species of which forty-nine species occur in China alone. The genus occurs throughout South-east Asia from Korea and Japan in the north, to Madagascar and the Himalayas in the west, across to the Philippines in the east and south to Indonesia, Papua New Guinea, the Pacific Islands and eastern Australia. *Cymbidium* is possibly the oldest recorded orchid. The species, *Cymbidium ensifolum*, was first discussed in the herbal section of an ancient Chinese botanical manuscript written during the Chin dynasty (221–202 BC): 'the thickened root, when boiled in water and mixed with fermented glutinous rice, is said to be good for curing stomach ache'. Confucius (551–479 BC) referred to *Cymbidium* as 'the king of fragrant flowers'.

Cymbidium can be either an epiphytic, lithophytic or, rarely, a terrestrial herb. Stems are short, reduced to pseudobulbs covered with sheathing bracts or leaves. Leaves are long, coriaceous and channelled. Inflorescence is either erect, arching or pendulous, with one to many flowers, and the raceme grows up to 1.2m (4′) long. Sepals and petals are almost equal, free, spreading or erect. The labellum is tri-lobed, attached to the base of the column; side-lobes are erect around the column, the mid-lobe is concave above, and the lamina is recurved. The disc has ridges or pubescent lamellae. The column is erect, incurved or semi-terete.

Culture: Compost. *Cymbidium* species can roughly be divided into two groups: (a) Those from the tropics which require warm conditions; and (b) Those from highlands or temperate climates which require cooler conditions, specifically cool nights, but not below 3°C (36°F). Much contradictory information has been written about the requirements of the genus. Most growers treat *Cymbidiums* as semi-terrestrials, so use a quick-draining, porous compost mixture of 3 to 5cm (1 to 2″) cubes of tree-fern fibre, sphagnum moss, dust-free sterilised bark and washed shell grit; and when fertilised monthly, plants give excellent results.

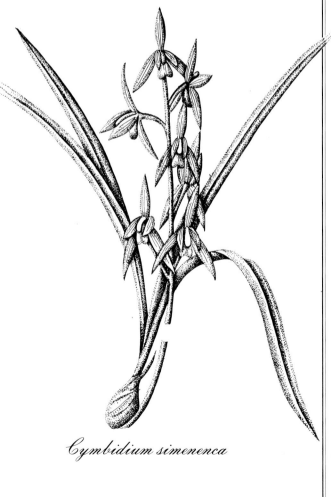

Cymbidium simenenca

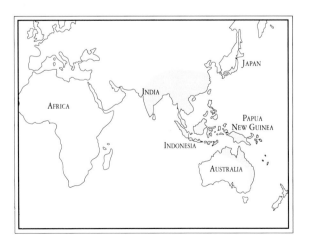

Cymbidium canaliculatum

COMMON NAME: White Tongued Cymbidium.
COLOUR: Flower colour variable, usually brown to green.
SIZE: An epiphytic plant, growing as high as 60cm (24″).
CLIMATE: Cool to hot.
DISTRIBUTION: Native to Australia. Sclerophyll forests, especially hollows of dead branches.
FLOWERING TIME: Spring.
DESCRIPTION: Pseudobulbs crowded, up to 20cm (8″) high. Leaves elongated, channelled, keeled, up to 60cm (24″) long. Inflorescence arching or pendulous. Numerous flowers, 3.5cm (1½″) across.

Cymbidium canaliculatum var. *sparksii*

Cymbidium canaliculatum

Cymbidium canaliculatum var. sparksii

COMMON NAME: Black orchid.
COLOUR: Dark purple to chocolate-red.
SIZE: Grows up to 60cm (2′) high.
CLIMATE: Warm.
DISTRIBUTION: Native to Australia (north-eastern Queensland only).
FLOWERING TIME: Spring.
DESCRIPTION: Same as type, except this colour variety gives a black appearance from a distance.

Cymbidium devonianum

COMMON NAME: None.
COLOUR: Flowers variable, olive-green, spotted and streaked with red-brown and purple. Labellum purple with darker blotches.
SIZE: Growing up to 40cm (16″) high.
CLIMATE: Cool.
DISTRIBUTION: Native to Himalayas, Khasia Hills, India. Altitude up to 1600m (5249′).
FLOWERING TIME: Summer.
DESCRIPTION: An epiphytic or lithophytic plant. Pseudobulbs obscure, ovoid, 4cm (1½″) high. Leaves oblong to oblanceolate, up to 35cm (14″) long. Inflorescence pendulous, flowers numerous.

Cymbidium devonianum

Cymbidium eburneum

Cymbidium eburneum

COMMON NAME: Ivory Orchid.
COLOUR: Flowers white. Labellum marked with yellow.
SIZE: Growing up to 60cm (24″) high.
CLIMATE: Cool.
DISTRIBUTION: Native to the Himalayas, Sikkim, Khasi Hills, Nepal, Bhutan, China and Burma. Altitudes 300 to 1600m (1000 to 5250′).
FLOWERING TIME: Autumn.
DESCRIPTION: Pseudobulbs obscure, covered by leaf-bracts. Leaves linear strap-shaped, up to 60cm (24″) long. One to two fragrant flowers, 7.5cm (3″) across.

Cymbidium grandiflorum

Cymbidium grandiflorum

COMMON NAME: None.
COLOUR: Flowers green. Labellum yellow with lines and spots of red-purple.
SIZE: Growing up to 60cm (24″) high.
CLIMATE: Cool.
DISTRIBUTION: Native to Nepal, Sikkim, Bhutan.
FLOWERING TIME: Early winter.
DESCRIPTION: Pseudobulbs ovoid. Leaves strap-like, acute, approximately 60cm (2′) long. Inflorescence arching, up to 75cm (30″) long. Flowers fragrant, up to 12.5cm (5″) across.

Cymbidium siamensis

COMMON NAME: None.
COLOUR: Flowers cream to green with longitudinal lines. Labellum pale yellow to green with red blotches, column yellow.
SIZE: Growing up to 35cm (14″) high.
CLIMATE: Cool to intermediate.
DISTRIBUTION: Native to Thailand; growing at elevations of 300 to 750m (1000 to 2500′).
FLOWERING TIME: Autumn to winter.
DESCRIPTION: Leaves strap-shaped, up to 35cm (14″) long. Inflorescence basal, erect, up to 30cm (12″) high, few blooms. Flowers up to 5cm (2″) across.

Cymbidium siamensis

Cymbidium suave

Cymbidium suave

COMMON NAME: None.
COLOUR: Flowers variable in colour from yellow to green. Labellum with brown markings.
SIZE: Grows up to 90cm (36″) high.
CLIMATE: Cool.
DISTRIBUTION: Native to coastal eastern Australia.
FLOWERING TIME: Spring to early summer.
DESCRIPTION: Grass-like epiphyte growing in dead trees. Leaves long and slender. Arching to pendulous and showy raceme. Small flowers with a sweet fragrance.

Cymbidium tracyanum

COMMON NAME: None.
COLOUR: Flowers greenish-yellow, veined with red-brown. Labellum yellowish-cream, veined and spotted red-purple.
SIZE: Growing up to 90cm (36″) high.
CLIMATE: Cool.
DISTRIBUTION: Native to Burma.
FLOWERING TIME: Autumn.
DESCRIPTION: A showy epiphyte. Pseudobulbs compressed, up to 15cm (6″) high. Leaves linear, strap-shaped, up to 75cm (30″) long. Inflorescence up to 1.2m (4′) long, pendulous. Flowers up to 12.5cm (5″) across.

Cymbidium tracyanum

DENDROBIUM
(den-droe-be-um)

Dendrobium from the Gk *dendron* (a tree) *biss* ('life) with reference to the aerial existence of the species (life in a tree). This genus of some 1500 species is the second-largest genus in Orchidaceae, excelled in species numbers only by *Bulbophyllum.* The genus extends from Korea and Japan south through South-east Asia, west to the Himalayas, east into the Philippines, and south through Indonesia, the Pacific Islands, New Zealand and Australia, with the highest concentration of more than 150 species in Papua New Guinea. *Dendrobium* habitats range from the steaming tropical coastal jungles of Malaya to the wind- and snow-swept mountains of the Himalayas, with a tremendous diversity of both plant and flower structure. *Dendrobiums* may be divided into four groups: those whose stems are: (a) rhizomatous; (b) erect having many nodes; (c) erect having one or two nodes with rhizomes of many nodes, and (d) without rhizomes, the new stem growing from the base of the old stem and having many nodes.

This is a genus of sympodial epiphytes having an immense variation in vegetative characteristics. Rhizomes may be tufted or creeping. Stems are either tall, erect to 3m (10′), creeping, pendulous or reduced to small roundish pseudobulbs of 2.5mm (1″). The leaves are of various shapes and sizes, and are either apical or distichous along the stem, flat, thin, thick, terete, papery or coriaceous. Inflorescence is erect, arching or pendulous. The flowers are usually showy, but can be either small or large. Sepals are sub-equal, with lateral sepals obliquely dilated at base and joined to foot of column to form spur under labellum. Petals are similar to sepals and are as long or longer. The labellum is articulate at end of column foot, tri-lobed or entire, erect, concave near base, with margins extending into lateral lobes to embrace the column; the mid-lobe is recurved or spreading, and the lamina has longitudinal ridges. The column is winged or toothed.

Culture: Depends on the species you intend to grow. Grow according to natural habitat. Compost in pots for upright species, and in a basket or on a tree-fern fibre slab for the pendulous variety. Consult your local orchid society about the care and treatment of the particular species you are growing.

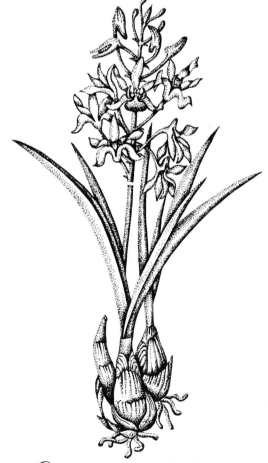

Dendrobium canaliculatum

Dendrobium aemulum

COMMON NAME: Iron Bark Orchid, Brush Box Orchid.
COLOUR: Flowers white. Labellum marked with purple.
SIZE: Growing up to 25cm (10″) high.
CLIMATE: Cool.
DISTRIBUTION: Native to eastern Australian coast and nearby mountains. Growing on Iron Bark (*Eucalyptus sideroxylon*) or Brush Box Trees (*Lophostemon confertus*).
FLOWERING TIME: Spring.
DESCRIPTION: Pseudobulbs up to 25cm (10″) long. Leaves two, terminal, oval. Flowers fragrant and showy, up to 3.5cm (1½″) across. This species has two vegetative forms: (a) those growing on Iron Bark have stout cigar-shaped pseudobulbs; (b) those growing on Brush Box have slender pencil-shaped pseudobulbs. The flowers of both forms appear to be identical.

Dendrobium aemulum

Dendrobium agrostophyllum

COMMON NAME: None.
COLOUR: Flowers bright yellow.
SIZE: Growing up to 70cm (28″) high.
CLIMATE: Cool to intermediate.
DISTRIBUTION: Native to far north-eastern Australia. Altitudes 1000m (3250′), cloud forest.
FLOWERING TIME: Late winter to spring.
DESCRIPTION: Pseudobulbs cylindrical, stem-like, slender fusiform canes up to 60cm (24″) long. Leaves narrow-ovate, emarginate, up to 10cm (4″) long. Racemes short. Flowers up to 2cm (¾″) across.

Dendrobium agrostyophyllum

Dendrobium aggregatum

COMMON NAME: None.
COLOUR: Flowers deep yellow. Labellum orange-yellow.
SIZE: Growing up to 20cm (8″) high.
CLIMATE: Intermediate.
DISTRIBUTION: Native to India, Burma, east to southern China and south to Malaysia, Indo-China, Thailand and Laos.
FLOWERING TIME: Spring.
DESCRIPTION: Pseudobulbs somewhat fusiform, angled, up to 7.5cm (3″) high. Leaf solitary, oblong, obtuse, up to 15cm (6″) long. Inflorescence borne apical. Flowers honey-scented, 3.5cm (1½″) across.

Dendrobium aggregatum

Dendrobium albosanguineum

COMMON NAME: None.
COLOUR: Flowers white, cream or lemon. Labellum has a crimson-purple spot each side of base.
SIZE: Growing up to 40cm (16″) high.
CLIMATE: Intermediate.
DISTRIBUTION: Native to Burma.
FLOWERING TIME: Spring.
DESCRIPTION: Stems pseudobulbous, cylindrical, stout and swollen at the base, up to 28cm (11″) high. Leaves deciduous, linear-lanceolate up to 15cm (6″) long. Short inflorescences borne from upper nodes of stem. Flowers fragrant, 9cm (3½″) across.

Dendrobium albosanguineum

Dendrobium amethystoglossum

COMMON NAME: None.
COLOUR: Flowers white. Labellum lilac, amethyst colour.
SIZE: Growing up to 75cm (30″) high.
CLIMATE: Intermediate to warm.
DISTRIBUTION: Native to the Philippines, Luzon; growing at high elevation.
FLOWERING TIME: Autumn to winter.
DESCRIPTION: Pseudobulbs cylindrical, stem-like, often flexuose up to 75cm (30″) high. Leaves lanceolate, deciduous, up to 10cm (4″) long. Flowers fragrant, 3.5cm (1½″) across. Labellum lobed.

Dendrobium amethystoglossum

Dendrobium amoenum

Dendrobium amoenum

COMMON NAME: None.
COLOUR: Flower colour variable, usually white with floral segments tipped red-purple. Labellum white, marked and veined with purple and yellow.
SIZE: Growing up to 75cm (30″) long.
CLIMATE: Intermediate.
DISTRIBUTION: Native to the Himalayas to Burma.
FLOWERING TIME: Spring.
DESCRIPTION: Pseudobulbs slender, stem-like, slightly swollen at the nodes, arching to pendulous, up to 75cm (30″) long. Leaves linear-lanceolate, acuminate, up to 12.5cm (5″) long; margins undulate. Inflorescences borne from leafless pseudobulbs. Flowers have a violet perfume. Labellum velvety.

Dendrobium antennatum

Dendrobium anosmum syn. D. superbum

COMMON NAME: None.
COLOUR: Flowers pink-purple, darker blotches in throat. Several colour varieties are to be found. The pure white variant is rare.
SIZE: Growing up to 150cm (5′) in length.
CLIMATE: Warm.
DISTRIBUTION: Native to Malay Peninsula, Laos, Vietnam, Philippines, Indonesia and Papua New Guinea.
FLOWERING TIME: Late winter to spring.
DESCRIPTION: Stem-like pseudobulbs, pendulous up to 150cm (5′) long (usually shorter). Leaves deciduous, linear-lanceolate, up to 18cm (7″) long. Flowers borne from leafless stems, up to 10cm (4″) across.

Dendrobium aphrodite syn. *D. nodatum*

Dendrobium antennatum

COMMON NAME: Antelope Orchid.
COLOUR: Sepals white with petals light green. Labellum white marked with red-purple.
SIZE: Growing up to 67.5cm (27″) high.
CLIMATE: Hot.
DISTRIBUTION: Native to Papua New Guinea, New Ireland, Solomon Islands and Australia (Cape York Peninsula). Altitude up to 800m (2600′).
FLOWERING TIME: Summer.
DESCRIPTION: Pseudobulbs up to 60cm (24″) high. Leaves fleshy. Flower up to 7.5cm (3″) long, erect, twisted.

Dendrobium atroviolaceum

Dendrobium anosmum syn. *D. superbum*

Dendrobium aphrodite syn. D. nodatum

COMMON NAME: None.
COLOUR: Flower white. Labellum white, may be blotched with purple and orange.
SIZE: Growing up to 30cm (12″) high.
CLIMATE: Intermediate.
DISTRIBUTION: Native to Thailand and Burma.
FLOWERING TIME: Spring.
DESCRIPTION: Pseudobulbs branching, swollen at the nodes, up to 30cm (12″) high. Leaves deciduous, oblong, obtuse, up to 7.5cm (3″) long. Flower solitary, borne from nodes of leafless pseudobulbs, fragrant, 7.5cm (3″) across.

Dendrobium atroviolaceum

COMMON NAME: None.
COLOUR: Flowers cream-white or yellow, spotted purple. Labellum green and purple.
SIZE: Growing up to 40cm (16″) high.
CLIMATE: Warm.
DISTRIBUTION: Native to Papua New Guinea.
FLOWERING TIME: Spring.
DESCRIPTION: Pseudobulbs clavate-fusiform, about 20cm (8″) high. Leaves apical, elliptic, up to 18cm (7″) long. Flowers fragrant, 6.5cm (2½″) across.

Dendrobium beckleri

COMMON NAME: Pencil Orchid.
COLOUR: White flowers tinged with green.
Labellum white, marginal fringed and streaked
with purple.
SIZE: An epiphyte growing to 2m (6'6") long.
CLIMATE: Cool.
DISTRIBUTION: Native to eastern Australia,
growing along coastal rivers and nearby
mountains. Altitude to 500m (1650').
FLOWERING TIME: Late spring.
DESCRIPTION: Leaves terete (pencil-like), from a
branched cane, tending to grow upwards, but
becoming pendulous to 15cm (6") long. Plant
bearing a mass of white flowers.

Dendrobium beckleri

Dendrobium bigibbum

COMMON NAME: Cooktown Orchid.
COLOUR: Flowers lilac-purple with dark purple
labellum.
SIZE: Growing up to 135cm (4'6") high.
CLIMATE: Warm.
DISTRIBUTION: Native to far north-eastern
Australia, Torres Strait Islands and Papua New
Guinea. Epiphytic plant growing on trees and
rocks often in exposed areas and monsoon vine
scrub.
FLOWERING TIME: Late summer to winter.
DESCRIPTION: Flower scape bears up to twenty
flowers, 8cm (3½") across. Pseudobulbs narrow,
cylindrical fusiform, to 120cm (48") long.
Leaves ovate-lanceolate, to 15cm (6") long.

dendrobium bigibbum

Dendrobium bifalce

COMMON NAME: None.
COLOUR: Flowers yellow-green, may be marked
with purple-brown. Labellum yellow-brown.
SIZE: Growing up to 45cm (18") high.
CLIMATE: Warm.
DISTRIBUTION: Native to Australia, Papua New
Guinea, Solomon Islands, Timor and New
Britain.
FLOWERING TIME: Usually summer.
DESCRIPTION: Pseudobulbs base stalked,
fusiform, up to 30cm (12") high. Leaves oblong,
obtuse, apical, up to 15cm (6") long.
Inflorescence borne from leaf axils. Flowers
4cm (¾") across.

Dendrobium bigibbum var. *alba*

Dendrobium bigibbum var. *alba*

COMMON NAME: White Cooktown Orchid.
COLOUR: Flower white:
SIZE: Similar to type form.
CLIMATE: Warm.
DISTRIBUTION: Same as type form. Australia.
FLOWERING TIME: Similar to type form.
DESCRIPTION: A showy slender ephiphyte or
lithophyte. Similar to type form, except for
flower colour.

Dendrobium bifalce

Dendrobium bigibbum ssp. *laratensis* syn. *D. biggibum* var. *phalaenopsis*

COMMON NAME: None.
COLOUR: Flowers purple, rose-purple or white.
SIZE: Similar to type form.
CLIMATE: Warm to hot.
DISTRIBUTION: Native to Tanimbar Islands (north
of Australia).
FLOWERING TIME: Autumn.
DESCRIPTION: Similar habit to type form, but
more robust, flower larger and more variable
than in type form.

Dendrobium bigibbum ssp. *laratensis* syn.,
D. bigibbum var. *phalaenopsis*

Dendrobium bracteosum

COMMON NAME: None.
COLOUR: Flowers white, pink or purple.
SIZE: Growing up to 40cm (16") high.
CLIMATE: Warm.
DISTRIBUTION: Native to Papua New Guinea, New Ireland and Rossel Island. Epiphyte growing from sea level to altitudes of 500m (1600'), in lowland rainforest and often on mangrove trees.
FLOWERING TIME: Spring.
DESCRIPTION: Stems slender, terete, erect or pendulous, up to 40cm (16") long. Leaves oblong, up to 7.5cm (3") long. Inflorescences dense. Flowers fragrant, up to 2.5cm (1") across.

Dendrobium bracteosum

Dendrobium bullenianum syn. D. topaziacum

COMMON NAME: None.
COLOUR: Flowers yellow to orange, with purple and red striations.
SIZE: Growing up to 60cm (2') high.
CLIMATE: Warm.
DISTRIBUTION: Native to the Philippines.
FLOWERING TIME: Spring.
DESCRIPTION: Stems up to 60cm (2') long. Leaves oblong, up to 7.5cm (3"). Inflorescence borne at the nodes on leafless stems. Flowers numerous, up to 2cm (¾") across.

Dendrobium bullenianum syn. *D. topaziacum*

Dendrobium canaliculatum

COMMON NAME: Tea-Tree Orchid, Onion Orchid.
COLOUR: Flower white tipped with yellow. Labellum marked with purple.
SIZE: Growing up to 20cm (8") high.
CLIMATE: Warm.
DISTRIBUTION: Native to north-eastern Australia and Papua New Guinea. An epiphyte, whose host is the *Melaleuca* species (Paper Bark trees).
FLOWERING TIME: Spring.
DESCRIPTION: Pseudobulbs ovate-elongate, up to 12.5cm (5") high, with sheathing bract. Leaves, linear, channelled, acute up to 20cm (8"). Flower up to 2.5cm (1") across.

Dendrobium chrysanthum syn. *D. paxonii*

Dendrobium chrysanthum syn. D. paxonii

COMMON NAME: None.
COLOUR: Flowers deep yellow. Labellum blotched red-brown.
SIZE: Growing up to 2m (6'6") high.
CLIMATE: Intermediate.
DISTRIBUTION: Native to upper Burma, Thailand, Himalayas, India and Nepal.
FLOWERING TIME: Spring and occasionally throughout the year.
DESCRIPTION: Fragrant flowers about 4cm (1½") across. Leaves ovate-lanceolate, acuminate, to 20cm (8") long. Pendulous stems to 2m (6'6") long with many nodes.

Dendrobium canaliculatum

Dendrobium chrysotoxum

COMMON NAME: None.
COLOUR: Flowers golden yellow. labellum throat has an orange band.
SIZE: Growing up to 32.5cm (13") high.
CLIMATE: Intermediate.
DISTRIBUTION: Native to Thailand, China (Yunnan), Laos, Burma and India (Assam).
FLOWERING TIME: Autumn to spring.
DESCRIPTION: Pseudobulbs clavate or fusiform, furrowed with age, clustered up to 20cm (8") high. Leaves apical oblong, up to 12.5cm (5") long. Flowers fragrant 4cm (1½") across. Labellum margins fringed.

Dendrobium chrysotoxum

Dendrobium chrysotoxum var. *suavissimum*

Dendrobium chrysotoxum var. *suavissimum*

COMMON NAME: None.
COLOUR: Flower golden yellow. Labellum throat has a large maroon blotch or band.
SIZE: Same as type form.
CLIMATE: Intermediate.
DISTRIBUTION: Same as type form.
FLOWERING TIME: Same as type form.
DESCRIPTION: Same as type form, except for flower colour.

Dendrobium conanthum

COMMON NAME: None.
COLOUR: Flowers yellow-brown, tinted and veined brown. Labellum red-purple, veined brown.
SIZE: An epiphytic plant, up to 90cm (3') high.
CLIMATE: Warm to hot.
DISTRIBUTION: Native to Papua New Guinea, Bougainville, Solomon Islands; growing on trees in lowland forest.
FLOWERING TIME: Autumn to winter.
DESCRIPTION: Pseudobulbs, cane-like stems, up to 2m (6'6") high. Leaves alternate, broad-lanceolate, 15cm (6") long. Inflorescence up to 40cm (16") long, flowers numerous. Flowers 5cm (2") across.

Dendrobium cruentum

COMMON NAME: None.
COLOUR: Flowers pale green. Labellum crimson and green.
SIZE: Growing up to 42.5cm (17") high.
CLIMATE: Warm.
DISTRIBUTION: Native to Burma, Thailand and northern Peninsula Malaysia.
FLOWERING TIME: Autumn.
DESCRIPTION: Erect stem-like pseudobulbs, cylindrical, up to 30cm (12") high. Leaves oblong, emarginate, deciduous, up to 12.5cm (5") long. Flowers up to 6.5cm (2½") across.

Dendrobium cruentum

Dendrobium cruttwellii

COMMON NAME: None.
COLOUR: Flowers whitish cream to whitish green, sepals flecked and spotted, maroon-purple on the outside. Labellum markings variable, green to white, spotted purple.
SIZE: Growing up to 25cm (10") high.
CLIMATE: Intermediate.
DISTRIBUTION: Native to Papua New Guinea, at elevations of 1800 to 2400m (5100 to 7850'). Growing on slopes in shaded forest, usually about 3m (10') above ground.
FLOWERING TIME: Throughout the year.
DESCRIPTION: An epiphytic plant. Pseudobulbs ovoid to fusiform, up to 12.5cm (5") high. Leaves borne at the apex of pseudobulbs, petiolate elliptic-lanceolate, acute up to 15cm (6") long. Inflorescence terminal and pendulous, up to 12.5cm (5") long. Flowers about 3cm (1½") across.

Dendrobium cruttwellii

Dendrobium crystallinum

COMMON NAME: None.
COLOUR: Flowers white, tipped with red-purple. Labellum orange.
SIZE: Growing up to 60cm (2') high.
CLIMATE: Intermediate.
DISTRIBUTION: Native to Himalayas, Burma, Thailand, Laos, Cambodia and Vietnam.
FLOWERING TIME: Summer.
DESCRIPTION: Pseudobulbs terete, 60cm (2') long. Leaves deciduous, falcate-lanceolate, 15cm (6") long.

Dendrobium crystallinum

Dendrobium conanthum

Dendrobium cucumerinum

COMMON NAME: Cucumber Ochid.
COLOUR: Flowers cream, streaked with maroon-purple.
SIZE: Creeping, mat forming.
CLIMATE: Cool.
DISTRIBUTION: Native to Australian eastern coast and mountains, growing along rivers and creeks on She Oaks (*Casuarina cunninghamiana*).
FLOWERING TIME: Erratic, summer to autumn.
DESCRIPTION: Epiphytic or lithophytic. Lacks pseudobulbs. Leaves gherkin-like, oblong-ovoid 4cm (1½″) long. Flowers up to 2.5cm (1″) across, borne in clusters.

Dendrobium cucumerinum

Dendrobium cuthbertsonii syn. *D. sophronites*

Dendrobium cuthbertsonii syn. *D. sophronites*

COMMON NAME: None.
COLOUR: Flower colour is variable—red, white, orange, yellow or purple.
SIZE: A diminutive plant up to 3cm (1¼″) high.
CLIMATE: Intermediate.
DISTRIBUTION: Native to Papua New Guinea in cloud forest above 2000m (6500′).
FLOWERING TIME: Throughout the year.
DESCRIPTION: Pseudobulbs small and oval. Leaves borne in pairs, linear, about 2cm (¾″) long, dark green, purple underneath. Flowers up to 2.5cm (1″) across. In this dwarf species, flowers can last up to nine months and sometimes longer. The new season's buds can appear before the last season's blooms fade.

Dendrobium dearei

COMMON NAME: None.
COLOUR: Flowers white, throat green.
SIZE: Growing up to 1m (40″) high.
CLIMATE: Warm.
DISTRIBUTION: Native to the Philippines.
FLOWERING TIME: Spring to summer.
DESCRIPTION: Stem-like pseudobulbs, up to 1m (40″) high. Leaves lanceolate, acute, deciduous, up to 15cm (6″) long. Flowers to 7.5cm (3″) across.

Dendrobium dearei

Dendrobium delacourii syn. *D. ciliatum*

COMMON NAME: None.
COLOUR: Flower cream. Labellum apricot-cream; side lobes veined red-brown.
SIZE: Stems up to 45cm (18″) high.
CLIMATE: Intermediate.
DISTRIBUTION: Native to Thailand and lower Burma. Elevations 800 to 1300m (2600 to 4250′).
FLOWERING TIME: Late winter to spring.
DESCRIPTION: Stems fusiform, up to 46cm (16″) long. Leaves linear-elliptic, up to 10cm (4″) long. Flower 3cm (1¼″) across. Labellum front margins are fringed cavate in shape.

Dendrobium X *delicatum*

COMMON NAME: Dainty Dendrobium.
COLOUR: Raceme erect, white or cream, often tinted pink. Labellum white marked with purple, callus yellow.
SIZE: Growing up to 45cm (18″) high.
CLIMATE: Cool.
DISTRIBUTION: Native to eastern Australia.
FLOWERING TIME: Spring.
DESCRIPTION: A natural hybrid between *D. kingianum* and *D. speciosum*. Pseudobulbs obclavate up to 45cm (18″) high. Leaves apical, lanceolate. Raceme erect.

Dendrobium X *delicatum*

Dendrobium delacourii syn. *D. ciliatum*

Dendrobium densiflorum

COMMON NAME: None.
COLOUR: Flowers yellow. Labellum orange-yellow.
SIZE: Growing up to 60cm (2') high.
CLIMATE: Intermediate.
DISTRIBUTION: Native to India, the Himalayas, Nepal, Burma, Sikkim and Assam. Altitude up to 1500m (5000').
FLOWERING TIME: Spring.
DESCRIPTION: Pseudobulbs tetragonal-fusiform, up to 50cm (20") high. Leaves elliptic, up to 15cm (6") long. Inflorescence pendulous, flowers dense and numerous. Flowers showy, up to 5cm (2") across. Labellum hairy.

Dendrobium devonianum syn. *D. pictum*

Dendrobium devonianum syn. D. pictum

COMMON NAME: None.
COLOUR: Sepals white-cream, suffusions pink, rarely tipped with red-purple. Petals lemon or white with orange blotch each side of disc.
SIZE: Growing up to 1.5m (5') high.
CLIMATE: Intermediate.
DISTRIBUTION: Native to the Himalayas, Burma, Thailand, China and Vietnam.
FLOWERING TIME: Spring to early summer.
DESCRIPTION: Pendulous, stem-like pseudobulbs, up to 1.5m (5') long. Leaves linear-lanceolate, acuminate, deciduous, up to 13cm (5") long. Flowers fragrant, 7.5cm (3") across. Petal margins fimbriate.

Dendrobium densiflorum

Dendrobium dicuphum

COMMON NAME: None.
COLOUR: Flowers white or with pinkish tinge.
SIZE: Up to 30cm (1').
CLIMATE: Intermediate to warm.
DISTRIBUTION: Top end of northern Australia.
FLOWERING TIME: Autumn to spring.
DESCRIPTION: Epiphyte. Pseudobulbs up to 30cm (1') long. Leaves 3 to 15cm (1 to 6") long on distal half of stem, deciduous. Inflorescence up to 50cm (20") long, arching, with as many as twenty flowers. Flowers are 2.5 to 5cm (1 to 2") across.

Dendrobium dicuphum

Dendrobium discolor syn. D. undulatum.

COMMON NAME: Golden Orchid.
COLOUR: Flowers usually yellow to brown.
SIZE: Growing up to 3m (10') high.
CLIMATE: Warm.
DISTRIBUTION: Native to north-eastern Australia, Papua New Guinea, Torres Strait Islands and Solomon Islands.
FLOWERING TIME: Throughout the year.
DESCRIPTION: Pseudobulbs cylindrical, up to 5m (15') high. Leaves oblong-lanceolate, 10cm (4") long. Inflorescence 60 cm (24") long, flowers numerous, 75cm (3") across.

Dendrobium discolor syn. *D. undulatum*

Dendrobium discolor var. *broomfieldii*

Dendrobium discolor var. broomfieldii

COMMON NAME: None.
COLOUR: Flowers vary from a pale yellow to golden yellow with a white keel on the labellum.
SIZE: Same as type form.
CLIMATE: Warm.
DISTRIBUTION: Same as type form.
FLOWERING TIME: Throughout the year.
DESCRIPTION: This plant differs from the type form in that the flowers vary from a pale yellow to golden yellow with a white keel on the labellum.

Dendrobium dixanthum

Dendrobium dixanthum

COMMON NAME: None.
COLOUR: Flowers yellow; streaked with red either side of labellum base.
SIZE: Erect stems, terete up to 1m (40″) high.
CLIMATE: Intermediate.
DISTRIBUTION: Native to Burma.
FLOWERING TIME: Spring.
DESCRIPTION: Leaves lanceolate or strap-shape, up to 17cm (6½″) long. Inflorescence short, borne at the nodes. Flowers up to 4cm (1½″) across.

Dendrobium farmeri

COMMON NAME: None.
COLOUR: Flowers white, flushed mauve-pink. Labellum yellow.
SIZE: Growing up to 30cm (12″) high.
CLIMATE: Intermediate.
DISTRIBUTION: Native to India, the Himalayas, Thailand and the Peninsula Malaysia.
FLOWERING TIME: Mostly spring.
DESCRIPTION: Pseudobulbs tetragonal, up to 30cm (12″) long. Leaves apical, three or four, up to 15cm (6″) long. Inflorescence arching to pendulous with numerous flowers. Flowers up to 5cm (2″) across. Labellum hairy.

Dendrobium farmeri var. *albaflorum*

Dendrobium farmeri var. albaflorum

COMMON NAME: None.
COLOUR: Flowers white. Labellum yellow.
SIZE: Same as type.
CLIMATE: Same as type.
DISTRIBUTION: Same as type.
FLOWERING TIME: Same as type.
DESCRIPTION: Same as type, except petals and sepals pure white.

Dendrobium farmeri

Dendrobium fimbriatum

COMMON NAME: None.
COLOUR: Flowers yellow.
SIZE: Growing up to 1.2m (4′) high.
CLIMATE: Cool to intermediate.
DISTRIBUTION: Native to India, the Himalayas, Nepal, Burma, Thailand, Indo-China, Vietnam and Malaysia.
FLOWERING TIME: Spring.
DESCRIPTION: Pseudobulbs terete, 1.2m (4′) high. Leaves acuminate, lanceolate. Flowers 7cm (3″) across. Labellum fringed.

Dendrobium fimbriatum

Dendrobium fimbriatum var. *oculatum*

Dendrobium fimbriatum var. oculatum

COMMON NAME: None.
COLOUR: Flowers cream-apricot. Labellum yellow-orange, blotched with crimson.
SIZE: Stems long, 1.2m (4′) high.
CLIMATE: Cool to intermediate.
DISTRIBUTION: Native to India, Burma and China.
FLOWERING TIME: Spring.
DESCRIPTION: Leaves oblong-lanceolate, acuminate, up to 20cm (8″) long. Flowers clustered, large, petals wider than typical form and margins untoothed.

Dendrobium findlayanum

COMMON NAME: None.
COLOUR: Petals and sepals are white with a lilac tint. Labellum has yellow throat, tipped with pink.
SIZE: Growing up to 60cm (24″) high.
CLIMATE: Intermediate.
DISTRIBUTION: Native to Burma and Thailand in a mountain climate.
FLOWERING TIME: Late summer.
DESCRIPTION: Canes swollen at the nodes, up to 60cm (24″) high. Leaves deciduous, oblong-lanceolate, unequally toothed, up to 10cm (4″) long. Flowers in pairs, 7.5cm (3″) across. Labellum heart-shaped.

Dendrobium flaviflorum

COMMON NAME: None.
COLOUR: Flower rich golden yellow.
SIZE: Growing up to 60cm (24″) high.
CLIMATE: Intermediate.
DISTRIBUTION: Native to Taiwan.
FLOWERING TIME: Summer.
DESCRIPTION: Cane-like pseudobulbs, up to 60cm (24″) high. Leaves oblong-lanceolate, up to 10cm (4″) long, alternating from top third of pseudobulb. Flower up to 5cm (2″) across, fimbriate.

Dendrobium flaviflorum

Dendrobium fleckeri

COMMON NAME: Yellow Moth Orchid.
COLOUR: Flowers apricot. Labellum marked with white and crimson.
SIZE: Growing up to 50cm (20″) high.
CLIMATE: Cool to intermediate.
DISTRIBUTION: Native to north-eastern Australia up to an altitude of 1000m (3300′).
FLOWERING TIME: Late winter to summer.
DESCRIPTION: Pseudobulbs slender, furrowed, cylindrical, up to 40cm (16″) high. Leaves terminal, two or three, lanceolate, up to 10cm (4″) long. Flowers large and terminal.

Dendrobium findlayanum

Dendrobium formosum

Dendrobium formosum

COMMON NAME: None.
COLOUR: Flower white. Throat of labellum yellow.
SIZE: Growing up to 50cm (20″) high.
CLIMATE: Intermediate to warm.
DISTRIBUTION: Native to the Himalayas, Burma and Thailand Peninsula.
FLOWERING TIME: Winter to early spring.
DESCRIPTION: Pseudobulbs ribbed, slightly fusiform, up to 37.5cm (15″) high. Leaves oblong-ovate, 12.5cm (5″) long. Flower size variable up to 13cm (5″) across.

Dendrobium fleckeri

Dendrobium friedericksianum var. oculatum

COMMON NAME: None.
COLOUR: Flowers pale yellow. Labellum marked with a medium purple blotch.
SIZE: Growing up to 1.2m (4') high.
CLIMATE: Cool to intermediate.
DISTRIBUTION: Native to Thailand.
FLOWERING TIME: Spring.
DESCRIPTION: Pseudobulbs stem-like. Leaves linear and deciduous. Flowers up to 6cm (2½") across.

Dendrobium friedericksianum var. *oculatum*

Dendrobium gibsoni syn. D. fuscatum.

COMMON NAME: None.
COLOUR: Flowers deep yellow. Labellum marked with two brown blotches.
SIZE: Growing up to 1.2m (4') high.
CLIMATE: Cool.
DISTRIBUTION: Native to the Himalayas, Burma, southern China and Yunnan.
FLOWERING TIME: Summer.
DESCRIPTION: Pseudobulbs cylindrical, 1.2m (4') long. Leaves lanceolate 15cm (6") long. Inflorescence apical and pendulous. Flowers 5cm (2") across.

Dendrobium gonzalesii

COMMON NAME: None.
COLOUR: Flowers white to mauve. Labellum marked with purple.
SIZE: Growing up to 50cm (20") high.
CLIMATE: Intermediate to warm.
DISTRIBUTION: Native to the Philippines, growing at an altitude of 860m (2800').
FLOWERING TIME: Spring.
DESCRIPTION: An epiphytic plant. Cane stems pendulous, clustered up to 50cm (20") long, may be branched. Leaves lanceolate, oblong, acute, up to 10cm (4") long. Flowers showy, about 5cm (2") across.

Dendrobium gordonii

COMMON NAME: None.
COLOUR: Flowers yellow to green, veined brown.
SIZE: Growing up to 45cm (18") high.
CLIMATE: Warm to hot.
DISTRIBUTION: Native to Fiji.
FLOWERING TIME: Winter.
DESCRIPTION: An epiphyte. Pseudobulbs fusiform, furrowed when matured, up to 30cm (12") high. Two to three apical leaves, broad-lanceolate, up to 20cm (8") long. Inflorescence terminal. Flowers 3.5cm (1½") across. Some botanists consider it syn. *D. macrophyllum.*

Dendrobium gibsoni syn. *D. fuscatum*

Dendrobium gonzalesii

Dendrobium gordonii

Dendrobium gouldii

COMMON NAME: Guadalcanal Gold Orchid.
COLOUR: Flower colour variable, mauve to yellow-brown with mauve veins. Labellum streaked red-brown. White to mauve colour forms readily found in Papua New Guinea, while yellow and brown forms are readily found on Guadalcanal Island. (Colour form in this photograph is Guadalcanal Gold.)
SIZE: Growing up to 1.2m (4') high.
CLIMATE: Warm to hot.
DISTRIBUTION: Native to Solomon Islands, northern and eastern coasts of Papua New Guinea, and Pacific Islands. Grows at sea level.
FLOWERING TIME: Autumn.
DESCRIPTION: Pseudobulbs stout, stem-like, canes up to 1.2m (4') and sometimes to 2.1m (7'). Leaves elliptic-ovate, distichous up to 15cm (6") long. Inflorescence apical, up to 60cm (24") long, six to twenty-five blooms. Flowers 6cm (2½") across.

Dendrobium gouldii

Dendrobium gracilicaule

Dendrobium gracilicaule

COMMON NAME: None.
COLOUR: Flowers are yellow and blotched with maroon.
SIZE: Growing up to 75cm (30″) high.
CLIMATE: Cool.
DISTRIBUTION: Native to Australia (north-eastern coast and mountains).
FLOWERING TIME: Spring.
DESCRIPTION: An epiphytic plant. Pseudobulbs erect, cylindrical, up to 75cm (30″) long. Three to six apical leaves, lanceolate to narrow-elliptic, slightly sinuate, up to 14cm (5½″) long. Five to sixteen flowers on raceme. Flowers 2cm (¾″) across.

Dendrobium gratiosissimum syn. *D. boxallii*

Dendrobium gratiosissimum syn. *D. boxalii* and *D. bullerianum*

COMMON NAME: None.
COLOUR: Flower white or mauve, floral segments tipped with pink-purple. Labellum white tipped with pink-purple; disc yellow marked with orange.
SIZE: Growing up to 1m (40″) high.
CLIMATE: Cool to intermediate.
DISTRIBUTION: Native to Burma and Thailand.
FLOWERING TIME: Spring.
DESCRIPTION: Pseudobulbs stem-like, canes cylindrical, generally 1m (40″) long. Leaves strap-like, deciduous, up to 10cm (4″) long. Inflorescence borne from leafless pseudobulbs. Flower 6cm (2½″) across.

Dendrobium griffithianum

COMMON NAME: None.
COLOUR: Flowers white. Labellum yellow.
SIZE: Growing up to 30cm (12″) high.
CLIMATE: Intermediate.
DISTRIBUTION: Native to Thailand and Burma.
FLOWERING TIME: Late spring to summer.
DESCRIPTION: Pseudobulbs tetragonal, up to 30cm (12″) high. Leaves oblong or ovate, up to 12.5cm (5″) long. Inflorescence erect to pendulous, numerous flowers, up to 4cm (1½″) across. Labellum margins ciliate.

Dendrobium griffithianum

Dendrobium guerreroi

COMMON NAME: None.
COLOUR: Flowers yellow to brown.
SIZE: Grows up to 75cm (30″) high.
CLIMATE: Intermediate to warm.
DISTRIBUTION: Native to the Philippines (Mindoro and Dinagat Islands).
FLOWERING TIME: Summer.
DESCRIPTION: An epiphytic plant. Canes long and generally leafless, clustered, elongate. Leaves deciduous, lanceolate-oblong, up to 10cm (4″) long. Inflorescence pendulous, loose raceme, bearing few flowers, up to 10cm (4″) long. Flowers about 2cm (¾″) across, bracts pink to purple.

Dendrobium bercoglossum syn. *D. linguella*

Dendrobium bercoglossum syn. *D. linguella*

COMMON NAME: None.
COLOUR: Flowers pinkish-mauve. Labellum white with a bright red-purple blotch at the apex.
SIZE: Growing up to 35cm (14″) high.
CLIMATE: Cool to intermediate.
DISTRIBUTION: Native to Thailand and Indo-China.
FLOWERING TIME: Spring to summer.
DESCRIPTION: Stems slender, clustered, up to 35cm (14″) high, almost hidden by leaf-sheaths. Leaves linear-lanceolate, unequally emarginate, distichous, up to 10cm (4″) long. Inflorescence flexuose. Flowers showy. Closely allied to *D. aduncum*; the separation of the two species is due mainly to differences in the labellum.

Dendrobium guerreroi

Dendrobium heterocarpum
syn. *D. aureum*

COMMON NAME: None.
COLOUR: Flowers creamy yellow. Labellum orange-yellow, veined with maroon.
SIZE: Growing up to 90cm (36") high.
CLIMATE: Cool to intermediate.
DISTRIBUTION: Native to India, Nepal, Burma, Assam, Sikkim, Sri Lanka, South-east Asia, Indonesia, the Philippines and Moluccas.
FLOWERING TIME: Spring to autumn.
DESCRIPTION: A variable plant. Pseudobulbs cylindrical, tapered at base, up to 90cm (3') high. Leaves deciduous, oblong-lanceolate, 12.5cm (5") long. Flowers fragrant, borne from the nodes, and up to 6cm (2½") across.

Dendrobium infundibulum syn. *D. moulmeinense*

Dendrobium infundibulum
syn. *D. moulmeinense*

COMMON NAME: None.
COLOUR: Flowers white. Labellum throat blotched yellow.
SIZE: Growing up to 100cm (40") high.
CLIMATE: Cool to intermediate.
DISTRIBUTION: Native to Thailand and Burma. Elevation 1100 to 2300m (3608 to 7000').
FLOWERING TIME: Spring to early summer.
DESCRIPTION: Pseudobulbs stem-like up to 100cm (40") high. Leaves linear-lanceolate, 8.5cm (3¼") long. Flowers up to 8.5cm (3¼") across. Closely allied species *D. formosum*, the main difference is in the sepals and spur.

Dendrobium heterocarpum syn. *D. aureum*

Dendrobium infundibulum
var. *jamesianum*, syn.
D. jamesianum

COMMON NAME: None.
COLOUR: As for type, with differences listed below.
SIZE: As for type.
CLIMATE: As for type.
DISTRIBUTION: Native to Burma.
FLOWERING TIME: Spring.
DESCRIPTION: Differing from the type in the following: pseudobulbs shorter; in shape of the labellum, lateral lobes and colour of the labellum throat, deeper yellow.

Dendrobium infundibulum var. *jamesianum*

Dendrobium kingianum

COMMON NAME: Pink Rock Orchid.
COLOUR: Flowers pinkish-mauve and rarely white.
SIZE: Growing up to 40cm (16") high.
CLIMATE: Cool.
DISTRIBUTION: Native to eastern half of Australia, coast and mountains.
FLOWERING TIME: Spring.
DESCRIPTION: A lithophytic orchid growing on rocks and cliff faces forming a mat-like growth. Very variable in colour and growth habit. Pseudobulbs clustered, clavate up to 40cm (16") high. Leaves terminal, lanceolate up to 10cm (4") long. Two to nine flowers per raceme.

Dendrobium kingianum

Dendrobium kingianum var.
silcockii

COMMON NAME: None.
COLOUR: Flowers white. Labellum purple.
SIZE: Growing up to 40cm (16") high.
CLIMATE: Cool.
DISTRIBUTION: Native to eastern Australia, coastal mountains.
FLOWERING TIME: Spring.
DESCRIPTION: Same as type, except flower colour.

Dendrobium kingianum var. *silcockii*

Dendrobium lasianthera 'May River Red'

Dendrobium lasianthera

COMMON NAME: May River Red.
COLOUR: Flowers red-bronze-brown, with yellow margins. Petal apex yellow. Labellum red-purple.
SIZE: Growing up to 3m (10') high.
CLIMATE: Hot.
DISTRIBUTION: Native to Papua New Guinea (along the May River), low altitudes.
FLOWERING TIME: Summer.
DESCRIPTION: Pseudobulbs terete, erect canes, up to 3m (10') high. Leaves up to 18cm (7") long, elliptic, alternate, emarginate. Inflorescence up to 60cm (24") long. Flowers large and showy. Petals erect and twisted.

Dendrobium lasianthera 'Veronica Somare'

Dendrobium lasianthera

COMMON NAME: Veronica Somare.
COLOUR: Flowers red-brown. Labellum white at base, pink-purple, apex yellow, yellow tint throughout flower.
SIZE: Canes up to 3m (10') high.
CLIMATE: Hot.
DISTRIBUTION: Native to Papua New Guinea; low altitudes, swamps.
FLOWERING TIME: Summer.
DESCRIPTION: Habit same as type. Flowers large, showy, petals somewhat erect and twisted.

Dendrobium lineale

COMMON NAME: Bougainville White.
COLOUR: Flowers white. Labellum flushed with mauve.
SIZE: Growing up to 1m (40") high.
CLIMATE: Hot.
DISTRIBUTION: Native to Papua New Guinea, New Ireland and Solomon Islands. Commonly growing in coastal trees and festooning the beech trees in many areas.
FLOWERING TIME: Autumn to winter.
DESCRIPTION: Pseudobulbs somewhat fusiform, slender, canes up to 1m (40") long. Flowers numerous, to about 5cm (2") across, petals quite erect and twisted.

Dendrobium linguiforme

Dendrobium linguiforme

COMMON NAME: Tongue Orchid.
COLOUR: Flower white. Labellum marked lemon.
SIZE: Creeping, mat forming.
CLIMATE: Cool.
DISTRIBUTION: Native to eastern Australia. Lithophytic growing on rock, or epiphytic on trees, especially growing on Paper Bark (*Melaleuca alternifolia*).
FLOWERING TIME: Late winter to spring.
DESCRIPTION: Creeping rhizomes, stem prostrate. Leaves numerous, thick, flattened, grooved, ovate or ovate-lanceolate, tongue-like, and up to 5cm (2") long. Raceme up to 12.5cm (5") long.

Dendrobium lineale

Dendrobium loddigesii

COMMON NAME: None.
COLOUR: Flower pastel, mauve to pink. Labellum white, fringed centre orange to yellow.
SIZE: A dwarf epiphyte with creeping, branching, soft canes to 20cm (8") long.
CLIMATE: Intermediate.
DISTRIBUTION: Native to Laos, China and Hainan Island.
FLOWERING TIME: Mid winter to spring.
DESCRIPTION: Stems bear small, ovate-elliptic, alternate, deciduous leaves. Flowers are fragrant, solitary, up to 2.5cm (1") across.

Dendrobium loddigesii

Dendrobium macrophyllum

COMMON NAME: None.
COLOUR: Flower yellow to yellow-green. Petals spotted with purple. Labellum green or yellow-green, veined purple.
SIZE: Growing up to 45cm (18″) high.
CLIMATE: Warm to hot.
DISTRIBUTION: Native to Papua New Guinea, the Philippines, Malaysia and Java.
FLOWERING TIME: Spring to early summer.
DESCRIPTION: Pseudobulbs clavate, often compressed, ribbed, 45cm (18″) high. Leaves up to 25cm (10″) long, elliptic, acute, shiny. Flower colour variable, grows to 5cm (2″) across.

Dendrobium macrophyllum

Dendrobium malbrownii

COMMON NAME: Mal Brown's Cane Orchid.
COLOUR: Flower fleshy apricot to creamy white. Labellum maroon or dark glossy purple.
SIZE: Growing up to 25cm (10″) high.
CLIMATE: Intermediate to warm.
DISTRIBUTION: Native to far north-eastern Australia and Papua New Guinea.
FLOWERING TIME: Late summer to autumn.
DESCRIPTION: Pseudobulbs grass-like, up to 25cm (10″) high. Leaves up to 6cm (2½″) long. Flowers solitary, about 8mm (under ½″).

Dendrobium malbrownii

Dendrobium margaritaceum

Dendrobium margaritaceum

COMMON NAME: None.
COLOUR: Flowers white. Labellum yellow and red.
SIZE: Stems subclavate, 5cm (2″) high.
CLIMATE: Warm.
DISTRIBUTION: Native to Thailand and Vietnam, Assam.
FLOWERING TIME: Spring.
DESCRIPTION: Leaves apical, lanceolate, 4cm (1½″) long. One to two flowers up to 3cm (1¼″) across.

Dendrobium mirbelianum syn. *D. wilkianum*

Dendrobium mirbelianum syn. D. wilkianum

COMMON NAME: None.
COLOUR: Flowers usually yellow-green, veined and may be finely spotted with purple-brown.
SIZE: Growing up to 50cm (20″) high.
CLIMATE: Warm to hot.
DISTRIBUTION: Native to Australia (Cape York Peninsula), Papua New Guinea, New Britain, Alor Islands, Hamahera, Timor and Moluccas.
FLOWERING TIME: Throughout the year, often more than once annually.
DESCRIPTION: Epiphytic growing in lowland forest. A variable plant in both vegetation and floral segments, resulting in many forms. Pseudobulbs fusiform, up to 40cm (16″) high. Leaves unusually oval obtuse, up to 10cm (4″) long. Flowers up to 5cm (2″) across.

Dendrobium miyakei

Dendrobium miyakei

COMMON NAME: None.
COLOUR: Flowers purple.
SIZE: Growing up to 1m (40″) high.
CLIMATE: Intermediate to warm.
DISTRIBUTION: Native to the Philippines (Bataan Island) and Taiwan in mountain areas.
FLOWERING TIME: Winter.
DESCRIPTION: Stems pendulous, clustered, terete, swollen at the nodes, up to 1m (40″) long. Leaves linear-lanceolate, acute, up to 10cm (4″) long. Inflorescence borne from leafless stems, in short raceme, four to eight blooms. Flowers about 2cm (¾″) across.

Dendrobium moblianum

Dendrobium moblianum

COMMON NAME: None.
COLOUR: Flowers orange.
SIZE: Growing up to 45cm (18″) high.
CLIMATE: Warm.
DISTRIBUTION: Native to Fiji, growing at altitudes above 800m (2500′).
FLOWERING TIME: Autumn.
DESCRIPTION: Epiphyte of the cloud forests with cane-like pseudobulbs to 45cm (18″) high, slightly hirsute. Leaves oblong-lanceolate to 10cm (4″) long. Flowers 1.5cm (½″) across, clustered on short inflorescence.

Dendrobium monophyllum

Dendrobium monophyllum

COMMON NAME: Lily of the Valley.
COLOUR: Flowers yellow-green.
SIZE: Growing up to 20cm (8″) high.
CLIMATE: Cool.
DISTRIBUTION: Native to Australia (north-eastern coast and nearby ranges) growing at altitudes of up to 900m (3000′).
FLOWERING TIME: Mainly spring.
DESCRIPTION: Pseudobulbs thick, narrow-conical, up to 10cm (4″) high, mature bulbs often furrowed. Leaf solitary, terminal, oblong to lanceolate, up to 10cm (4″) long. Raceme solitary, terminal, about as long as the leaf. Flowers on drooping pedicel, fragrant, up to 6mm (¼″) long.

Dendrobium moschatum

COMMON NAME: None.
COLOUR: Flowers pale apricot. Labellum inside orange with two red-brown blotches.
SIZE: Canes terete, erect or pendulous, up to 2.5m (8′6″) long.
CLIMATE: Cool to intermediate.
DISTRIBUTION: Native to the Himalayas, Burma, Thailand and Laos.
FLOWERING TIME: Spring to summer.
DESCRIPTION: Leaves oblong-ovate 20cm (8″) long. Flowers up to 10cm (4″) across, musk-scented. Labellum pouch shaped.

Dendrobium moschatum

Dendrobium moschatum var. colorum

COMMON NAME: None.
COLOUR: Flower apricot, tinged purple.
SIZE: Same as type.
CLIMATE: Same as type.
DISTRIBUTION: Native to India and Burma.
FLOWERING TIME: Spring to early summer.
DESCRIPTION: Same as type, except for colour variation.

Dendrobium moschatum var. *colorum*

Dendrobium nobile

COMMON NAME: None.
COLOUR: Flowers mauve. Labellum mauve and cream, throat crimson-purple.
SIZE: Growing up to 70cm (28″) high.
CLIMATE: Cool to intermediate.
DISTRIBUTION: Native to Nepal, Sikkim, Bhutan, Upper Burma, Assam, China, Laos, Vietnam and Taiwan.
FLOWERING TIME: Spring.
DESCRIPTION: Pseudobulbs clustered, terete, somewhat compressed, up to 60cm (24″) high. Leaves deciduous, oblong, slightly emarginate, up to 10cm (4″) long. Flowers borne from the nodes in short racemes; flowers are large, up to 7.5cm (3″) across. This plant is popular as a parent for hybridisation, and also for certain medicinal properties.

Dendrobium nobile

Dendrobium nobile var. *virginale*

COMMON NAME: None.
COLOUR: Flowers white.
SIZE: Same as type.
CLIMATE: Same as type.
DISTRIBUTION: Native to Burma, growing at high altitudes, liking sunny position.
FLOWERING TIME: Spring.
DESCRIPTION: This soft cane species is an alba variety of *D. nobile*. Habit same as type *D. nobile*, differing in that flowers are white.

Dendrobium nobile var. *virginale*

Dendrobium ochreatum syn. *D. cambridgeanum*

COMMON NAME: None.
COLOUR: Flowers deep yellow. Labellum yellow with maroon blotch.
SIZE: Growing up to 30cm (12″) high.
CLIMATE: Cool to intermediate.
DISTRIBUTION: Native to Thailand, India and the Himalayas; grows generally at high elevations.
FLOWERING TIME: Spring.
DESCRIPTION: Pseudobulbs pendulous, cylindrical, stout, 30cm (12″) long, swollen at the nodes. Leaves ovate-lanceolate, acute, deciduous, 5 to 10cm (2 to 4″) long. Inflorescence short, borne from the nodes. Flowers are 5cm (2″) across.

Dendrobium ochreatum syn. *D. cambridgeanum*

Dendrobium parishii

Dendrobium pendulum syn. *D. crassinode.*

COMMON NAME: None.
COLOUR: Flowers usually white, tipped with red-purple. Labellum carries yellow-orange blotches.
SIZE: Growing up to 45cm (18″) high.
CLIMATE: Intermediate.
DISTRIBUTION: Native to India, Burma and Thailand.
FLOWERING TIME: Spring.
DESCRIPTION: Pseudobulbs crassinode in shape, usually erect, swollen at the nodes, up to 45cm (18″) long. Leaves deciduous, linear-lanceolate 12.5cm (5″) long. Flowers borne on leafless pseudobulbs, 5 to 6cm (2 to 2½″) across.

Dendrobium petiolatum

Dendrobium parishii

COMMON NAME: None.
COLOUR: Flowers purple. Labellum throat blotched with two maroon spots.
SIZE: Growing up to 20cm (8″) high.
CLIMATE: Cool to intermediate.
DISTRIBUTION: Native to Burma, Thailand, Laos, Cambodia, Vietnam and China.
FLOWERING TIME: Spring.
DESCRIPTION: Pseudobulbs cylindrical; pendulous or prostrate canes up to 20cm (8″) long. Leaves oblong-lanceolate and deciduous. Flowers borne from the nodes along the canes, and are 5cm (2″) across.

Dendrobium pendulum syn. *D. crassinode*

Dendrobium petiolatum

COMMON NAME: None.
COLOUR: Flowers are pink. Labellum marked yellow.
SIZE: Growing up to 25cm (10″) high.
CLIMATE: Intermediate to warm.
DISTRIBUTION: Native to Papua New Guinea.
FLOWERING TIME: Spring.
DESCRIPTION: Pseudobulbs are cane-like, swollen at the nodes, up to 25cm (10″) high. Leaves oblong-lanceolate, sheathing at the base, up to 10cm (4″) long. Inflorescence short, flowers clustered, up to 2.5cm (1″) across.

Dendrobium pierardii

Dendrobium pierardii

COMMON NAME: None.
COLOUR: Flowers mauve. Labellum pale yellow, veined purple.
SIZE: Growing up to 1m (40″) long.
CLIMATE: Cool to intermediate.
DISTRIBUTION: Native to India, Himalayas, Burma, China, Thailand and Peninsula Malaysia.
FLOWERING TIME: Spring to early summer.
DESCRIPTION: Pseudobulbs are stem-like, slender, pendulous, up to 1m (40″) long. Leaves are deciduous, sessile lanceolate, up to 10cm (4″) long. Flowers are fragrant, semi-translucent, and grow up to 5cm (2″) across.

Dendrobium pierardii var. *alba*

Dendrobium pierardii var. *alba*

COMMON NAME: None.
COLOUR: Flowers are white.
SIZE: Same as type.
CLIMATE: Same as type.
FLOWERING TIME: Same as type.
DESCRIPTION: Same as type, but for white flower.

Dendrobium polysema

COMMON NAME: None.
COLOUR: Flower whitish cream, heavily spotted with maroon. Labellum warm yellow marked with maroon.
SIZE: Growing up to 45cm (18″) high.
CLIMATE: Hot.
DISTRIBUTION: Native to Papua New Guinea.
FLOWERING TIME: Spring.
DESCRIPTION: Pseudobulbs clavate, ribbed up to 40cm (16″) high. Leaves elliptic, acute, shiny, up to 20cm (8″) long. *D. polysema* is not a synonym of *D. macrophyllum*, differing in all floral segments, especially the narrow lateral lobes of the labellum. The column is also different.

Dendrobium prasinum

Dendrobium prasinum

COMMON NAME: None.
COLOUR: Flowers white.
SIZE: Growing up to 15cm (6″) long.
CLIMATE: Warm.
DISTRIBUTION: Native to Fiji; common in forest over 600m (2000′) in altitude.
FLOWERING TIME: Early spring.
DESCRIPTION: Pseudobulbs clavate, up to 7.5cm (3″) high. Leaves linear-oblong, up to 12.5cm (5″) long. Inflorescence short, four to five, clustered. Flowers inverted, and are up to 4cm (1½″) across.

Dendrobium polysema

Dendrobium pugioniforme

COMMON NAME: Dagger Orchid.
COLOUR: Flowers green to cream with purple marks.
SIZE: Growing to 2m (6′6″) long.
CLIMATE: Cool.
DISTRIBUTION: Native to Australia (central eastern coast and nearby mountains).
FLOWERING TIME: Spring.
DESCRIPTION: Pendulous epiphyte. Leaves ovate to lanceolate, tapering to a dagger-like point, up to 7.5cm (3″) long. Flowers up to 2.5cm (1″) across.

Dendrobium pugioniforme ·

Dendrobium pulchellum syn. *D. dalhousieanum*

Dendrobium pulchellum syn. D. dalhousieanum

COMMON NAME: None.
COLOUR: Flowers creamy yellow to pinkish yellow. Labellum creamy white with maroon blotch on each side of disc.
SIZE: Growing up to 1.5m (5′) high.
CLIMATE: Intermediate to warm.
DISTRIBUTION: Native to Thailand, Vietnam, Himalayas to Burma and Peninsula Malaysia.
FLOWERING TIME: Spring.
DESCRIPTION: Pseudobulbs terete, canes up to 1.5m (5′) or more high. Leaves linear-oblong, up to 20cm (8″) long. Basal leaves are heart-shaped. Flowers have a musk scent, up to 10cm (4″) across.

Dendrobium revolutum

Dendrobium revolutum

COMMON NAME: None.
COLOUR: Flower white. Labellum orange.
SIZE: Growing up to 60cm (24″) high.
CLIMATE: Warm to hot.
DISTRIBUTION: Native to Burma, Thailand, Laos, Vietnam, Peninsula Malaysia and Papua New Guinea.
FLOWERING TIME: Early summer.
DESCRIPTION: Pseudobulbs are cylindrical, up to 60cm (24″) high. Leaves are oblong. Solitary flower, 2.5cm (1″) long.

Dendrobium rhodopterygium syn. D. polyphlebium

COMMON NAME: None.
COLOUR: Flowers pale pink to purple, may be blotched white. Labellum throat blotched with purple.
SIZE: Growing up to 20cm (8″) high.
CLIMATE: Intermediate.
DISTRIBUTION: Native to Burma.
FLOWERING TIME: Spring.
DESCRIPTION: Pseudobulbs are long, cylindrical canes up to 20cm (8″) high. Inflorescence borne from leafless canes. Flowers are fragrant and 7.5cm (3″) across. Labellum fringed.

Dendrobium rhodopterygium syn. *D. polyphlebium*

Dendrobium rhodostictum

COMMON NAME: None.
COLOUR: Flowers white. Labellum throat veined and speckled with mauve.
SIZE: Growing up to 25cm (10″) high.
CLIMATE: Warm.
DISTRIBUTION: Native to Papua New Guinea in rainforest above 1500m (5000′).
FLOWERING TIME: Spring to early summer.
DESCRIPTION: Pseudobulbs are slender clavate, up to 20cm (8″) high. Leaves are apical oval, obtuse, up to 6.5cm (2½″) long. Flowers are waxy and fragrant.

Dendrobium rhodostictum

Dendrobium ruginosum

Dendrobium ruginosum

COMMON NAME: None.
COLOUR: Flowers white. Labellum veined purple-red.
SIZE: Growing up to 37cm (14½″) high.
CLIMATE: Hot.
DISTRIBUTION: Native to Solomon Islands and Bougainville, growing in montane forests.
FLOWERING TIME: Summer.
DESCRIPTION: An epiphytic or lithophytic plant. Pseudobulbs clustered, tetragonal, clavate, up to 25cm (10″) high. Leaves broad-lanceolate, acute, up to 12cm (4½″) long. Inflorescence up to 20cm (8″) long. Flowers grow up to 4cm (1½″) across.

Dendrobium ruppianum

COMMON NAME: None.
COLOUR: Flowers white. Labellum marked with purple lines.
SIZE: Growing up to 45cm (18″) high.
CLIMATE: Cool to warm.
DISTRIBUTION: Native to Australia (far north-east); common in rainforest.
FLOWERING TIME: Late winter to spring.
DESCRIPTION: Pseudobulbs fusiform, furrowed, up to 30cm (12″). Two to seven leaves, up to 15cm (6″) long, ovate-oblong, and apical margins may be undulate. Raceme erect; flowers numerous and fragrant.

Dendrobium sanderae

Dendrobium sanderae

COMMON NAME: None.
COLOUR: Flowers white. Labellum marked with purple and green.
SIZE: Stems erect up to 80cm (32″) high.
CLIMATE: Warm.
DISTRIBUTION: Native to the Philippines and Luzon.
FLOWERING TIME: Usually autumn to winter.
DESCRIPTION: Leaves ovate to linear-ovate, 12.5cm (5″) long. Flowers are large, showy, and 10cm (4″) across.

Dendrobium schuetzei

Dendrobium ruppianum

Dendrobium sanderae var. major

COMMON NAME: None.
COLOUR: Flowers white. Labellum veined light purple.
SIZE: Growing up to 70cm (28″) or more high.
CLIMATE: Warm.
DISTRIBUTION: Native to the Philippines (Baguio).
FLOWERING TIME: Spring to summer.
DESCRIPTION: Stems clustered, elongate, up to 70cm (28″) long. Leaves lanceolate, slightly notched at the apex, up to 10cm (4″) or more long. Flowers are large and showy, about 10cm (4″) across. Labellum tri-lobed. *Dendrobium Sanderae* var. *major* is similar in habit to *D. sanderae*, but is much longer in every aspect.

Dendrobium schuetzei

COMMON NAME: None.
COLOUR: Flowers white. Labellum green, spotted at the base.
SIZE: Ephiphytic plant, 35cm (14″) high.
CLIMATE: Warm.
DISTRIBUTION: Native to the Philippines (Mindanao).
FLOWERING TIME: Autumn. It has a long flower life.
DESCRIPTION: Pseudobulbs are robust and stem-like. Flowers are large, borne in clusters of four or more, white, up to 7.5cm (3″) across and are fragrant. Labellum tri-lobed.

Dendrobium secundum

Dendrobium schuleri

COMMON NAME: None.
COLOUR: Flowers green-yellow. Labellum green-white with purple markings.
SIZE: Growing up to 1.2m (4′) high.
CLIMATE: Hot.
DISTRIBUTION: Native to northern Papua New Guinea; growing alongside swamps, creeks and lagoons.
FLOWERING TIME: Usually autumn.
DESCRIPTION: Pseudobulbs cylindrical, swollen near the base, up to 1.2m (4′) high. Leaves lanceolate, alternate, up to 17cm (6¾″) long. Inflorescence long, flowers are numerous and grow up to 6cm (2½″) across.

Dendrobium schuleri

Dendrobium sanderae var. *major*

Dendrobium secundum

COMMON NAME: Toothbrush Orchid.
COLOUR: Flowers pink. Labellum orange.
SIZE: Growing up to 1m (40″) high.
CLIMATE: Warm.
DISTRIBUTION: Native to Burma, Thailand, Vietnam, Malaysia, the Philippines, Java, Sumatra and Borneo.
FLOWERING TIME: Spring to early summer.
DESCRIPTION: Pseudobulbs erect or semi-pendulous, fusiform, 1m (40″) long or more. Leaves oblong-lanceolate, unequally emarginate, up to 10cm (4″) long. Inflorescence borne from upper nodes, with numerous, small and waxy flowers.

Dendrobium smilliae

COMMON NAME: Bottle Brush Orchid.
COLOUR: Flower colour varies from pink-mauve at the base to green-white. Labellum dark shining green.
SIZE: Growing up to 1m (40″) high.
CLIMATE: Warm to hot.
DISTRIBUTION: Native to Australia (northern Queensland), Papua New Guinea; mainly coastal and lowland forest.
FLOWERING TIME: Late winter to spring.
DESCRIPTION: Pseudobulbs cylindrical, furrowed when mature, up to 90cm (3′) high. Leaves ovate or oblong-lanceolate, up to 15cm (6″) long. Flowers dense in short raceme.

Dendrobium speciosum var. *hillii*

Dendrobium speciosum var. hillii

COMMON NAME: King Rock Orchid
COLOUR: Flowers creamy white, yellow.
SIZE: Growing up to 1.2m (4′) high.
CLIMATE: Cool.
DISTRIBUTION: Native to Australia (eastern rainforests).
FLOWERING TIME: Spring.
DESCRIPTION: Pseudobulbs up to 1.2m (4′) high. Leaves apical, thick, ovate to oblong 30cm (12″) long. Long raceme with numerous flowers and strongly perfumed. This giant epiphytic and lithophytic plant gives a showy display.

Dendrobium smilliae

Dendrobium spectabile syn. D. tigrinum

COMMON NAME: None.
COLOUR: Flowers cream, margin pale green-cream, veined and mottled purple-red.
SIZE: Growing up to 60cm (2′) high.
CLIMATE: Warm to hot.
DISTRIBUTION: Native to Papua New Guinea and Solomon Islands.
FLOWERING TIME: Winter to early spring.
DESCRIPTION: Pseudobulbs clavate, up to 60cm (2′) high. Leaves lanceolate to ovate, up to 20cm (8″) long. Floral segments margins crinkled.

Dendrobium spectabile syn. *D. tigrinum*

Dendrobium X superbiens

COMMON NAME: None.
COLOUR: Flowers purple to rose, mottled with purple.
SIZE: Growing up to 1.2m (4′) high.
CLIMATE: Warm.
DISTRIBUTION: Native to Australia (north-east, and Torres Strait Islands)
FLOWERING TIME: Autumn to early winter.
DESCRIPTION: A natural hybrid between *D. bigibbum* and *D. discolor*. Pseudobulbs up to 1.2m (4′) high. Flowering scape up to 93cm (3′) long. Flowers are 7.5cm (3″) across.

Dendrobium sutepense

COMMON NAME: Ueang Mali.
COLOUR: Flowers white. Labellum marked with yellow and veined orange.
SIZE: Growing up to 30cm (12″) high.
CLIMATE: Intermediate.
DISTRIBUTION: Native to Burma, Thailand and Indo-China, growing at elevations from 1500 to 1700m (5000 to 5600′).
FLOWERING TIME: Spring.
DESCRIPTION: A common epiphytic plant. Pseudobulbs cane-like, stems linear, cylindrical, narrow at the base, becoming flexuose, about 30cm (12″) high. Leaves alternate, borne at nodes, lanceolate, unequally emarginate at the apex, about 7.5cm (3″) long. Inflorescence short. Flowers borne at the leaf axis, and grow up to 3cm (1¼″) across.

Dendrobium sutepense

Dendrobium X *superbiens*

Dendrobium tangerinum

COMMON NAME: Tangerine Dendrobium.
COLOUR: Petals tangerine, sepals and labellum are cream marked and veined red-purple.
SIZE: Growing up to 2m (6′6″) high.
CLIMATE: Warm to hot.
DISTRIBUTION: Native to Papua New Guinea.
FLOWERING TIME: Winter.
DESCRIPTION: Pseudobulbs cane-like stems, up to 2m (6′6″). Leaves alternate, broad-lanceolate. Inflorescence erect arching up to 60cm (2′) high. Flowers to 10cm (4″) across.

Dendrobium tangerinum

Dendrobium taurinum

Dendrobium taurinum

COMMON NAME: None.
COLOUR: Sepals yellow-green. Petals purple. Labellum white to purple.
SIZE: Growing up to 1.2m (4′) high.
CLIMATE: Warm.
DISTRIBUTION: Native to the Philippines.
FLOWERING TIME: Autumn to winter.
DESCRIPTION: Pseudobulbs fusiform to cylindrical, up to 1.2m (4′) high. Leaves oblong or elliptic, emarginate, up to 15cm (6″) long. Flowers are waxy and 6cm (2½″) across. Labellum margins wavy.

Dendrobium teretifolium

COMMON NAME: Bridal Veil or Pencil Orchid.
COLOUR: Flowers white to cream with purple-brown markings.
SIZE: Pendulous epiphyte hanging to 2m (6′6″) long.
CLIMATE: Cool.
DISTRIBUTION: Native to Australia (on east coast) and Papua New Guinea.
FLOWERING TIME: Spring.
DESCRIPTION: Leaves are pencil-like and grow up to 60cm (2′) long. Flowers are about 5cm (2″) across.

Dendrobium teretifolium

Dendrobium tetragonum

COMMON NAME: Spider Orchid.
COLOUR: Flowers yellow-cream margined maroon.
SIZE: Pendulous to 60cm (2′) long.
CLIMATE: Cool to intermediate.
DISTRIBUTION: Native to Australia (eastern coast).
FLOWERING TIME: Mostly spring.
DESCRIPTION: Pseudobulbs pendulous, tetragonal, fusiform. Leaves sinuate, apical, broadly oblanceolate, 10cm (4″) long. Flowers are variable, 5cm (2″) long, and borne in clusters.

Dendrobium tetragonum (Island form)

Dendrobium tetragonum (Island form)

COMMON NAME: None.
COLOUR: Flower colour yellow-brown, barred maroon.
SIZE: Same as type.
CLIMATE: Cool.
DISTRIBUTION: Native to Australia (eastern coast lowlands), growing on Paper Barks (*Melaleuca* sp.) along rivers, creeks and on estuarine islands.
FLOWERING TIME: Late winter to spring.
DESCRIPTION: Same as its type, but a superior form. Flowers much larger. Raceme terminal, densely flowered, up to fifteen blooms. Known to many botanists as *D. melaleucaphilum*.

Dendrobium tetragonum

Dendrobium tetragonum var. gigantum

COMMON NAME: Large Spider Orchid.
COLOUR: Flowers marked maroon. Labellum white.
SIZE: Same as type.
CLIMATE: Intermediate.
DISTRIBUTION: Native to Australia (north-eastern).
FLOWERING TIME: Late autumn to spring.
DESCRIPTION: Same as type, except flowers much larger.

Dendrobium tokai

Dendrobium thyrsiflorum

COMMON NAME: None.
COLOUR: Flowers white. Labellum yellow-orange.
SIZE: Growing up to 50cm (20″) high.
CLIMATE: Intermediate.
DISTRIBUTION: Native to Himalayas, Thailand and Burma.
FLOWERING TIME: Spring.
DESCRIPTION: Pseudobulbs tetragonal-fusiform to 50cm (20″) high. Inflorescence arching to pendulous. Flowers numerous and approximately 5cm (2″) across, fragrant.

Dendrobium thyrsiflorum

Dendrobium tetragonum var. *gigantum*

Dendrobium tokai

COMMON NAME: None.
COLOUR: Flowers yellow to brown.
SIZE: Up to 1.2m (4′) high.
CLIMATE: Warm to hot.
DISTRIBUTION: Native to Fiji.
FLOWERING TIME: Late autumn to spring.
DESCRIPTION: A large, common epiphyte, with cane-like pseudobulbs to 1.2m (4′) high, leaves alternating on upper one-third of cane, to 10cm (4″) long. Flowers to 6cm (2.5″) across, sepals and petals slightly twisted.

Dendrobium transparens

Dendrobium tortile

COMMON NAME: None.
COLOUR: Flowers mauve to purple. Labellum white or cream, veined mauve.
SIZE: Growing up to 30cm (12″) high.
CLIMATE: Intermediate to warm.
DISTRIBUTION: Native to Thailand, Burma, Vietnam and Peninsula Malaysia.
FLOWERING TIME: Spring.
DESCRIPTION: Pseudobulbs fusiform-cylindrical, erect, furrowed when matured, up to 30cm (12″) high. Leaves linear-oblong, deciduous, up to 10cm (4″) long. Inflorescence short, borne from the nodes of leafless pseudobulbs. Flowers are fragrant and up to 7.5cm (3″) across.

Dendrobium tortile

Dendrobium transparens

COMMON NAME: None.
COLOUR: Flowers lilac to pink with a transparent look. Labellum veined and blotched purple.
SIZE: Growing up to 70cm (28″) high.
CLIMATE: Intermediate.
DISTRIBUTION: Native to the Himalayas through to Burma; common in Nepal, Sikkim and Assam. Grows at an altitude of 1300m (4265′).
FLOWERING TIME: Spring to early summer.
DESCRIPTION: Pseudobulbs up to 70cm (28″) high. Leaves linear-lanceolate, acute, up to 10cm (4″) long. Inflorescence short, borne from leafless pseudobulbs. Flowers are 4cm (1½″) across.

Dendrobium trigonopsis

Common Name: None.
Colour: Flowers are golden yellow. Labellum often has red transverse lines on both sides with greenish centre.
Size: Growing up to 30cm (1′) high.
Climate: Intermediate to warm.
Distribution: Native to Burma, China (Yunnan), Thailand and Laos.
Flowering Time: Spring.
Description: Pseudobulbs are clustered, fusiform, up to 20cm (8″) high. Leaves are oblong or strap-like, acute, up to 10cm (4″) long. Flowers are up to 5cm (2″) across.

Dendrobium trigonopsis

Dendrobium victoriae-reginae

Dendrobium victoriae-reginae

Common Name: None.
Colour: Flowers white, apical blotched and veined blue-mauve.
Size: Growing up to 60cm (2′) high.
Climate: Intermediate.
Distribution: Native to the Philippines. Grows in damp mossy forests at altitudes of 1800 to 2400m, (3300 to 8000′).
Flowering Time: Throughout the year.
Description: Pseudobulbs pendulous, cylindrical, stem-like, swollen at the nodes, up to 60cm (24″) high. Leaves oblong-lanceolate, up to 8cm (3½″) long. Inflorescence short, borne from leafless pseudobulbs.

Dendrobium wassallii

Common Name: None.
Colour: Flowers white. Labellum marked with yellow.
Size: Grows up to 10cm (4″) high.
Climate: Intermediate.
Distribution: Native to Australia (far north-east).
Flowering Time: Late autumn to winter and sometimes late summer.
Description: Leaves semi-terete on creeping rhizomes. Mat-forming epiphyte or lithophyte. Raceme densely flowered. Flowers are spidery and about 2.5cm (1″) across.

Dendrobium wassallii

DIMORPHORCHIS
(dye-morf-or-kis)

*D*imorphorchis from the Gk *dimorphus* (having two forms) *orchi(s), orchid(eus)*(orchid-like), with reference to the two distinct forms of flowers on the same inflorescence spike. This is a genus of two extraordinary epiphytic species from Borneo. Stems multiply from the roots, erect or arching, up to 2m (7') tall, and are densely leafy. Leaves are up to 1m (3') long, unequally lobed at apex. Inflorescence is pendulous and many-flowered. The flowers have two distinct forms: basal flowers are usually more fleshy than remaining flowers. The labellum is identical in structure in both forms, and is slipper-shaped. *Dimorphorchis lowii* is much more spectacular than *D. rohaniana*. This is one of the most sought after orchidaceous plants and is found in choice collections.

Culture: Compost as for tropical *Vandas*. The plant requires support on maturing. Use well-drained pots, water regularly, and provide humidity and moderate shade.

Dimorphorchis lowii

Dimorphorchis lowii

COMMON NAME: None.
COLOUR: Flowers yellow with red-brown blotches. Labellum yellow spotted with purple.
SIZE: Growing up to 2.3m (7') high.
CLIMATE: Hot.
DISTRIBUTION: Native to Borneo.
FLOWERING TIME: Autumn to early winter.
DESCRIPTION: Stems unusually erect, up to 2.1m (7') high in mature plants. Leaves strap-shaped, apical, unequally emarginate up to 90cm (3') long. Inflorescence long, pendulous, carrying two forms of flowers: basal one third, sepals and petals are broad, yellow and speckled with maroon; distal two thirds flowers, sepals and petals are yellow and heavily blotched with maroon. Flowers are numerous and grow up to 7.5cm (3") across.

Dimorphorchis lowii

DIPODIUM
(due-poe-dee-um)

Dipodium from the Gk *di* (two) *podion* (foot as in a vase) with possible reference to the two stipes of the pollinia. This genus of over twenty species is widely distributed from China through South-east Asia, the Philippines, Malaysia, Indonesia, Papua New Guinea to New Caledonia and Australia. It is a genus of extremely diverse growing habits. Some species are leafless terrestrial herbs, some are leafy terrestrial, and others start as terrestrials and develop a long, climbing epiphytic stem which continues to grow from the apex producing roots and branching. With the decay of the primary roots, the plant simulates the monopodial habit of the *Vanda*. The leafless species have a *mycorrhizal* association with Honey Fungus. The fungus is attached to both the roots of the orchid and another plant; thus, the fungus feeds the orchid on food obtained from the other plant. Flowers occur in a terminal raceme on a long stem. Sepals and petals are equal. The labellum is tri-lobed and is attached to the column foot.

Culture: The leafy terrestrial species grow as for *Phaius*, i.e. coarse compost, good drainage, shade, cool conditions and less water when growth is complete. The species with the monopodial habit grow as *Arachnis*. The leafless saprophytic species are very difficult to cultivate. Treat as for *Galeola*.

Dipodium punctatum

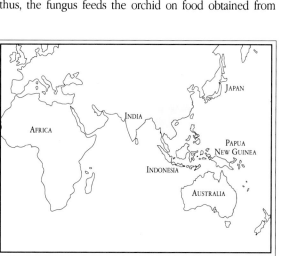

Dipodium punctatum

COMMON NAME: Hyacinth Orchid.
COLOUR: Flowers are pink to dark mauve with red spots.
SIZE: Leafless, rhizomeous. Inflorescence to 1.5m (5′) high.
CLIMATE: Cool.
DISTRIBUTION: Native to eastern Australia.
FLOWERING TIME: Spring.
DESCRIPTION: A variable saprophytic terrestrial living off subterranean fungi. The leafless stem carries a raceme of up to sixty flowers. Flowers are 1 to 3.1cm (½ to 1¼″) across.

Dipodium punctatum

DIURIS
(dye-yewr-is)

Diuris from the Gk *di* (two) *ura* (a tail) with reference to the two tail-like lateral sepals. This genus of about forty delightful species is found mainly in Australia extending to Timor and Java. It is a glabrous terrestrial herb with ovoid tubers. Leaves are few to numerous, and are linear. There are several flowers in a terminal raceme. The dorsal sepal is erect or reflexed, and broad; lateral sepals are more or less deflexed, linear or petaloid, and long. Petals are broad. The labellum is deeply tri-lobed, with the mid-lobe often longer and broader than lateral lobes. The column comprises a separate style and stamen.

Culture: As for *Caladenia*.

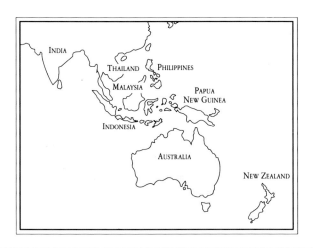

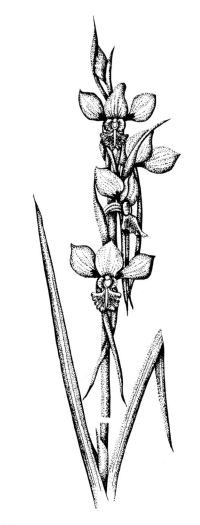

Diuris punctata forma *blakneyae*

Diuris sulphurea

Diuris sulphurea

COMMON NAME: Donkey Orchid or Clown Orchid.
COLOUR: Flowers yellow with brown markings.
SIZE: Growing up to 60cm (2′) high.
CLIMATE: Cool.
DISTRIBUTION: Native to eastern Australia.
FLOWERING TIME: Spring.
DESCRIPTION: A terrestrial plant up to 60cm (2′) high. Leaves long and flat. Labellum 15mm (½″) long, tri-lobed. Dorsal sepal shorter and broader than the petals. Flowers to 6cm (2½″) across.

DORITIS
(doh-rye-tis)

Doritis The derivation of the name is obscure, possibly it is from the Gk *dory* (a spear) with reference to the shape of the labellum, or after Doritis, one of the names of Aphrodite the goddess of love and beauty in Greek mythology. This is a genus of several species, or variants of a single species, and occurs from India, Burma, Sri Lanka, Thailand, Malaysia to Sumatra. This epiphytic or terrestrial monopodial herb with a clump forming habit, continuously grows then blooms, reaching ever upwards producing beautiful mauve-purple blossoms all the year round. It is pseudobulbless, with leafy stems. Leaves are distichous and coriaceous. Inflorescence is erect and up to 90cm (3') long, and has many flowers in a dense raceme. Flowers are variable in size and colour, and grow up to 5cm (2") across; they are showy and blooms remain open for long periods. Sepals and petals are free, and spreading; lateral sepals form a spur-like mentum with column foot. The labellum is tri-lobed, adnate to column foot and clawed; side-lobes are erect; mid-lobe is veined with white lines, geniculate about the middle, with two antennae behind the lateral lobes at base of the labellum; the disc has a forked callus.

Culture: Compost in pots or baskets. It shoots from the base forming clumps. Roots will grow over the side of the pots or baskets. The plant requires plenty of shade, humidity in well-drained pots, and plenty of water. Do not allow the plants to become dry, but reduce the watering when plant is not growing.

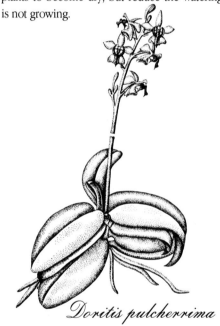

Doritis pulcherrima

Doritis pulcherrima

COMMON NAME: None.
COLOUR: Flowers light pink-purple. Labellum darker.
SIZE: Growing up to 25cm (10") wide.
CLIMATE: Warm.
DISTRIBUTION: Native to Burma, Thailand, Laos, Cambodia, Vietnam, Peninsula Malaysia and Sumatra.
FLOWERING TIME: Mainly autumn to winter or throughout the year.
DESCRIPTION: Leaves spreading 15cm (6") long. Inflorescence about 90cm (3') high, raceme dense. Flowers vary from 1 to 5cm (½ to 2") across.

Doritis pulcherrima

DRACULA
(dray-cula)

Dracula Gk *draco* (dragon). The whimsical name dracula means 'little dragon', having reference to the monster-like appearance of some of the hairy flowers with their bizarre markings and long tails; they are often described as grotesque. In 1978 Dr C. A. Luer separated species from the genus *Masdevallia* to form a new genus, *Dracula*. *Dracula* differs from *Masdevallia* in having keeled leaves, and it has a mobile labellum hinged to the foot of the column and partitioned into epichile and hypochile; the petals are divided at the apex with knob-like nodules.

Culture: Plant in hanging baskets of well-drained, good moisture-retaining compost. It requires frequent watering. The leaves are prone to spotting, known as apical necrosis. Treat the disfiguration with fungicidal spray. Check the air movement and hygiene of your orchid house.

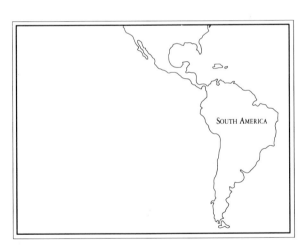

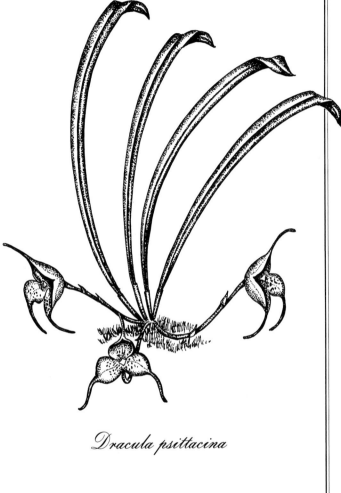

Dracula psittacina

Dracula sibundoyensis syn. *Masdevallia sibundoyensis*

Dracula sibundoyensis syn. *Masdevallia sibundoyensis*

COMMON NAME: None.
COLOUR: Flower cream, speckled maroon and tips maroon. Labellum cream.
SIZE: Growing to 16cm (6″) or more high.
CLIMATE: Warm.
DISTRIBUTION: Native to Colombia (Andes), growing in cloud forests.
FLOWERING TIME: Spring.
DESCRIPTION: A tufted epiphytic or lithophytic herb. Leaves are narrow-lanceolate, keeled, acute, up to 15cm (6″) high. Flower scape shorter than the leaves. Solitary flower grows to 10cm (4″) or more long, spreading to 3.5cm (1¼″) across.

DRYADELLA
(dry-ad-ella)

Dryadella is named after the dryads (wood nymphs), the mythological semi-divine maidens inhabiting the forests and trees. This genus comprises four species from Brazil and one from Central America; it was removed from genus *Masdevallia* by Dr C. A. Luer. *Dryadella* differ from *Masdevallia* in that their leaves are narrow, fleshy with longitudinal grooves. The flowers differ from *Masdevallia* in having a thick fold near the base of the lateral sepals; the sepals are joined forming a mentum below the column foot. The labellum is long and tongue-like.

Culture: As for *Masdevallia*. Compost, in well-drained pots. Water carefully and do not overwater.

SOUTH AMERICA

Dryadella zebrina

Dryadella zebrina syn. *Masdevallia zebrina*

COMMON NAME: Partridge in the Grass Orchids.
COLOUR: Flowers yellow, spotted maroon. Labellum orange-brown.
SIZE: Growing up to 6cm (2¼″) high.
CLIMATE: Intermediate.
DISTRIBUTION: Native to Brazil.
FLOWERING TIME: Spring.
DESCRIPTION: Leaves are lanceolate, green with purple tinges, up to 6cm (2¼″) long. Flowers are small, 4.5cm (1¾″) long.

Dryadella zebrina syn. *Masdevallia zebrina*

ENCYCLIA

(en-sik-lee-ah)

Encyclia from the Gk *enkyklin* (to encircle) with reference to side lobes of the labellum encircling the column. This genus of about 150 species is found in Mexico, West Indies and the tropics of South America. It is an epiphytic and occasionally lithophytic herb. Stems form pseudobulbs and are ovoid-conical, pyriform, ellipsoid or fusiform, clustered or spaced along creeping rhizomes. Leaves are coriaceous, fleshy, lanceolate, lingulate, broad or ovate. Inflorescence panicles or racemose, erect, arching or pendulous. Flowers are showy and often delightfully fragrant. Sepals and petals are free, spreading and sub-similar. The labellum is tri-lobed or entire, free from the column, may be part adnate but never completely adnate. The genus *Encyclia* was first described in 1828, but continued to be included in *Epidendrum* by many taxonomists until 1961. *Encyclia's* features distinguishing it from *Epidendrum* are the presence of pseudobulbs and the labellum being only partially adnate to the column.

Culture: Use compost in well-drained pots or pans. Plants require moderate shade, humidity and water. Watch carefully for over watering in plants with soft stems.

Encyclia cochleata

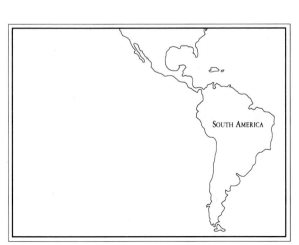

SOUTH AMERICA

Encyclia baculus syn. *Epidendrum baculus*

COMMON NAME: None.
COLOUR: Flowers are whitish cream. Labellum veined with purple.
SIZE: Growing up to 60cm (2') high.
CLIMATE: Warm.
DISTRIBUTION: Native to Mexico, found as far south as Colombia.
FLOWERING TIME: Spring.
DESCRIPTION: Pseudobulbs borne on rhizome, somewhat compressed, fusiform, up to 30cm (1') high. Leaves lanceolate or strap-shape, up to 30cm (1') long. Inflorescence short. Flowers usually grow in pairs, borne back to back, and are up to 9cm (3½") across.

Encyclia baculus syn. *Epidendrum baculus*

Encyclia chacaoensis syn. *Epidendrum chacaoense*

COMMON NAME: None.
COLOUR: Flowers greenish yellow. Labellum marked with purple.
SIZE: Growing up to 37.5cm (15") high.
CLIMATE: Intermediate to warm.
DISTRIBUTION: Native to Panama and Mexico.
FLOWERING TIME: Winter to spring.
DESCRIPTION: Pseudobulbs are compressed, ovoid to fusiform, 7.5cm (3") long. Leaves are narrow-obtuse, 30cm (12") long. Short inflorescence. Flowers are fragrant, inverted and 5cm (2") across.

Encyclia chacaoensis syn. *Epidendrum chacaoense*

Encyclia chondylobulbon

COMMON NAME: None.
COLOUR: Flowers whitish cream. Labellum white or pale green, with purple veins.
SIZE: Grows up to 1.2m (4') high.
CLIMATE: Intermediate to warm.
DISTRIBUTION: Native to Mexico.
FLOWERING TIME: Spring.
DESCRIPTION: Pseudobulbs up to 25cm (10") high, 3cm (1") apart. The three to five leaves are narrow-lanceolate and up to 1m (40") long. Four or more flowers grow on a long peduncle and are up to 7.5cm (3") wide.

Encyclia citrina syn. *Epidendrum citrinum, Cattleya citrina*

COMMON NAME: None.
COLOUR: Flowers yellow.
SIZE: Growing pendulous to 30cm (12") long.
CLIMATE: Intermediate.
DISTRIBUTION: Native to Mexico at an altitude of 1300 to 2200m (4265 to 7200') and growing in pine and oak forests.
FLOWERING TIME: Spring.
DESCRIPTION: Pseudobulbs are pendulous in clusters, often hanging in tufts, conical ovoid or fusiform, up to 6cm (2½") long. Leaves are pendulous, elliptic to 25cm (10") long. Inflorescence 10cm (4") long. The fragrant flowers grow up to 7.5cm (3") long.

Encyclia citrina syn. *Epidendrum citrinum, Cattleya citrina*

Encyclia chondylobulbon

Encyclia bractescens syn. *E. acicularis*

Encyclia bractescens syn. *E. acicularis*

COMMON NAME: None.
COLOUR: Flowers greenish yellow. Nerves red-brown. Labellum white with maroon-brown throat.
SIZE: Growing up to 20cm (8") high.
CLIMATE: Intermediate to warm.
DISTRIBUTION: Native to Mexico, Bahamas, British Honduras and Guatemala.
FLOWERING TIME: Spring.
DESCRIPTION: Pseudobulbs clustered, up to 2.5cm (1") high. Leaves linear-lanceolate, 20cm (8") long. Inflorescence five to twenty flowers, 15cm (6") long. Fragrant flowers are 2.5cm (1") across.

Encyclia cochleata syn. *Epidendrum cochleatum*

Encyclia cochleata syn. *Epidendrum cochleatum*

COMMON NAME: Cockleshell Orchid.
COLOUR: Flower petals lemon-green. Labellum has purple markings.
SIZE: Growing up to 50cm (20″) high.
CLIMATE: Intermediate.
DISTRIBUTION: Native to Venezuela, Colombia, South Mexico, Florida (USA), Cuba, Brazil and West Indies. Grows at an altitude of 1000 to 2000m (3280 to 6561′).
FLOWERING TIME: All year, ever-blooming.
DESCRIPTION: Pseudobulbs ovoid-ellipsoid, compressed, 5 to 20cm (2 to 8″) long. Leaves oblong-lanceolate up to 37cm (15″) long. Flowers up to 9cm (3½″) long. Labellum inverted.

Encyclia cordigera var. *alba* 'Henrique' syn. *Epidendrum atropurpurea*

Encyclia cordigera var. *alba* syn. *Epidendrum atropurpurea*

COMMON NAME: None.
COLOUR: Flowers light green. Labellum white.
SIZE: Growing up to 56cm (23″) high.
CLIMATE: Intermediate to warm.
DISTRIBUTION: Native to Mexico and Peru, growing from sea level to 900m (2952′) in dry forest.
FLOWERING TIME: Spring.
DESCRIPTION: Pseudobulbs clustered, erect, ovoid-conical, up to 10cm (4″). Leaves are strap-shaped, up to 45cm (18″). Inflorescence long, paniculate, with large flowers. The species *E. cordigera* has many colour variations. Many growers consider it to be one of the best Mexican *Encyclia* for cultivation.

Encyclia fragrans syn. *Epidendrum fragrans*

Encyclia fragrans syn. *Epidendrum fragrans*

COMMON NAME: None.
COLOUR: Labellum creamy white with purple streaks.
SIZE: Grows up to 30cm (12″) high.
CLIMATE: Intermediate.
DISTRIBUTION: Native to Mexico, Central America, northern South America, West Indies, Ecuador, Peru and Brazil. Grows at altitudes from sea level up to 1800m (3300′).
FLOWERING TIME: Winter to spring.
DESCRIPTION: A variable species. Pseudobulbs ellipsoid 5 to 11.5cm (2 to 4½″) long. Leaves are oblong-lanceolate to 20cm (8″) long. Flower inverted and grows to 5cm (2″) across.

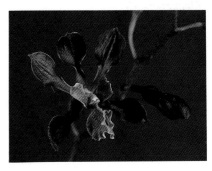

Encyclia hanburii syn. *Epidendrum hanburii*

Encyclia hanburii syn. *Epidendrum hanburii*

COMMON NAME: None.
COLOUR: Flowers red-brown. Labellum white or pink with purple veins.
SIZE: Growing up to 30cm (12″) high.
CLIMATE: Intermediate.
DISTRIBUTION: Native to Mexico. Grows at altitudes of 1200 to 1800m (4000 to 6000′) in scrub oak forests.
FLOWERING TIME: Summer to autumn.
DESCRIPTION: Pseudobulbs are clustered, conical-ovoid, up to 8cm (3¼″) high. Leaves are elliptic-lanceolate to oblong, up to 23cm (9″) long. Inflorescence paniculate, with ten to thirty-five blooms, grows up to 90cm (3′) long. Flowers are up to 5cm (2″) across.

Encyclia linkiana syn. *Epidendrum linkianum*

Encyclia linkiana syn. *Epidendrum linkianum*

COMMON NAME: None.
COLOUR: Flowers olive-green, veined maroon. Labellum white, marked with green and maroon.
SIZE: Growing up to 30cm (12″) high.
CLIMATE: Intermediate.
DISTRIBUTION: Native to Mexico, Venezuela and Peru. Growing at elevations of 500 to 2300m (1650 to 6600′).
FLOWERING TIME: Spring to summer and probably most of the year.
DESCRIPTION: Pseudobulbs fusiform borne on creeping rhizome. Leaves are strap-like and flowers are sparse.

Encyclia livida syn. *E. tessellata*

COMMON NAME: None.
COLOUR: Flowers outside greenish-yellow, inside brown and streaked with a darker brown. Labellum pale yellow streaked with purple.
SIZE: Grows up to 30cm (12″) high.
CLIMATE: Intermediate to warm.
DISTRIBUTION: Native from Mexico to Panama, Venezuela and Colombia.
FLOWERING TIME: Generally summer.
DESCRIPTION: Pseudobulbs are compressed, fusiform, ellipsoid or ovoid, up to 7.5cm (3″). Leaves are ligulate-elliptic, growing up to 22.5cm (9″) long. Flowers grow up to 2cm (¾″) across.

Encyclia livida syn. *E. tessellata*

Encyclia microbulbon

COMMON NAME: None.
COLOUR: Flowers light green, may be veined brown. Labellum white spotted pink.
SIZE: A small plant, growing up to 15cm (6″) high.
CLIMATE: Intermediate.
DISTRIBUTION: Native to Mexico.
FLOWERING TIME: Late spring.
DESCRIPTION: Pseudobulbs are clustered, conical, up to 4cm (1½″) high. Leaves are strap-shaped, up to 12.5cm (5″) long. Flowers grow up to 4cm (1½″) across.

Encyclia tampensis syn. *Epidendrum tampense*

COMMON NAME: None.
COLOUR: Flowers light yellow-brown or yellow-green, suffused and veined brownish purple. Labellum white, blotched red-purple.
SIZE: Growing up to 45cm (18″) high.
CLIMATE: Intermediate to warm.
DISTRIBUTION: Native to Bahamas, Florida (USA) and with *Encyclia tampense* var. *amessianum* in Cuba.
FLOWERING TIME: Spring to winter.
DESCRIPTION: Pseudobulbs are clustered, ovoid, up to 7.5cm (3″) high and are mat-forming. Leaves are linear-lanceolate and grow up to 37.5cm (15″) long. Flowers are fragrant and may measure up to 5cm (2″) across, but are generally smaller; their colour is most variable.

Encyclia microbulbon

Encyclia odoratissima syn. *Epidendrum odoratissium*

COMMON NAME: None.
COLOUR: Flowers green. Labellum yellow-cream, veined red.
SIZE: Growing up to 30cm (12″) high.
CLIMATE: Intermediate.
DISTRIBUTION: Native to Brazil.
FLOWERING TIME: Summer.
DESCRIPTION: Pseudobulbs are erect, elongate-ovoid, up to 30cm (12″) high. Leaves are long and linear. Inflorescence branched. Flowers are fragrant, growing to about 2.5cm (1″) across.

Encyclia tampensis syn. *Epidendrum tampense*

Encyclia odoratissima syn. *Epidendrum odoratissium*

EPIDENDRUM
(eh-pi-den-drum)

Epidendrum from the Gk *epi* (upon) *dendrum* (tree) with reference to epiphytic habit of the plants. From their discovery in the early 1700s, all epiphytes were called *Epidendrum*. Since that time, researchers have revised the genus on several occasions, with the result that today we have *Amblostoma, Arachnis, Barkeria, Brassavola, Cymbidiums, Encyclia* together with many other genera all originally included in *Epidendrum*. Today *Epidendrum* is still an extremely large genus of over one thousand species spread throughout Central America, Florida, the West Indies, and northern South America. This is a genus of epiphytic or perhaps lithophytic or terrestrial plants; they are variable, either small or large, erect or on creeping rhizomes not always conspicuous, sympodial, and stems which rarely develop pseudobulbs. Leaves vary almost as much as the stems, being thick, fleshy, coriaceous, linear or terete, apical on pseudobulbs, alternate on reed-like stems, and few to many.

The inflorescence is terminal and can be one or many-flowered. Flowers are 2 to 7.5cm (1 to 3″) across. Sepals and petals are similar—uniform, equal, reflexed or spreading. The labellum is tri-lobed, with lateral lobes adnate to column, and the mid-lobe broad, lobed, fringed or with serrate margins.

Culture: Compost. The pseudobulb group do best in pots. The creeping rhizome group grow best in pans or mounted on tree-fern fibre. The reed-like group do well in pots or grown as terrestrials. Plants require shade, especially during the summer months, and regular watering while growing, less during the rest period.

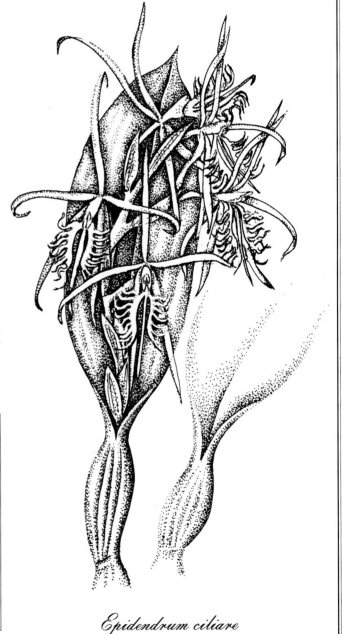

SOUTH AMERICA

Epidendrum ciliare

Epidendrum anceps

COMMON NAME: None.
COLOUR: Flowers yellow-brown to green-brown. Labellum pale green, flushed pink.
SIZE: Growing up to 70cm (28″) high.
CLIMATE: Intermediate.
DISTRIBUTION: Native to Mexico, southern Florida (USA), tropical America to Brazil, Peru and Ecuador.
FLOWERING TIME: Throughout the year, nearly always in bloom.
DESCRIPTION: An epiphytic, and at times, lithophytic plant. Stems are clustered and erect up to 70cm (28″) high. Leaves are oblong-elliptic, up to 15cm (6″) long. Inflorescence terminal. Flowers grow up to 1.5cm (½″) across.

Epidendrum anceps

Epidendrum ciliare

COMMON NAME: None.
COLOUR: Flowers yellow-green. Labellum white.
SIZE: Grows up to 30cm (12″) high.
CLIMATE: Intermediate.
DISTRIBUTION: Native to Mexico, West Indies, tropical America, Colombia, the Guyanas and Brazil.
FLOWERING TIME: Autumn to spring.
DESCRIPTION: A common epiphytic or lithophytic plant. Creeping rhizome, pseudobulbs fusiform, up to 20cm (8″). Leaves are oblong-lanceolate, growing to 12.5cm (5″) long. Flowers spreading to 7.5cm (3″) across.

Epidendrum ciliare

Epidendrum coriifolium

COMMON NAME: None.
COLOUR: Flowers pale green-brown, sepals and petals narrow. Labellum darker.
SIZE: Growing up to 35cm (14″) high.
CLIMATE: Intermediate.
DISTRIBUTION: Native to Mexico and Peru.
FLOWERING TIME: Autumn to winter.
DESCRIPTION: Epiphyte. Pseudobulb cane-like up to 30cm (12″). Leaves are fleshy, rigid, channelled, growing up to 25cm (10″) long. Inflorescence zig-zag, 25cm (10″) long. Flowers are narrow with a broad labellum.

Epidendrum difforme syn. *E. latilabre*

Epidendrum difforme syn. E. latilabre

COMMON NAME: None.
COLOUR: Flowers white, yellow or green.
SIZE: Growing up to 50cm (20″) high.
CLIMATE: Intermediate.
DISTRIBUTION: Native to Mexico, southern Salvador, West Indies, Central America to Brazil and Peru.
FLOWERING TIME: Almost throughout the year.
DESCRIPTION: This is a wide-ranging variable species. Stems are erect and numerous and grow up to 50cm (20″) high. Leaves are oblong-lanceolate, growing up to 10cm (4″) long. Inflorescence terminal and short.

Epidendrum coriifolium

Epidendrum nocturnum

Epidendrum nocturnum

COMMON NAME: None.
COLOUR: Flowers light green. Labellum white with yellow markings.
SIZE: Growing up to 1m (40") high.
CLIMATE: Intermediate.
DISTRIBUTION: Native to Brazil, Peru, tropical America, Ecuador, Mexico and Florida (USA); introduced to tropical West Africa.
FLOWERING TIME: Summer to autumn.
DESCRIPTION: A variable epiphyte. Stem canes, clustered up to 1m (40") high, with papery-sheaths bearing shiny distichous, oval to lanceolate leaves, 18cm (7") long. Compact inflorescence with flowers variable in size and colour; white is rare.

Epidendrum parkinsonianum syn. *E. falcatum*

Epidendrum paniculatum syn. E. floribundum

COMMON NAME: None.
COLOUR: Flowers pale green. Labellum white to cream.
SIZE: Growing up to 2.5m (10') tall.
CLIMATE: Intermediate to warm.
DISTRIBUTION: Native throughout tropical America.
FLOWERING TIME: Generally summer, and usually more than once annually.
DESCRIPTION: A common variable epiphytic or terrestrial plant. Stems are terete, clustered and covered in leaf sheaths. Leaves are lanceolate, up to 20cm (8") long. Inflorescence paniculate with numerous flowers, sometimes up to 250 blooms. The flower is about 1cm (½") across.

Epidendrum paniculatum syn. *E. floribundum*

Epidendrum parkinsonianum syn. E. falcatum

COMMON NAME: None.
COLOUR: Flowers white or creamy green and may be tinted with mauve. Labellum white with disc blotched yellow.
SIZE: A large pendulous epiphytic.
CLIMATE: Intermediate to warm.
DISTRIBUTION: Native to Mexico, Guatemala, Honduras, Panama and Costa Rica.
FLOWERING TIME: Summer to autumn, usually several times annually.
DESCRIPTION: Pseudobulbs are clustered, terete, curved-ascending, and up to 10cm (4") long. Leaves are fleshy, linear, channelled, acuminate, up to 75cm (30") long. Flowers, borne from new growth on short peduncles, are fragrant and grow up to 15cm (6") across.

Epidendrum schlechterianum

Epidendrum schlechterianum

COMMON NAME: None.
COLOUR: Flowers yellow-green, brown-green to pink-purple.
SIZE: Small epiphyte, mat-forming.
CLIMATE: Intermediate.
DISTRIBUTION: Native to Peru, Central America, Mexico to Panama, West Indies and Brazil. Altitude 670 to 1700m (2000 to 3000'). Found in dense forest.
FLOWERING TIME: Summer.
DESCRIPTION: A variable dwarf species. Stem enclosed by leaf sheaths, up to 5cm (2"). Numerous elliptic-oblong leaves, growing up to 3.2cm (1¼") long. Flowers are small, about 1.2cm (½") across.

Epidendrum stamfordianum

Epidendrum stamfordianum

COMMON NAME: None.
COLOUR: Flowers green-yellow, spotted purple-red. Labellum yellow with mid-lobe margins red.
SIZE: Growing up to 40cm (16") high.
CLIMATE: Intermediate to warm.
DISTRIBUTION: Native to Venezuela, Colombia and Mexico to Panama.
FLOWERING TIME: Winter to spring.
DESCRIPTION: Pseudobulbs are clustered, fusiform, up to 25cm (10") high. Leaves apical, oblong-linear, obtuse, growing up to 15cm (6") long. Inflorescence borne from base of pseudobulbs, occasionally one may be borne apical, and often branching. Flowers are numerous, showy, fragrant and are 4cm (1½") long. Labellum tri-lobed.

EPIGENEIUM

(eh-pi-jee-nee-um)

Epigeneium from the Gk *epi* (upon) *geneion* (chin) meaning 'on the chin' with reference to the sepals and petals on the column foot. This is a genus of about thirty rare species scattered across South-east Asia, from China in the north to India in the west, as far as the Philippines in the east, and to Papua New Guinea in the south. It is a medium-sized erect epiphytic herb. Pseudobulbs are angular, occurring at intervals along elongated creeping rhizomes. Leaves are apical, coriaceous, oblong to obovate. Pseudo-terminal with one to few flowers. The flowers are attractively showy and are medium to large. The dorsal sepal encloses the column; lateral sepals form a mentum with column foot. Petals are deltoid, decurrent along the mentum. The labellum is tri-lobed and pandurate; lateral lobes are erect and the callus has a ridge or lobulate. Column is short with a long foot.

Culture: Mount the plant on a tree-fern slab or in a shallow basket. Allowance must be made for the creeping habit of the elongated rhizome. It requires warm, humid, shady conditions. Potted plants are easily set back by stale or sour conditions at the roots. Perfect drainage is essential. The fleshy foliage will burn from over exposure if left in a sunny spot. Plants from this genus are rare in collections.

Epigeneium coelogyne

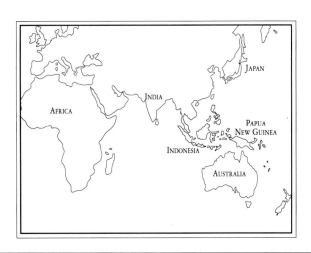

Epigeneium coelogyne

Epigeneium coelogyne

COMMON NAME: None.
COLOUR: Flowers brownish yellow with purple markings. The mid-lobe is almost purple-black.
SIZE: Growing up to 10cm (4″) high.
CLIMATE: Intermediate.
DISTRIBUTION: Native to Thailand and Burma.
FLOWERING TIME: Autumn.
DESCRIPTION: Pseudobulbs are borne on a stout creeping rhizome, ellipsoid, tetragonal, up to 6cm (2½″) high. Leaves grow in pairs, oblong-elliptic, emarginate to 7.5cm (3″) long. The fragrant flower grows to 10cm (4″) across.

ERIA
(ear-ee-a)

Eria from the Gk *erion* (wool) with reference to the woolly covering of the perianth. This is one of the larger aggregations of orchids into one genus in Orchidaceae. It has about five hundred species divided into thirteen groups, spread across tropical Asia from the Himalayas, China, the Philippines, Indonesia, Papua New Guinea, Pacific Islands to Fiji. Habitats range from hot humid coastal rainforests to the snow-line of the Himalayas. Primarily epiphytic, often lithophytic and rarely terrestrial, the genus has a variable habit. Stems are pseudobulbous, round, along creeping rhizomes, or often lengthy, cylindrical, fleshy, leafy stems, others short and heavily tomentose. The plant has two or many leaves often carpeted with hairs. Inflorescence is terminal or axillary, possessing either single flowers or dense racemes. Flowers have a distinctive shape and range from small to medium size. Sepals are free, hirsute or glabrous; lateral sepals adnate to elongate column foot; mentum saccate or spur-like; petals are similar, but smaller. The labellum is entire or tri-lobed, with the disc one to five keeled.

Culture: Depends on the species. Certain species do well in pans, while others grow best when mounted on tree-fern fibre slabs. Most plants require humid, shady conditions. Others may be grown outdoors even in cool climates. Make sure plants have good drainage and water with care. Consult your local orchid society about caring for these plants.

Eria vestita

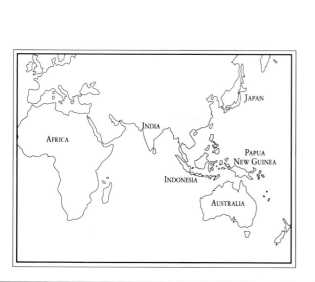

Eria albido-tomentosa

COMMON NAME: None.
COLOUR: Flowers yellowish green. Labellum marked with red.
SIZE: Growing up to 30cm (12″) high.
CLIMATE: Intermediate.
DISTRIBUTION: Native to Thailand, Burma, Java, Sumatra, Laos and Cambodia.
FLOWERING TIME: Autumn.
DESCRIPTION: Pseudobulbs are borne on a creeping rhizome, ovoid, up to 12.5cm (5″) high. Leaves are apical from pseudobulb, are narrow-lanceolate and grow up to 20cm (8″) long. Inflorescence basal, 15cm (6″) or more long, stem very white and tomentose. Flowers grow up to 2.5 cm (1″) across.

Eria albido-tomentosa

Eria inornata

COMMON NAME: None.
COLOUR: Flowers pale yellow.
SIZE: Growing up to 40cm (16″) high.
CLIMATE: Warm.
DISTRIBUTION: Native to far north-eastern Australia.
FLOWERING TIME: Late winter to spring.
DESCRIPTION: An epiphytic-lithophytic plant. Pseudobulbs are stout, ovate, conical, up to 20cm (8″) high. Leaves are 20cm (8″) long, or more. Raceme is vertical and grows up to 25cm (10″) long. Flowers are numerous.

Eria javanica

Eria javanica

COMMON NAME: None.
COLOUR: Flowers whitish cream. Labellum white with side lobes spotted red.
SIZE: Growing up to 37.5cm (15″) high.
CLIMATE: Intermediate to warm.
DISTRIBUTION: Native to Himalayas, Burma, Thailand, Indonesia and the Philippines.
FLOWERING TIME: Autumn.
DESCRIPTION: Pseudobulbs are ovoid, sheathed, up to 7.5cm (3″) high. Leaves are shiny, linear, growing up to 30cm (12″) long. Inflorescence pubescent, nodding, and longer than the leaves. Flowers are fragrant. The labellum is tri-lobed.

Eria aliciae

Eria undicaulius

COMMON NAME: None.
COLOUR: Flowers creamy white. Labellum marked with rosy pink.
SIZE: Growing up to 30cm (12″) high.
CLIMATE: Intermediate.
DISTRIBUTION: Native to Taiwan.
FLOWERING TIME: Spring to summer.
DESCRIPTION: Pseudobulbs are clustered, elongate, up to 25cm (10″) high. Leaves are broad-lanceolate, and grow up to 12.5cm (5″) long. Inflorescence arching to 15cm (6″) long, with dense numerous flowers, up to 2.5cm (1″) across.

Eria inornata

Eria aliciae

COMMON NAME: None.
COLOUR: Flowers whitish pink and marked with pink.
SIZE: Growing up to 1.5m (5′) high.
CLIMATE: Intermediate to warm.
DISTRIBUTION: Native to the Philippines, growing at an altitude of 1500m (4920′).
FLOWERING TIME: Autumn to winter.
DESCRIPTION: Long cane-like pseudobulbs, up to 1.5m (5′) long. Leaves are alternate, linear, acute, up to 25cm (10″) long. Inflorescence short, clustered and produced at the leaf axis. Flowers are small and numerous.

Eria undicaulius

EUANTHE
(yew-*an*-thee)

Euanthe from the Gk *euanthes* (blooming) with reference to the showy inflorescence. A monotypic genus established in 1914 by Schlechter. This is an extremely popular monopodial epiphytic orchid from the Philippines. Originally, it was labelled *Vanda sanderiana*. The distinction from *Vanda* is based on the structure of the flattened flower, in particular the formation of the labellum which is bipartite not tri-lobed as in other *Vanda* species.

Culture: As for *Vanda*. Use compost in large, well-drained pots or baskets. In the wild, *Euanthe* grows on trees close to the ocean, often on branches overhanging waves, and in tropical sunshine.

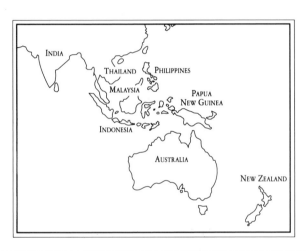

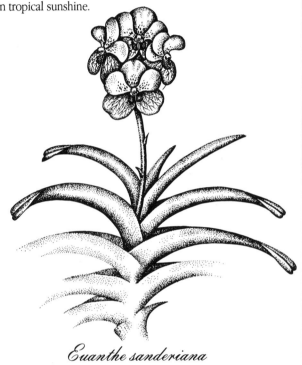

Euanthe sanderiana

Euanthe sanderiana syn. *Vanda sanderiana*

COMMON NAME: None.
COLOUR: Flowers are a blend of white-pink, mauve to dull yellow, suffused with white.
SIZE: Growing up to 1m (3') high.
CLIMATE: Warm.
DISTRIBUTION: Native to the Philippines, south-east Mindanao (Davao).
FLOWERING TIME: Autumn to spring.
DESCRIPTION: A large showy epiphytic species. Stems are elongated, generally solitary, branching from the base. Leaves are strap-shaped, unequally emarginate, growing up to 40cm (16") long. Inflorescence generally shorter than leaves, with up to ten blooms. Flowers are variable in size and colour, but are generally large and fragrant. *Euanthe* is separate from *Vanda* by having no spur.

Euanthe sanderiana

GALEOLA
(gal-ee-oh-la)

Galeola from the Lat. *galeaola* (a small helmet) with reference to the helmet or hood-like dorsal appendage of the anther. This is a genus of about seventy species of leafless epiphytes or saprophytes whose distribution extends through India, Japan, Malaysia, Indonesia, Papua New Guinea, New Caledonia and Australia. This genus includes some of Orchidaceae's most spectacular and unusual species. *Galeola foliata* is the tallest-growing orchid in the world; with its sucker-like roots biting deep into the bark, its vine-like stem attains heights of 20 to 30m (60 to 100'), producing panicles of flowers often measuring as much as 180cm (6') in length, with thousands of handsome blooms.

Culture: It is almost impossible to keep this gigantic saprophytic vine alive for more than several years. Several growers have had interesting but limited success by taking a very young plant together with a large quantity of *mycelium* and its host to a specially prepared and selected site, and by continuing to duplicate original growing conditions, and to feed the *mycelium*.

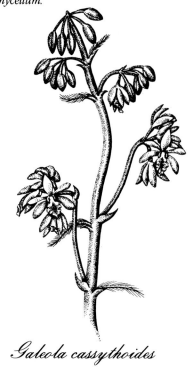

Galeola cassythoides

Galeola cassythoides

Galeola cassythoides

COMMON NAME: Climbing Orchid.
COLOUR: Flowers yellow-brown with green-brown markings.
SIZE: This saprophyte climbs as high as 6m (20') with the aid of sucker-like roots.
CLIMATE: Cool.
DISTRIBUTION: Native to the Australian eastern coast.
FLOWERING TIME: Spring to summer.
DESCRIPTION: Flowers are numerous and measure about 3cm (1¼") across. Stems are leafless and coloured chocolate brown.

GOMESA
(go-mee-sa)

*G*omesa was named in honour of Dr Bernardino Antonio Gomes, a Portuguese naval physician and botanist. This is a genus of about twenty species of dwarf epiphytic plants from Brazil. The genus is closely allied to *Oncidium* and is often confusing for the novice. The unusual shape of the flower segments and the labellum is distinctive. *Gomesa* are commonly called the 'little men orchids'. Pseudobulbs are nearly elliptical and flattened, grow up to 10cm (4″) long, and are closely spaced along the rhizome. The plant has one or two leaves, which are apical, elongate, soft and arching. Inflorescence comes from the base of the pseudobulb, is short and arching with up to twenty or more flowers. Flowers are small, very fragrant, and are off-white, yellow or pale green in colour. Dorsal sepal and petals are free and spreading; the lateral sepals are adnate for half their length forming an inverted 'Y' beneath the labellum. Sepals and petals are similar in size and length. The labellum is tri-lobed, short, curved and u-shaped sectionally, with lateral lobes erect; the mid-lobe is fixed to the base of column foot, and is spurless; the disc has two prominent keels.

Culture: Compost. Plants grow well in pots, but be careful with watering. They require good drainage, shade and humidity.

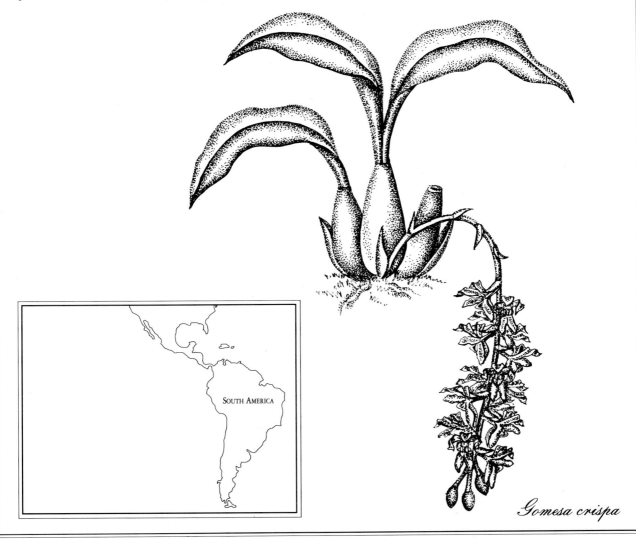

SOUTH AMERICA

Gomesa crispa

Gomesa barkerii

COMMON NAME: None.
COLOUR: Flowers are yellow.
SIZE: Growing up to 30cm (12″) high.
CLIMATE: Intermediate.
DISTRIBUTION: Native to Brazil.
FLOWERING TIME: Spring.
DESCRIPTION: Pseudobulbs are compressed,
smooth, ovoid-elongate, up to 10cm (4″) high.
Leaves grow up to 30cm (12″) long and are
oblong-lanceolate. Inflorescence is basal from
sheaths of new growth, is arching, and grows up
to 20cm (8″) long. Flowers are 2.5cm (1″) long.

Gomesa barkerii

Gomesa recurva syn. Rodriguezia recurva

Gomesa crispa

COMMON NAME: None.
COLOUR: Flowers are yellow-green.
SIZE: Growing up to 30cm (12″) high.
CLIMATE: Intermediate.
DISTRIBUTION: Native to Brazil.
FLOWERING TIME: Spring to early summer.
DESCRIPTION: Pseudobulbs are compressed,
oblong and 10cm (4″) high. Leaves are strap-
shaped, growing up to 20cm (8″) long.
Inflorescence is up to 22cm (8¾″) long.
Flowers are dense and numerous, are fragrant,
and grow to 2cm (¾″) long. Floral segment
margins are undulate.

Gomesa crispa

Gomesa recurva syn. Rodriguezia recurva

COMMON NAME: None.
COLOUR: Flowers are yellow-green. Labellum has
a yellow basal streak.
SIZE: Growing up to 30cm (12″) high.
CLIMATE: Intermediate.
DISTRIBUTION: Native to Brazil.
FLOWERING TIME: Spring to autumn.
DESCRIPTION: Pseudobulbs are compressed,
narrowly ovoid, up to 7.5cm (3″) high. Leaves
are linear-oblanceolate, acute, growing up to
30cm (12″) long. Inflorescence is up to 35cm
(14″) long. Flowers are densely numerous,
small and fragrant.

GONGORA
(gon-gor-uh)

Gongora is named in honour of Don Antonio Caballero Gongora, Viceroy of New Granada, and later Bishop of Cordova, Spain. This genus of about fifteen species of monopodial epiphytes, and their variants, is distributed through the tropical Americas, from Mexico to Peru and Brazil. The genus is divided into two groups by several workers: (a) *eugongora* (e.g. *G. quinquenervis*), and (b) *acropera* (e.g. *G. armeniaca* var. *biconuta*). Fundamentally, the difference is the floral shapes.

This is a most extraordinary small epiphyte. The short stems develop into strongly ridged pseudobulbs. The two leaves are apical, soft and plicate. Inflorescence rises from the base of the pseudobulbs and is pendulous and flexuous. The flowers are most unusual being intricate, 'grotesque' and 'fascinating'. The dorsal sepal is adnate to the column foot for one third of its length; lateral sepals are attached to the column foot. Petals emerge from the middle of the column and appear like wings. The extreme complexity of the fleshy labellum makes description difficult. The labellum is continuous with the column foot, is narrow and fleshy, complex and tri-lobed; the lateral lobes form a hypochile, erect, saccate and bear horns or bristle-like appendages; the mid-lobe (epichile) is complicate-saccate or laterally compressed, the apex is bi-lobed, elongate, lanceolate, acute or acuminate. The column is more or less clavate above.

Culture: Use moisture-retaining compost. Grow in a hanging basket as for *Stanhopea.* The plant requires high humidity, shade, plenty of water and good drainage. The winter temperature should be a minimum of 10°C (50°F).

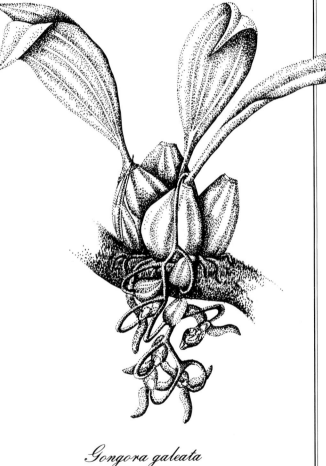

Gongora galeata

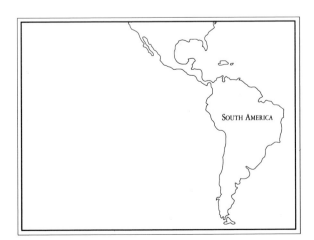

SOUTH AMERICA

Gongora galeata

COMMON NAME: None.
COLOUR: Flowers are brown-buff to greenish cream, mottled orange. Labellum yellow-brown with spotted purple column.
SIZE: Growing up to 30cm (12″) high.
CLIMATE: Intermediate.
DISTRIBUTION: Native to Mexico.
FLOWERING TIME: Summer to early autumn.
DESCRIPTION: An epiphytic species. Pseudobulbs are ovoid to pyriform with sheaths, up to 5cm (2″) long. Leaves are broad-lanceolate, growing up to 30cm (12″) long. Pendulous inflorescence grows up to 30cm (12″) long.

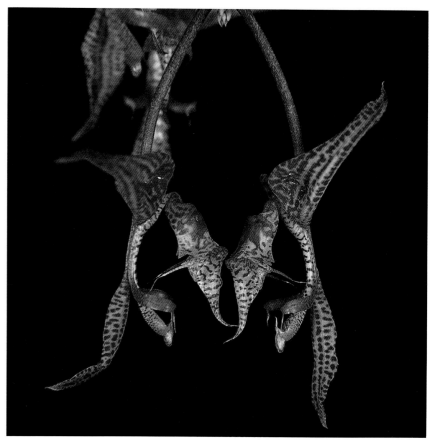

Gongora quinquenervis

Gongora galeata

Gongora quinquenervis

COMMON NAME: None.
COLOUR: Flowers are generally yellow, spotted maroon.
SIZE: Growing up to 40cm (16″) high.
CLIMATE: Intermediate.
DISTRIBUTION: Native to Peru, Ecuador, Trinidad, Mexico, Guyana, Venezuela and Colombia.
FLOWERING TIME: Autumn.
DESCRIPTION: Pseudobulbs are oblong-ovoid to conical, up to 8cm (3¼″). Leaves occur in apical pairs, strap-like, acute, plicate, margins undulate, and grow up to 40cm (16″) long. The inflorescence is long and pendulous. The numerous flowers are fragrant.

Gongora truncata

Gongora truncata

COMMON NAME: None.
COLOUR: Flowers are white with red marks. Labellum yellow.
SIZE: Growing up to 40cm (16″) high.
CLIMATE: Intermediate.
DISTRIBUTION: Native to Mexico.
FLOWERING TIME: Summer.
DESCRIPTION: Pseudobulbs are angular, up to 7.5cm (3″) high. Leaves are broad-lanceolate, growing up to 40cm (16″) long. Inflorescence pendulous, 60cm (2′) long. Flowers are numerous, fragrant, and are 5cm (2″) across.

GRAMMATOPHYLLUM
(gram-mat-o-fill-um)

*G*rammatophyllum from the Gk *gramma* (a letter) *phyllum* (leaf) with reference to the dark markings on the sepals and petals. This genus of about eight species has several varieties of sympodial epiphytic orchids. It is scattered throughout Burma, Thailand, Malaysia, the Philippines, Indonesia, Papua New Guinea and Polynesia. The genus has two distinct growth forms: (a) *Gabertia* has very elongated pseudobulbs which are really fleshy stems with many leaves, for example, *G. speciosum*, which has plants as large as 12.75m (42.5') high; and (b) *Pattonia* with short ovoid or ellipsoidal pseudobulbs with two to eight apical leaves, for example, *G. scriptum*.

Leaves are lanceolate with a pronounced mid-rib on the underside, are flexible and grow up to 60cm (2') long. Erect or arching inflorescence rises from the base of pseudobulbs, with spikes up to 2.4m (8') long, bearing up to a hundred flowers. Flowers are distinctive, being yellow-green or olive-green with purple markings, and growing 5 to 15cm (2 to 6") in diameter. Sepals and petals are sub-similar. The labellum is small, tri-lobed, with lateral lobes partially enclosing the column, and the mid-lobe small with three low brown-purple keels.

Culture: In native habitat, the plant grows in full sunlight as well as in partial shade. If potted, it requires a very large container. Compost as suggested for other large species. Humid, sticky heat is needed at all times. The genus produces gigantic inflorescences and requires a very large area. Fertilise monthly, and pay attention to drainage and fresh compost.

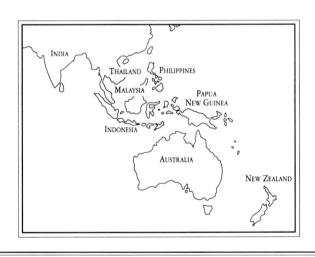

Grammatophyllum speciosum

Grammatophyllum scriptum

COMMON NAME: None.
COLOUR: Flowers are yellow-green, blotched with brown.
SIZE: Growing up to 75cm (30") high.
CLIMATE: Warm to hot.
DISTRIBUTION: Native to Papua New Guinea, Solomon Islands, the Philippines, Moluccas, Celebes and Borneo.
FLOWERING TIME: Usually summer.
DESCRIPTION: An extremely epiphytic plant in all parts. Pseudobulbs are clustered, ellipsoidal, up to 25cm (10") high. Leaves are usually apical, lanceolate, undulate, growing up to 50cm (20") long. Inflorescence long, up to 2m (6'), with numerous flowers and as many as a hundred fragrant blooms.

Grammatophyllum scriptum

ISABELIA
(is-a-bell-ee-a)

Isabelia is named in honour of Isabel, Countess d'Eu, patroness of science and floriculture in Brazil during the reign of Pedro II. *Isabelia* is now referred to as *Neolauchea* (q.v.). This single species genus comes from the damp humid forests of Brazil. It is a rare genus in orchid collections. It is a dwarf-growing, mat-forming epiphytic plant. Pseudobulbs are tightly clustered and are covered with a fine network of grey fibres; the rhizome forms a mat. Leaves are needle-like. Inflorescence is a single snow-white flower. Sepals form a sac with labellum.

Culture: Grow in a shallow pan or on a flat slab of tree-fern fibre. The plant has a creeping, mat-forming habit. Water carefully; plant needs to be kept just damp—not too wet or too dry.

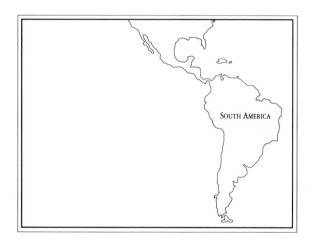

SOUTH AMERICA

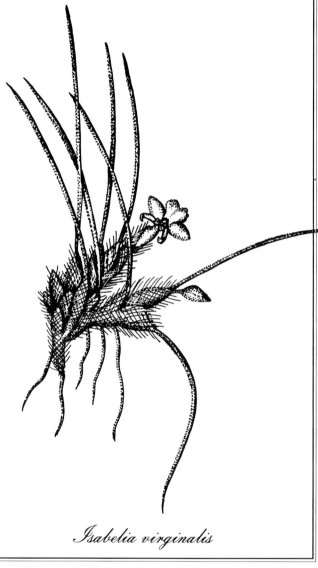

Isabelia virginalis

Isabelia virginalis

COMMON NAME: None.
COLOUR: Flowers white and may have a flush of rose or lilac.
SIZE: Growing up to 7.5cm (3″) high.
CLIMATE: Intermediate.
DISTRIBUTION: Native to Brazil.
FLOWERING TIME: Winter.
DESCRIPTION: This small rare species grows in humid forests. Pseudobulbs clustered on a creeping rhizome are tiny and ovoid-conical. Pseudobulbs are densely covered in brown to grey networks of fibres. Leaves are solitary, needle-like and grow up to 7.5cm (3″) long.

Isabelia virginalis

ISOCHILUS

(eye-so-kye-lus)

Isochilus from the Gk *isos* (equal) *chilos* (a lip) with reference to the labellum which is more or less equal to the sepals in size. This genus of just two species and four varieties is found in West Indies, Central and northern South America, and from Mexico to Argentina and Jamaica. *Isochilus* is a sympodial, epiphytic, lithophytic or terrestrial creeping herb, which forms dense masses. Stems grow up to 60cm (2′) tall, are reed-like, with the upper two thirds clothed with small soft leaves. Leaves are flat, sub-coriaceous or soft, distichous, green, linear, base stem-clasping, and grow to about 6cm (2.5″) long. Inflorescence is terminal with one to several flowers. The flowers do not open fully, and are coloured pink to magenta. Sepals and petals are alike in shape, size and colour and are concave, forming a tube around the labellum. The labellum is tri-lobed, shortly clawed, sigmoid. It has a different shade of colour to the sepals and petals, and two pronounced dark dots close to the lateral lobes. The column is erect. The anther cap is partially enclosed by the lateral lobes at the apex.

Culture: Compost using mainly tree-fern fibre in pots or pans. *Isochilus* requires moderate humidity and shade and regular fertilisation. Water carefully as roots will rot with too much water and shrivel with too little water.

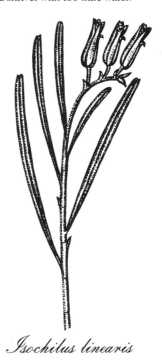

Isochilus linearis

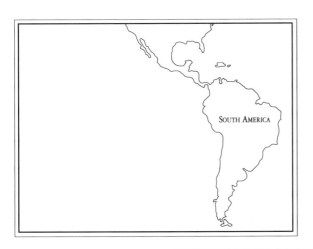

SOUTH AMERICA

Isochilus linearis

Isochilus linearis

COMMON NAME: None.
COLOUR: Flower colour variable from white to pink-purple, but is usually pink-purple.
SIZE: Variable in height, up to 60cm (2′) high.
CLIMATE: Intermediate.
DISTRIBUTION: Native to Cuba, Argentina and Mexico.
FLOWERING TIME: Throughout the year and usually more than once.
DESCRIPTION: A terrestrial, epiphytic or lithophytic plant. Stems form clumps, covered by verrucose leaf sheaths. Leaves are linear, obtuse, measuring up to 6.5cm (2½″) long.

KINGIDIUM
(king-ee-de-um)

Kingidium is named in honour of Sir George King, co-author with R. Pantling of *Orchids of the Sikkim-Himalaya*. This genus was previously known as *Kingiella*. In 1970, P. F. Hunt established the genus as *Kingidium* in the *Kew Bulletin*, explaining that under the International Code of Botanical Nomenclature the name *Kingiella* was invalid.

The genus is closely allied to *Phalaenopsis*, and is much confused with *Doritis*. *Kingidium* is a small genus of about six species of epiphytic monopodial orchids. They are distributed from India, east to the Philippines, and south to Indonesia. Stems are free rooting. The succulent leaves are 12 to 18cm (5 to 7″) long. Inflorescence is erect with numerous small flowers which do not open fully. The dorsal sepal and petals are free; lateral sepals unite with the base of the labellum to form a spur-like mentum. The labellum is tri-lobed, saccate at base without a claw, with side lobes erect, and mid-lobe widening from the base.

Culture: Compost as for *Phalaenopsis* and *Doritis*, that is with coarse 5cm (2″) chunks in baskets where roots can grow exposed to the air. Plants require humidity and shade, with plenty of water while growing and less on maturity.

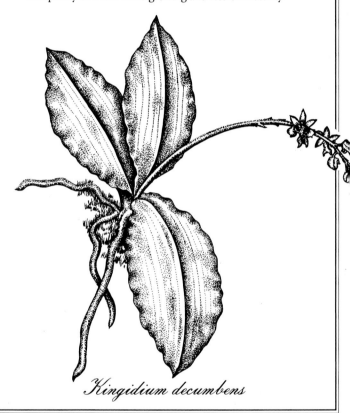

Kingidium decumbens

Kingidium decumbens syn. *Kingiella decumbens*, *Phalaenopsis decumbens*

Kingidium decumbens syn. *Kingiella decumbens*
COMMON NAME: None.
COLOUR: Flowers white with the dorsal sepal spotted purple.
SIZE: Growing up to 25cm (10″) across.
CLIMATE: Warm.
DISTRIBUTION: Native to India, throughout eastern Asia, Malaysia, Indonesia and the Philippines.
FLOWERING TIME: Varies, usually flowering more than once annually.
DESCRIPTION: This is a variable epiphytic species. Short stems, up to 1cm (½″) high. Oblong-obovate leaves grow up to 15cm (6″) long. Inflorescence erect, may be branching, up to 20cm (8″) long with numerous, small flowers.

LAELIA
(lay-lee-a)

Laelia is thought to be dedicated to Laelia, one of the Vestal Virgins, or possibly the name derives from Laelius, the name given to the female members of Roman families. The genus of about sixty species is widespread from Mexico, West Indies and Panama, through Peru to Venezuela and Brazil. This genus is often divided into subdivisions, such as the following:

Cattleyoides—those resembling *Cattleyas*, e.g. *L. lobata*, *L. tenebrosa*;

Hadro-laelia—those with heteroblastic pseudobulbs and with a prominent labellum-keel, e.g. *L. jongheana*;

Eu-laelia—those with homoblastic pseudobulbs, e.g. *L. speciosa*;

Micro-laelia—similar to *Eu-laelia* but having sepals and petals of equal width, e.g. *L. lundii*;

Podo-laelia—those whose stems are articulate, e.g. *L. rubescens.*

Laelia is a genus of epiphytic, lithophytic or terrestrial herbs. Pseudobulbs develop along creeping rhizomes, varying considerably in shape and size; they may be fusiform, egg-shaped or ovoid, flat, cylindrical or almost reed-like. The one or several leaves per pseudobulb are apical, coriaceous, entire and varying in length. Inflorescence is terminal, and occurs either singly, close to apex of pseudobulb, or in a cluster of up to twenty flowers, or in a spike up to 1.5m (5′) in length. Flowers are large and showy, and display various colours, such as white, cream, yellow, orange, pink, red or purple. Sepals are narrow and spreading. Petals are generally broader, but are the same colour as sepals. The labellum is the longest and most showy segment of the flower; it is free or adnate to column base, tri-lobed, with lateral lobes forming a tube around the column. The mid-lobe is flat and spreading, and the apex is colourful. The column is toothed at the apex.

Culture: Compost. Most species grow well in pots, others do better in hanging baskets, while some grow well on tree-fern slabs. All require moderate shade, humid conditions and good drainage. Mexican species, however, need cooler conditions than Brazilian species. Fertilise monthly. With this genus it is a good idea to consult your local orchid club for more guidance.

Laelia anceps

SOUTH AMERICA

Laelia anceps

COMMON NAME: None.
COLOUR: Flower colour is variable with the typical form being pale rose-purple. Labellum dark purple.
SIZE: Growing up to 30cm (12″) high.
CLIMATE: Intermediate.
DISTRIBUTION: Native to Mexico and Honduras.
FLOWERING TIME: Summer.
DESCRIPTION: Pseudobulbs are borne on a creeping rhizome, ovoid-oblong, compressed, up to 7.5cm (3″) high. Leaves are oblong-lanceolate, leathery, generally solitary, growing up to 20cm (8″) long. Inflorescence terminal long. Flowers measure up to 10cm (4″) across.

Laelia anceps var. *chamberlainiana*

Laelia anceps var. chamberlainiana

COMMON NAME: None.
COLOUR: Flower pale pink-mauve. Labellum pink-purple. Throat yellow with maroon veining.
SIZE: Growing up to 30cm (12″) high.
CLIMATE: Intermediate.
DISTRIBUTION: Native to Mexico and Honduras. Habitat same as its type.
FLOWERING TIME: Same as type.
DESCRIPTION: Same as type except for colour variation in the flower.

Laelia anceps

Laelia anceps var. williamsiana

COMMON NAME: None.
COLOUR: This variety is the white form. Labellum has a flush of yellow and maroon veining.
SIZE: Growing up to 30cm (12″) high.
CLIMATE: Intermediate.
DISTRIBUTION: Native to Mexico. Habitat same as its type.
FLOWERING TIME: Same as type.
DESCRIPTION: Same as type except for the flower colour variation.

Laelia anceps var. *williamsiana*

Laelia crispa var. candissima

COMMON NAME: None.
COLOUR: Flowers are white. Labellum throat yellow veined red-purple.
SIZE: Growing up to 45cm (18″) high.
CLIMATE: Intermediate.
DISTRIBUTION: Native to Brazil.
FLOWERING TIME: Autumn.
DESCRIPTION: Pseudobulbs are compressed, furrowed, clavate, up to 22cm (10″) high. Solitary leaves are broad-oblong, up to 20cm (8″) long. Inflorescence terminal, up to 15cm (6″) long. Flowers are large and showy, measuring 12.5cm (5″) across.

Laelia crispa var. grandiflora

COMMON NAME: None.
COLOUR: Flowers are lilac. Labellum veined dark purple with throat white.
SIZE: Growing up to 60cm (24″) high.
CLIMATE: Intermediate.
DISTRIBUTION: Native to Brazil. Altitudes 800 to 1150m (2500 to 4000′).
FLOWERING TIME: Summer.
DESCRIPTION: Pseudobulbs are compressed, clavate, up to 30cm (12″) high. Leaf is solitary, erect, lanceolate-oblong, and grows up to 30cm (12″) long. Flower margins are undulate crisped; the flowers are fragrant and grow up to 12.5cm (5″) across.

Laelia crispa var. *grandiflora*

Laelia crispa var. *candissima*

Laelia esalqueana

COMMON NAME: None.
COLOUR: Flowers are yellow.
SIZE: A diminutive plant.
CLIMATE: Intermediate.
DISTRIBUTION: Native to Brazil.
FLOWERING TIME: Summer.
DESCRIPTION: Pseudobulbs are compressed, up to 3cm (1¼″) high. Leaf apical from the pseudobulbs, fleshy, up to 5cm (2″) long. Flower scape up to 4.5cm (1½″) long. There are usually four flowers, growing up to 3cm (1¼″) across.

Laelia esalqueana

Laelia gouldiana

Laelia gouldiana

COMMON NAME: None.
COLOUR: Flowers are rose-pink.
SIZE: Growing up to 30cm (12″) high.
CLIMATE: Intermediate.
DISTRIBUTION: Native to Mexico.
FLOWERING TIME: Summer.
DESCRIPTION: Pseudobulbs are oblong-elliptic, up to 15cm (6″) high. The two leaves are oblong or strap-shaped, growing up to 17.5cm (7″) long. The flower scape is up to 80cm (32″) long. Inflorescence has three to five flowers, each flower growing up to 10cm (4″) across.

Laelia harpophylla

COMMON NAME: None:
COLOUR: Flowers are orange-red.
SIZE: Growing up to 65cm (26″) high.
CLIMATE: Intermediate.
DISTRIBUTION: Native to Brazil.
FLOWERING TIME: Autumn.
DESCRIPTION: Pseudobulbs are long, erect, canes up to 45cm (18″) high; membranous sheaths. Leaf is solitary, ensiform up to 20cm (8″) long. Inflorescence has clustered flowers, each being 5 to 7.5cm (2 to 3″) across.

Laelia harpophylla

Laelia lindeyanum

Laelia lindeyanum

COMMON NAME: None.
COLOUR: Flowers are creamy white and may be tinted and spotted with lilac. Labellum tinted lilac, throat lemon and blotched.
SIZE: Growing up to 25cm (10″) high.
CLIMATE: Intermediate.
DISTRIBUTION: Native to Brazil.
FLOWERING TIME: Spring.
DESCRIPTION: Pseudobulbs are cylindrical, up to 20cm (8″) high. Leaves are linear-lanceolate, acute, slightly channelled, and grow up to 15cm (6″) long. Inflorescence short. Flowers are showy, measuring up to 10cm (4″) across.

Laelia purpurata var. carnea

COMMON NAME: Lady Godiva.
COLOUR: Flowers are white. Labellum crimson and throat yellow.
SIZE: Growing up to 50cm (20″) high.
CLIMATE: Intermediate.
DISTRIBUTION: Native to southern Brazil. It is an epiphyte growing in jungle conditions.
FLOWERING TIME: Spring.
DESCRIPTION: Pseudobulbs are up to 15cm (6″) high, fusiform, somewhat compressed and furrowed when matured. The solitary leaf is strap-shaped and grows up to 35cm (14″) long. Inflorescence short. Fragrant flowers measure up to 15cm (6″) across.

Laelia tenebrosa

Laelia purpurata var. carnea

Laelia reginae

COMMON NAME: None.
COLOUR: Flowers are pink. Labellum white and yellow.
SIZE: Growing to 7.5cm (3″) or more high.
CLIMATE: Intermediate to hot.
DISTRIBUTION: Native to Brazil.
FLOWERING TIME: Spring.
DESCRIPTION: A small epiphytic plant. Pseudobulbs are ovoid, up to 3.5cm (1½″) high. Leaves are solitary, apical, ovate-lanceolate, acute, growing to 3.5cm (1½″) or more long. Inflorescence short, up to 6.5cm (2½″) long. Flowers measure 4cm (1½″) across.

Laelia tenebrosa

COMMON NAME: None.
COLOUR: Flowers are a coppery bronze to yellow. Labellum pink-mauve, veined dark purple.
SIZE: An epiphytic plant up to 50cm (20″) high.
CLIMATE: Intermediate.
DISTRIBUTION: Native to Brazil.
FLOWERING TIME: Spring.
DESCRIPTION: Pseudobulbs are compressed, furrowed, fusiforme, up to 15cm (6″) high. Leaves are erect, up to two, apical from pseudobulb, narrow to broad and oblong, emarginate, growing up to 30cm (12″) long. Inflorescence short, with usually three blooms. Flowers measure up to 15cm (6″) across. Labellum trumpet-shaped. It has a beautiful flower and is a parent for many cultivated hybrids.

Laelia wendlandii

Laelia wendlandii

COMMON NAME: None.
COLOUR: Flowers are green-brown. Labellum green-white to pale yellow, marked with purple.
SIZE: Growing up to 40cm (16″) high.
CLIMATE: Intermediate to warm.
DISTRIBUTION: Native to Guatemala, Honduras and Nicaragua.
FLOWERING TIME: Summer.
DESCRIPTION: Pseudobulbs are fusiform, grooved, up to 17.5cm (7″) high. Leaves are apical oblong-elliptic, up to 22.5cm (9″) long. Inflorescence erect, up to 2.1m (7′) long. Flowers are fragrant and measure 5cm (2″) across. Petal margins are undulate.

Laelia reginae

LYCASTE

(lye-kass-tee)

*L*ycaste is named after Lycaste, the beautiful daughter of King Priam of Troy. The genus is distributed throughout the West Indies, Mexico and south to Peru and Bolivia. Many of the species have at one time or another been transferred into the *Maxillaria* genus then back to *Lycaste*. The distinguishing feature is the plicate leaves of *Lycaste*. This genus is divided into two groups: (a) those in which the mid-lobe of the labellum is fimbriate and the callus is bifid; and (b) those in which the mid-lobe of the labellum is not fimbriate and the callus is entire (finger-like). *Lycaste* plants are epiphytic, terrestrial or may be lithophytic herbs with short thick pseudobulbs. Leaves are plicate and apical. Inflorescence comes from the base of the pseudobulb and is erect. Flowers are showy, large, and usually fragrant. Sepals are spreading, forming saccate mentum with column foot. Petals are similar but smaller than the sepals, and are often of a different colour. Labellum is tri-lobed.

Culture: Compost in well-drained pots, or on a tree-fern slab. *Lycaste* requires shade and humidity. Provide plenty of water only while the plant is growing, that is, after new shoots appear and while new pseudobulbs are forming. During the rest period use less water.

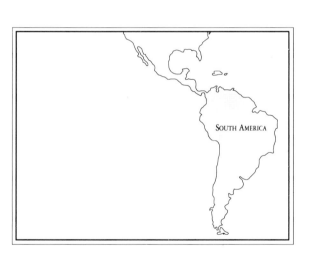

SOUTH AMERICA

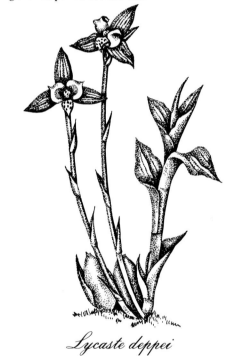

Lycaste deppei

Lycaste cruenta

COMMON NAME: None.

COLOUR: Sepals yellow-green with maroon flecks and a crimson blotch.

SIZE: Growing up to 50cm (20″) high.

CLIMATE: Cool to intermediate.

DISTRIBUTION: Native to Costa Rica, Mexico, Guatemala and El Salvador. Altitude up to 2200m (7250′).

FLOWERING TIME: Spring.

DESCRIPTION: Pseudobulbs are ovoid, compressed, and grow up to 10cm (4″) high. Leaves are deciduous, elliptic-lanceolate, plicate, growing up to 38cm (15″) long. Flowers are large, waxy and fragrant.

Lycaste cruenta

MALLEOLA
(mal-ee-oh-la)

Malleola The name's derivation is uncertain. It is a small genus of about thirty species found from India and Burma, through Malaysia and Indonesia to Papua New Guinea. Little is known of its genetic affinities, but it is thought to be closely allied to *Sarcanthus*. *Malleola* is an epiphytic herb. Stems are pendulous and branching. Leaves are fleshy, often with a waxy appearance. Inflorescence is pendulous with many flowers. The flowers are small, less than 1.2cm (½″); they look insignificant, but are exceedingly fragrant. The labellum is erect, fleshy and tri-lobed; lateral lobes are short with tips incurved, almost joining. The mid-lobe is short and fleshy, and almost closes the spur entrance. The spur is pendulous.

Culture: Compost in well-drained pots, as for *Vandas*. Water carefully, making sure not to over water. This genus is uncommon in collections.

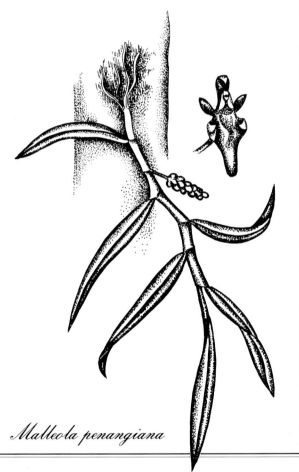

Malleola penangiana

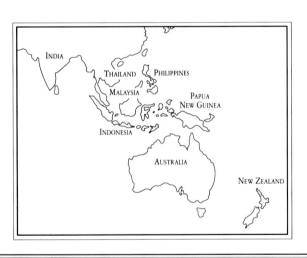

Malleola witteana

Malleola witteana

COMMON NAME: None.
COLOUR: Flowers greenish yellow, mottled and marked brown-red. Labellum white-cream.
SIZE: Pendulous, to 30cm (12″) long.
CLIMATE: Warm.
DISTRIBUTION: Native to Sumatra, Java and Malaysia.
FLOWERING TIME: Spring to summer.
DESCRIPTION: Stems are pendulous, up to 30cm (12″) long. Leaves are elliptic, may be purple-green, up to 8.5cm (3½″) long. Inflorescence is pendulous and 20cm (8″) long.

MASDEVALLIA
(maz-de-val-lee-a)

Masdevallia is named after Dr Jose Masdevall, a Spanish physician and botanist. This is a large genus of almost three hundred species classified. It is distributed throughout Mexico, Panama and tropical South America to Peru and Venezuela with the greatest development in the cloud forests of the Andes of Colombia. Here, three-quarters of the known species occur. *Masdevallia* is a small to medium-sized epiphytic herb with creeping rhizomes. Stems are short, erect with an apical leaf, without pseudobulbs. Leaf is erect, fleshy, coriaceous, and is oblong to linear. Inflorescence is either erect, arching or pendulous, and is racemose with several flowers. These flowers are unusual; they are showy and have various vivid colours. Sepals are connate forming a tube at the base, with the upper part free, spreading with long or short filaments. Petals are small, as is the labellum which is parallel to the column. The petals and labellum are often hidden in the tube formed by the sepals. The short column is also hidden and is either winged or has a narrow margin. The sepals are the showy segments of the flower.

Culture: Compost in well-drained pots. Plants require moist, shady situations. Water carefully: neither too little nor too much water. This genus is very popular in collections.

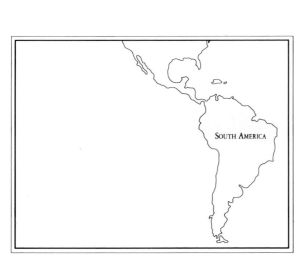

SOUTH AMERICA

Masdevallia pandurilabia

Masdevallia burfordensis

COMMON NAME: None.
COLOUR: Flowers yellowish orange, speckled and marked heavily with maroon.
SIZE: Growing up to 14cm (5½") high.
CLIMATE: Intermediate to cool.
DISTRIBUTION: Native to Peru.
FLOWERING TIME: Autumn.
DESCRIPTION: A tufted herb. Leaves are lanceolate-oblong, up to 14cm (5½") high. Inflorescence is shorter than the leaves. The solitary flower is triangular in shape and up to 8cm (3¼") across.

Masdevallia floribunda

Masdevallia burfordensis

Masdevallia floribunda

COMMON NAME: None.
COLOUR: Flowers pale yellow, spotted brown-purple. Labellum white with red-brown blotch.
SIZE: Small plant, growing up to 10cm (4") high.
CLIMATE: Cool to intermediate.
DISTRIBUTION: Native to Costa Rica, Mexico, Guatemala and Honduras. Altitude 900 to 1300m (3000 to 4500').
FLOWERING TIME: Spring.
DESCRIPTION: A tufted herb. Leaves are oblong-lanceolate and grow up to 10cm (4") long. Inflorescence is up to 7.5cm (3") high.

Masdevallia infracta

COMMON NAME: None.
COLOUR: Flower colour variable, pink-purple to red-brown and flushed yellow outside; purple-red inside with pale yellow tails.
SIZE: A small epiphytic plant, up to 20cm (8") high.
CLIMATE: Cool.
DISTRIBUTION: Native to Brazil and Peru. Altitude 200m (6561'), growing on mountain slopes, covered by grass steppe.
FLOWERING TIME: Winter.
DESCRIPTION: Leaves are lanceolate, shiny green, petiolate, and grow up to 10cm (4") long. Flowers are bell-shaped, up to 6cm (2½") long.

Masdevallia infracta

Masdevallia mezae

COMMON NAME: None.
COLOUR: Flower cream-yellow, spotted dark pink, tips ochre-yellow.
SIZE: Growing to 15cm (6") or more high.
CLIMATE: Intermediate to warm.
DISTRIBUTION: Native to Mexico.
FLOWERING TIME: Late winter to spring.
DESCRIPTION: A tufted epiphytic or lithophytic herb. Leaves are lanceolate, emarginate, growing to 15cm (6") or more high. Flower scape is shorter than the leaves. Flowers are solitary and about 9cm (3½") long.

Masdevallia mezae

Masdevallia torta

COMMON NAME: None.
COLOUR: Flower pale greenish yellow, spotted and striped red.
SIZE: Growing up to 22cm (8½″) high.
CLIMATE: Cool.
DISTRIBUTION: Native to Mexico; growing on mossy trees in damp forests, at altitudes of 2000 to 2400m (7150 to 7800′).
FLOWERING TIME: Winter to spring.
DESCRIPTION: Leaves are lanceolate, the mid rib is prominent and it grows up to 22cm (8½″) long. Petiole is long. Inflorescence is erect and short, up to 7.5cm (3″) long. Flower is solitary, bell shaped and about 15cm (6″) long.

Masdevallia torta

Masdevallia tovarensis

COMMON NAME: None.
COLOUR: Flowers white.
SIZE: Growing up to 15cm (6″) high.
CLIMATE: Cool.
DISTRIBUTION: Native to Venezuela.
FLOWERING TIME: Summer.
DESCRIPTION: Leaves clustered, shiny, green, elliptic-spathulate, growing up to 15cm (6″) long. Scapes are long, carrying up to five waxy, white flowers, about 7.5cm (3″) long. Sepals are tri-nerved with short tails.

Masdevallia tovarensis

Masdevallia veitchiana

COMMON NAME: None.
COLOUR: Flowers orange-red within, outer bluish sheen with numerous red-purple papillae.
SIZE: Growing up to 30cm (12″) high.
CLIMATE: Cool.
DISTRIBUTION: Native to Peru, common at the Inca ruins of Macchu-Picchu; altitude 2200 to 4000m (11 000 to 13 000′).
FLOWERING TIME: Winter.
DESCRIPTION: A large tufted, showy, lithophytic species. Leaves are linear-oblong, up to 30cm (12″). Flower scape is longer than leaves. Flowers grow up to 12.5cm (5″) long.

Masdevallia ventricularia

COMMON NAME: None.
COLOUR: Flower maroon with darker markings, inside yellowish brown.
SIZE: Growing up to 15cm (6″) high.
CLIMATE: Cool.
DISTRIBUTION: Native to Colombia and Ecuador, growing at altitudes of 1800 to 2200m (5095 to 7100′) on trunks of forest trees.
FLOWERING TIME: Spring to summer.
DESCRIPTION: Leaves are oblong-lanceolate, clustered and up to 15cm (6″) long. Flower scape is about the same length as the leaves. Flowers are terminal, solitary, tubular and up to 12.5cm (5″) long.

Masdevallia ventricularia

Masdevallia veitchiana

MAXILLARIA

(max-il-lair-ee-a)

Maxillaria derives from the Lat. *maxillae* (jaw-bone) because the labellum and column of some species reminded Ruiz and Pavon of the jaws of insects. This genus of over three hundred species is found in tropical and subtropical America, from Mexico to Peru and Brazil. The plant is epiphytic or lithophytic, very rarely terrestrial, and has short, matted or creeping rhizomes. Pseudobulbs are tightly clustered, flattened, smooth or fluted. Leaves are coriaceous, with one or more per pseudobulb. Inflorescence rises from the base of the pseudobulb. The flower is solitary, but several scapes may rise from the base of one pseudobulb. Sepals are alike in size and colour with the dorsal sepal erect. Petals are smaller than sepals, but have the same colour. The labellum is tri-lobed and is attached to the column by a short claw. Lateral lobes are incurved and almost surround the column; the mid-lobe is decurved.

Culture: Compost in well-drained pots or mount on a tree-fern slab. Water freely and fertilise regularly.

Maxillaria picta syn. *M. fuscata*

Maxillaria densa syn. *Ornithidium densum*

COMMON NAME: None.

COLOUR: Flower colour variable, green-white, yellow-white, tinged purple to maroon.

SIZE: Growing up to 38cm (15″) high.

CLIMATE: Cool to warm.

DISTRIBUTION: Native to Mexico, Guatemala, and British Honduras. An epiphyte or terrestrial plant, growing at low elevations in damp woodlands of altitudes up to 2500m (8400′) in cloud forest; also occurs in pine forests where it has a terrestrial habit.

FLOWERING TIME: Usually late winter to spring.

DESCRIPTION: Pseudobulbs are oblong-elliptic on a creeping rhizome, compressed-ancipitous, up to 7.5cm (3″) high. Leaf is solitary, apical, linear to lanceolate, 30cm (12″) long. Flower grows 1cm (¼″) long.

Maxillaria densa syn. *Ornithidium densum*

Maxillaria luteo-alba

Maxillaria luteo-alba

COMMON NAME: None.

COLOUR: Flowers variable in colour and size, but generally white outside, yellow inside.

SIZE: Growing up to 50cm (20″) high.

CLIMATE: Intermediate to warm.

DISTRIBUTION: Native to Ecuador, Costa Rica, Panama, Colombia and Venezuela.

FLOWERING TIME: Spring to early summer.

DESCRIPTION: Pseudobulbs clustered, somewhat compressed, oblong-ovoid to elliptic-ovoid, up to 5cm (2″) high. Solitary leaf is shiny, linear-lanceolate, acute, growing up to 50cm (20″) long. Inflorescence is numerous, growing up to 15cm (6″) long. Flowers are variable in size, but about 10cm (4″) across.

Maxillaria picta syn. *M. fuscata*

COMMON NAME: None.

COLOUR: Flowers yellow with purple spots. Labellum yellow-white; column purple.

SIZE: Growing up to 45cm (18″) high.

CLIMATE: Intermediate.

DISTRIBUTION: Native to Brazil.

FLOWERING TIME: Autumn.

DESCRIPTION: Pseudobulbs mostly clustered on a creeping rhizome, compressed, ovoid, furrowing when old, growing up to 8cm (3″) high. Leaf is usually solitary, leathery, shiny, narrow, strap-shaped, acute, growing up to 38.5cm (15″) long. Flowers measure about 6.5cm (2½″) across.

Maxillaria picta syn. *M. fuscata*

Maxillaria porphyrostele

Maxillaria porphyrostele

COMMON NAME: None.

COLOUR: Flowers yellow with purple stripe near base of petals. Labellum column purple.

SIZE: Growing up to 25cm (10″) high.

CLIMATE: Intermediate.

DISTRIBUTION: Native to Brazil.

FLOWERING TIME: Late winter to spring.

DESCRIPTION: Pseudobulbs are clustered, compressed, orbicular-ovoid, up to 4.5cm (1¾″) high. Leaves are usually paired, linear, obtuse at the apex, growing up to 20cm (8″) long. Inflorescence is up to 7.5cm (3″) long. Flowers measure about 3.5cm (1¼″) across. Labellum is tri-lobed.

Maxillaria tenuifolia

COMMON NAME: None.
COLOUR: Flowers dark red, mottled yellow. Labellum dark red; the apical yellow with purplish spots.
SIZE: Growing up to 40cm (16″) high.
CLIMATE: Intermediate to warm.
DISTRIBUTION: Native to Mexico, Honduras, British Honduras, Guatemala, Nicaragua and Costa Rica.
FLOWERING TIME: Spring and summer.
DESCRIPTION: Pseudobulbs are about 2.5cm (1″) apart on ascending rhizome, compressed, ovoid, about 2.5cm (1″) long and are produced further along the stem than preceding pseudobulbs. Leaves are linear, acuminate, grass-like, measuring up to 38.5cm (15″) long. Inflorescence is usually numerous and about 5cm (2″) long. Flowers are up to 5cm (2″) across. The tropical species has a creeping rhizome, growing in a vertical position with oval pseudobulbs; its scent is similar to the coconut.

Maxillaria tenuifolia

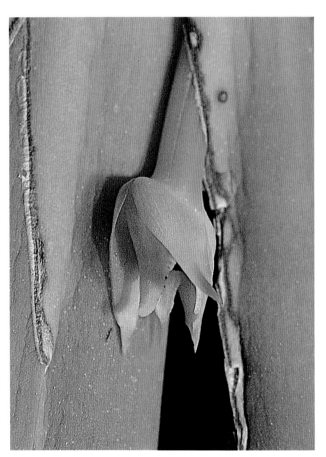

Maxillaria valenzuelana

Maxillaria valenzuelana

COMMON NAME: None.
COLOUR: Flowers light green or green-yellow. Labellum light brown, spotted purple.
SIZE: Pendulous to 20cm (8″) long.
CLIMATE: Warm.
DISTRIBUTION: Native to central and southern tropical America and West Indies.
FLOWERING TIME: Summer.
DESCRIPTION: An epiphytic species with short stems. Leaves are compressed, falcate, acute (fan-like), pendulous, measuring up to 20cm (8″) long. Flowers are about 2cm (¾″) long.

MENADENIUM

(men-a-dee-nee-um)

Menadenium This is a genus of four exceptionally rare and beautiful epiphytes from Venezuela and northern Brazil. *Menadenium* are rare, even in the best collections, and are scarce even in their native land. The genus is thought to be rather closely allied to *Zygopetalum*. It is truly an epiphytic plant; rhizomes branch frequently forming a large mass. Pseudobulbs occur at regular intervals along rhizomes, usually with leaf-like bracts, and become shrivelled with age. The one or two leaves are apical, glossy, and five to seven nerves are prominent. Inflorescence from the base of the pseudobulb is erect. Flowers are large, showy, fragrant and variable in colour. Sepals and petals are free and spreading. The labellum is entire with a thickened basal part; the callus is semi-circular and fleshy. The column has two antenna-like projections.

Culture: For this truly epiphytic plant use compost in a hanging basket or shallow fern-pan. It does best mounted on a tree-fern slab. The plant requires warm, humid conditions at all times. Allow it to rest for several weeks after flowering.

SOUTH AMERICA

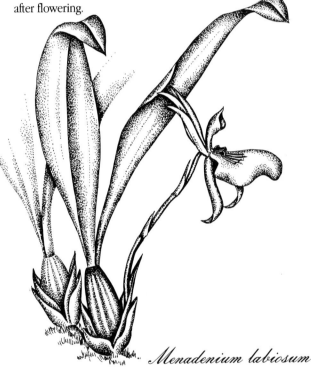

Menadenium labiosum

Menadenium labiosum

COMMON NAME: None.
COLOUR: Colour variable, usually green-yellow, suffused with pink or grey. Labellum white with purple-red callus and veins.
SIZE: Growing up to 35cm (14″) high.
CLIMATE: Intermediate to warm.
DISTRIBUTION: Native to northern Brazil, Venezuela and Guyana.
FLOWERING TIME: Spring to early summer.
DESCRIPTION: Pseudobulbs borne at wide intervals, compressed, ovoid-oblong. One to two leaves are lanceolate, strap-shaped, acuminate and grow up to 30cm (12″) long. Flowers are fragrant, large and handsome.

Menadenium labiosum

MILTONIA
(mil-toh-nee-a)

Miltonia is named after Earl Fitzwilliam Viscount Milton. This small genus of about twenty species is found from the Andes to south-east Brazil, with one species from Panama and Costa Rica. *Miltonia* are characterised as having scandent rhizomes, compressed pseudobulbs with leaves, and an auriculate column. In 1977, *Miltonia* was divided into two groups: (a) those having terete peduncles, e.g. *M. clowesii*; and (b) those having compressed ancipitous peduncles, e.g. *M. spectabilis. Miltonia* is a genus of epiphytic plants, which have very small pseudobulbs at intervals along creeping, climbing rhizomes. The two leaves are apical and coriaceous. Inflorescence emerges from the base of the pseudobulb, and is short, erect or arching, with one or many flowered racemes. Flowers are medium to large and are showy. Sepals are free and spreading. Petals are similar to sepals, though often broader. The labellum is entire, broad and spreading. The column has ear-like appendages.

Culture: Compost. These plants have creeping, climbing rhizomes, so grow in shallow pans or baskets, or mount on tree-fern slabs. They require frequent watering and moderate shade. Provide warm but not hot conditions.

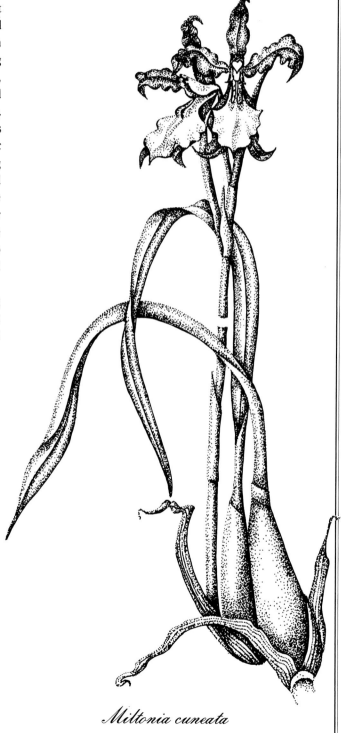

Miltonia cuneata

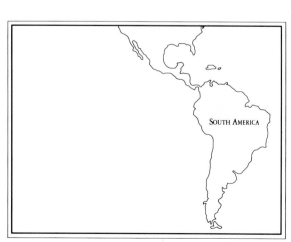

SOUTH AMERICA

Miltonia X *bluntii*

COMMON NAME: None.
COLOUR: Flowers red-purple. Labellum pink-purple.
SIZE: Growing up to 30cm (12″) high.
CLIMATE: Intermediate.
DISTRIBUTION: Native to Brazil.
FLOWERING TIME: Spring.
DESCRIPTION: A natural hybrid between *M. clowesii* and *M. spectabilis*. Two leaves. Inflorescence sheathing. Flowers are handsome, fragrant, usually produced one at a time and measure about 7.5cm (3″) across.

Miltonia X *bluntii*

Miltonia candida

Miltonia candida

COMMON NAME: None.
COLOUR: Flowers red-brown, tipped and spotted with yellow. Labellum white marked with purple.
SIZE: Growing up to 50cm (20″) high.
CLIMATE: Intermediate.
DISTRIBUTION: Native to Brazil.
FLOWERING TIME: Spring.
DESCRIPTION: Pseudobulbs are somewhat compressed, elongated, narrow-ovoid, up to 10cm (4″) high. Leaves grow in pairs, are linear-oblanceolate, acute and up to 38.5cm (15″) long. Flowers are fragrant, waxy and 7.5cm (3″) across.

Miltonia clowesii

COMMON NAME: None.
COLOUR: Flowers red-brown, barred and tipped yellow. Labellum purple and white.
SIZE: Growing up to 45cm (18″) high.
CLIMATE: Intermediate.
DISTRIBUTION: Native to Brazil.
FLOWERING TIME: Spring.
DESCRIPTION: An epiphytic plant. Pseudobulbs are compressed, narrowly ovate-oblong, up to 10cm (4″) high. Leaves are apical in pairs, strap-shaped, up to 46cm (18″) long. Inflorescence up to 45cm (18″) long with seven to ten blooms. Flowers measure up to 7.5cm (3″) across.

Miltonia clowesii

Miltonia cuneata

Miltonia cuneata

COMMON NAME: None.
COLOUR: Flowers red-brown, tipped with lemon, may have yellow streaks at the base.
SIZE: Growing up to 45cm (18″) high.
CLIMATE: Intermediate.
CLIMATE: Native to Brazil.
FLOWERING TIME: Summer to autumn
DESCRIPTION: Robust creeping rhizome. Pseudobulbs are compressed, oblong-ovoid and up to 10cm (4″) high. Two leaves are narrow-lanceolate, acute and grow up to 38.5cm (15″) long. Inflorescence is up to 60cm (2′) long. Flower measures 7.5cm (3″) across.

Miltonia flavescens

COMMON NAME: None.
COLOUR: Flowers ochre yellow. Labellum white with purple-red streaks on basal area.
SIZE: Growing up to 45cm (18″) high.
CLIMATE: Intermediate.
DISTRIBUTION: Native to Paraguay and Brazil.
FLOWERING TIME: Spring.
DESCRIPTION: Rhizome creeping. Pseudobulbs are compressed, oblong-oval, up to 12.5cm (5″) high. Two leaves are linear, strap-shaped and grow up to 30cm (12″) long. Flowers are fragrant. Petals and sepals are narrow, star-shaped and are about 10cm (4″) across.

Miltonia flavescens

Miltonia regnellii

Miltonia regnellii

COMMON NAME: None.
COLOUR: Flowers white with basal pink tint, streaked with pink, and purple-pink and white margins, and crest has yellow lines. Labellum pink and veined purple.
SIZE: Growing up to 45cm (18″) high.
CLIMATE: Intermediate.
DISTRIBUTION: Native to Brazil.
FLOWERING TIME: Spring.
DESCRIPTION: Pseudobulbs are compressed, oblong-ovoid and grow up to 10cm (4″) high. Two leaves are linear, strap-shaped, acute and 40cm (16″) long. Inflorescence is erect and grows up to 60cm (2′) long. Flowers measure about 7.5cm (3″) across. Labellum is tri-lobed.

Miltonia spectabilis

Miltonia spectabilis

COMMON NAME: None.
COLOUR: Flower colour variable, usually cream-white, may be tinted with pink near the base. Labellum red-purple, with deeper hue on longitudal veins.
SIZE: Growing up to 25cm (10″) high.
CLIMATE: Intermediate.
DISTRIBUTION: Native to Brazil.
FLOWERING TIME: Autumn.
DESCRIPTION: Creeping rhizome. Pseudobulbs are compressed, oblong-ovoid and measure up to 10cm (4″) high. Leaves are linear, strap-shaped, growing up to 25cm (10″) long. Inflorescence is erect and about 20cm (8″) high. Solitary flower is about 7.5cm (3″) long.

Miltonia spectabilis var. moreliana

COMMON NAME: Parsley Orchid.
COLOUR: This variant differs from its type in that it has a larger plum-purple flower. Labellum rose colour with darker veins.
SIZE: Growing up to 25cm (10″) high.
CLIMATE: Intermediate.
DISTRIBUTION: Native to Brazil.
FLOWERING TIME: Autumn.
DESCRIPTION: Pseudobulbs borne on a creeping rhizome, compressed, oblong-ovoid, up to 10cm (4″) high. Strap-shaped leaves grow in pairs up to 25cm (10″) long. Inflorescence is short. Flowers are solitary measuring up to 10cm (4″) long. It is more common in cultivation than is the type.

Miltonia spectabilis var. *moreliana*

MILTONIOPSIS
(mil-toh-nee-opsis)

Miltoniopsis from the Gk *opsis* (appearance) with reference to the flower's similarity to that of genus *Miltonia.* This is an epiphytic genus of six species and is found in the central Americas, Panama, Costa Rica, Venezuela, Colombia and Ecuador. The genus was first established in 1889, but failed to gain approval by many authors. In 1976 when describing a new species, Garay and Dunsterville revived the name for four other central American species previously in the *Miltonia* group of Brazil. *Miltoniopsis* is different from *Miltonia* in that the pseudobulbs are bilaterally flat in clusters, the single apical leaf and the exauriculate column is joined to the labellum by a raised ridge and is not excavate at the base.

Culture: Mount the plant on a tree-fern slab.

SOUTH AMERICA

Miltoniopsis vexillaria

Miltoniopsis vexillaria syn. *Miltonia vexillaria*

COMMON NAME: None.
COLOUR: Flowers pink, white, or white striped and flushed pink. Labellum rose pink, white at base, marked with red and yellow.
SIZE: An epiphytic plant up to 30cm (12″) high.
CLIMATE: Cool to intermediate.
DISTRIBUTION: Northern Ecuador and Colombia, growing at an altitude of 1300 to 2150m (4265 to 7053′), in marginal areas of montane forests.
FLOWERING TIME: Spring.
DESCRIPTION: Pseudobulbs are conical-ovoid, compressed, up to 7.5cm (3″) high. Leaves are apical, strap-like, growing up to 25cm (10″) long. Inflorescence is borne from the base of the pseudobulbs, and is up to 30cm (12″) long. Flowers are showy and large, up to 10cm (4″) long.

Miltoniopsis vexillaria syn. *Miltonia vexillaria*

NEOBENTHAMIA
(nee-o-ben-tham-ee-a)

Neobenthamia is named after George Bentham, an English botanist. This single species genus is from tropical eastern Africa. It is a terrestrial orchid often cultivated in domestic gardens. The handsome robust plant often grows to 2.5m (8′) tall, with leaves to 20cm (8″) long. Inflorescence is a terminal cluster of white flowers, each 2.5cm (1″) across, in a hemisphere up to 30cm (12″) diameter on a tall leafy stem.

Culture: As for *Phaius*. Grows best in full sun. The plant requires water, a coarse moisture-retaining soil with very good drainage, and careful fertilising. *Neobenthamia* is a must for all orchidists.

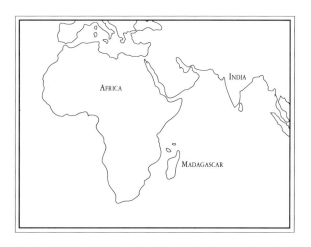

Neobenthamia gracilis

Neobenthamia gracilis

Neobenthamia gracilis

COMMON NAME: None.
COLOUR: Flowers white. Labellum white, with yellow stripe and red-purple markings either side.
SIZE: Growing up to 1.8m (6′) high.
CLIMATE: Intermediate.
DISTRIBUTION: Native to tropical eastern Africa.
FLOWERING TIME: Throughout the year.
DESCRIPTION: A robust species. Stems are slender, often branching and variable in size but usually up to 1.8m (6′) high. Leaves are shiny, linear-lanceolate, acute and grow up to 20cm (8″) long. Terminal inflorescence, up to 12.5cm (5″) high. Flowers are numerous and measure up to 2.5cm (1″) across.

NEOFINETIA
(nee-o-fi-net-ee-a)

*N*eofinetia is named after M. Achille Finet, a French botanist, who worked in China and Japan. This single species genus from China, Japan and Korea is a dwarf epiphytic monopodial plant. Leaves are distichous, fleshy and channelled above. Inflorescence is in the form of an axillary raceme with several white flowers. Sepals and petals are free and spreading. The labellum is tri-lobed, erect with arcuate spur at base. This species has some eight synonyms and several hybrids.

Culture: Compost. Grow in a small pot or basket. The plant requires humid conditions, light shade, frequent watering and good drainage. (Same treatment as for dwarf *Vandas.*)

Neofinetia falcata

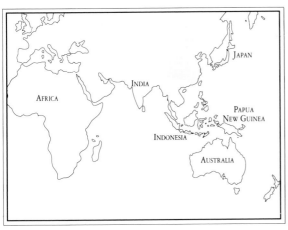

Neofinetia falcata

COMMON NAME: None.
COLOUR: Flowers white.
SIZE: Growing up to 15cm (6″) high.
CLIMATE: Intermediate.
DISTRIBUTION: Native to Korea and Japan.
FLOWERING TIME: Summer to autumn.
DESCRIPTION: A genus of one species, with many varieties. Small plant, stems branching from base, about 15cm (6″) high. Leaves are curving, linear, acute and grow up to 15cm (6″) long. Flowers are fragrant at night and measure about 3cm (1¼″) across. Sepals and petals are linear. Labellum is triangular with a long curved spur, up to 10cm (4″) long. Inflorescences short, bearing three to seven flowers.

Neofinetia falcata

NEOLAUCHEA
(nee-o-lau-chee-a)

Neolauchea may be named after Lauche, or after the Spanish *lauchea* (struggling) as the plant is difficult to establish. This single species genus comes from southern Brazil and is a most uncommon dwarf epiphytic orchid. The plant has small pseudobulbs at intervals along creeping rhizomes. Leaves are terete and coriaceous. Inflorescence is terminal with attractive rose-red flowers. This genus is found in only the most comprehensive collections. Nothing is known of its genetic affinities.

Culture: Use compost of finely chopped fibre, tightly packed, in a small basket. *Neolauchea* is difficult to handle because all vegetative parts of the plant are exceedingly fragile; however, once established it grows readily. The plant requires frequent watering, perfect drainage, a shady and perpetually moist situation, and warm but never hot conditions. Disturb as little as possible.

Neolauchea pulchella

SOUTH AMERICA

Neolauchea pulchella

Neolauchea pulchella

COMMON NAME: None.
COLOUR: Flowers rose-red or mauve.
SIZE: Growing up to 7.5cm (3″) high.
CLIMATE: Intermediate.
DISTRIBUTION: Native to southern Brazil.
FLOWERING TIME: Summer.
DESCRIPTION: Pseudobulbs are narrow ovoid, 1cm (½″) high, borne at intervals on a creeping rhizome. Leaf is solitary, linear to almost terete, up to 6cm (2½″). Inflorescence is terminal and short. Flowers are about 1cm (¼″) long.

NEOMOOREA

(nee-o-moor-ee-a)

Neomoorea is named after F. W. Moore, curator at Glasnevin Botanic Gardens in Dublin. The genus has two epiphytic or terrestrial species and comes from Colombia and Panama. *Neomoorea* is closely allied to *Stanhopea*, but the labellum hypochile of *Neomoorea* is not saccate-concave like *Stanhopea*. Pseudobulbs are ovoid. The two leaves are apical and plicate. Inflorescence is erect from the base of the pseudobulb. Flowers are large and showy. Sepals and petals are free and spreading, with petals narrower at the base. The labellum is tri-lobed; lateral lobes are large and spreading, and the mid-lobe is concave with two lateral erect and spreading wings.

Culture: Use a compost of finely chopped tree-fern fibre, rich loam, gritty sand, and add sphagnum moss (ratio 5:1:1:1). If bark is used, sift out all the dust and use well-drained pots. Water frequently during growth periods and restrict watering during rest periods. New growth is very sensitive to over watering and stale compost. *M. irrorata*, a magnificent epiphytic orchid, is highly prized by orchidists. These majestic orchids deserve and require the best care and attention.

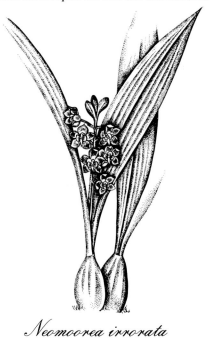

Neomoorea irrorata

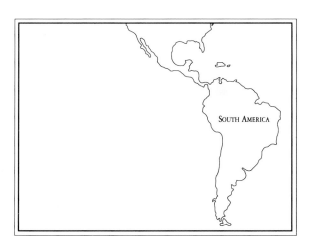

SOUTH AMERICA

Neomoorea irrorata

Neomoorea irrorata

COMMON NAME: None.
COLOUR: Flowers red-brown with white bases. Labellum lemon, marked and banded with brown-purple. Mid-lobe is lemon, spotted with red.
SIZE: Growing up to 1m (40") high.
CLIMATE: Warm.
DISTRIBUTION: Native to Colombia and Panama.
FLOWERING TIME: Spring.
DESCRIPTION: Pseudobulbs are ovoid-ovate, compressed, furrowed and up to 12.5cm (5") high. Two leaves are lanceolate-elliptic, folded and are about 1m (40") long. Inflorescence is erect with many fragrant, waxy flowers about 6cm (2½") across. Labellum is tri-lobed.

OCTOMERIA
(ok-toh-may-ree-a)

Octomeria from the Gk *octo* (eight) *meros* (part) with reference to the eight pollinia which are characteristic of the species in this genus. This is a relatively little known genus of about seventy species of epiphytic or lithophytic orchids. Mostly they originate from Brazil with widespread representation from the Honduras, Costa Rica, West Indies, Colombia and Guyana. The plant is small and insignificant in appearance. It has creeping rhizomes as the primary stem, with erect secondary stems, each with a single apical leaf. The leaf is coriaceous to fleshy, and flat to terete. Inflorescence arises from the base of the leaf. It has one to many flowers. The sepals and petals are connate at the base, or free and spreading. The labellum is very short and either tri-lobed or entire. The column also is very short with eight pollinia.

The *Octomeria* genus is a highly diverse plant, which is poorly known and exceptionally scarce in collections. Although quite small, many species are attractive with white, yellow or green flowers.

Culture: Use a fine compost in small pots. Depending on its place of origin, each species requires individual attention. Basically, treat as for *Pleurothallis*. Plants require shade and humidity during growth. Apply water regularly to roots and fertilise monthly. Always check with your local orchid club for advice when growing these species.

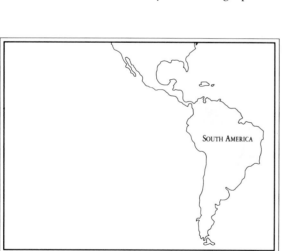

SOUTH AMERICA

Octomeria semiconnata

Octomeria gracilis

COMMON NAME: None.
COLOUR: Flowers lemon.
SIZE: A small plant, growing up to 18cm (7″) high.
CLIMATE: Intermediate.
DISTRIBUTION: Native to Brazil.
FLOWERING TIME: Throughout the year.
DESCRIPTION: Leaves are needle-like on a linear petiole. Flowers are clustered, small and up to 7mm (¼″) across.

Octomeria gracilis

ODONTOGLOSSUM

(o-don-toh-gloss-um)

*O*dontoglossum from the Gk *odonto* (tooth) *glossa* (tongue) with reference to the tooth-like crest of the labellum callus. This is a genus of over two hundred polymorphic species having several distinct forms. Its distribution extends from Mexico in the north down through the central Americas to Bolivia and Brazil. The larger number of species occur in the mountains of Ecuador, Peru and Venezuela. The genus is highly diverse in both appearance and vegetation; it is epiphytic or lithophytic, but rarely terrestrial. Rhizomes are short. Pseudobulbs are compressed, often with leaf-like distichous bracts, with one to three apical leaves. Leaves are fleshy or coriaceous and may be rigid or flexible. Inflorescence arises from the base of the pseudobulb, is erect or arching, and pendulous in several species. Flowers are large and either showy or small and inconspicuous. Sepals and petals are spreading. The labellum is often complex, tri-lobed or entire, erect or parallel to column, with lateral lobes erect or revolute; the mid-lobe is spreading.

The column is long with two pollinia. The genus is freely compatible genetically, hence the reports of thousands of hybrids. This genus is extremely popular with breeders.

Culture: Depends heavily on the place of origin of the specimen. Genus habitats range from sea level to 3000m (10 000′) elevation. Species from the coastal lowlands require moist humid conditions, while those from the Andes of Peru and Bolivia need 'cool-house' conditions. The roots must never be allowed to dry out. Fresh moving air is essential. Check with your local orchid society concerning growing conditions, such as use of fertiliser.

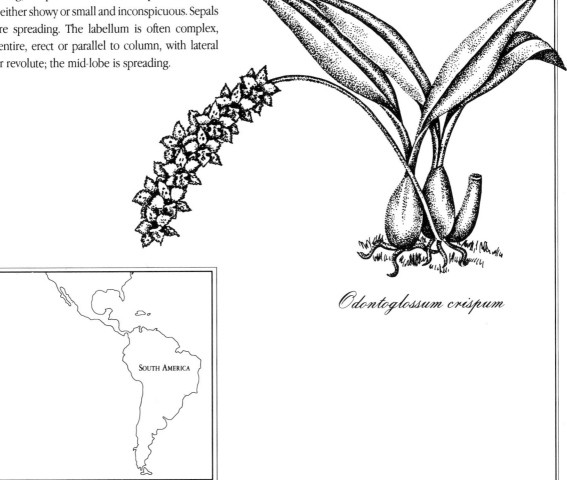

Odontoglossum crispum

SOUTH AMERICA

Odontoglossum bictoniense

COMMON NAME: None.
COLOUR: Flowers yellow-green, banded with red-brown. Labellum white, streaked purple.
SIZE: Growing up to 60cm (2') high.
CLIMATE: Warm.
DISTRIBUTION: Native to Mexico, El Salvador and Guatemala.
FLOWERING TIME: Winter to spring.
DESCRIPTION: Pseudobulbs are compressed, ovoid to ellipsoid, up to 17.5cm (7") high and are mostly concealed by leaf sheaths. Two to three leaves are oblong-elliptic to linear, acute and measure 45cm (18") long. Inflorescence is up to 90cm (3') high. Flowers are numerous, fragrant and 4cm (1½") across.

Odontoglossum bictoniense

Odontoglossum cariniferum

COMMON NAME: None.
COLOUR: Flowers red-brown with tips and margins yellow. Labellum white.
SIZE: Growing up to 50cm (20") high.
CLIMATE: Intermediate to warm.
DISTRIBUTION: Native to Colombia, Venezuela and Costa Rica, found growing in montane forest.
FLOWERING TIME: Autumn to spring.
DESCRIPTION: Pseudobulbs are compressed, oblong-elliptic and up to 10cm (4") high. Leaves are linear, strap-like, up to 45cm (18") long. Inflorescence is branching with many flowers, up to 1.2m (4'). Flowers measure up to 5cm (2") across.

Odontoglossum pulchellum

Odontoglossum pulchellum

COMMON NAME: None.
COLOUR: Flowers white. Labellum has yellow blotch.
SIZE: Growing up to 45cm (18") high.
CLIMATE: Warm.
DISTRIBUTION: Native to Mexico, Costa Rica, El Salvador and Guatemala.
FLOWERING TIME: Winter.
DESCRIPTION: Pseudobulbs are clustered, compressed, ovoid to ovoid-elliptic, up to 10cm (4") high. Leaves are strap-like, linear, acute and up to 40cm (16") long. Flowers are fragrant and 4cm (1½") long.

Odontoglossum cariniferum

Odontoglossum rossii

COMMON NAME: None.
COLOUR: Flowers lemon, white or pink; sepals barred red-brown. Labellum white with yellow callus.
SIZE: Growing up to 20cm (8") high.
CLIMATE: Warm.
DISTRIBUTION: Native to Mexico, Honduras, Guatemala and Nicaragua.
FLOWERING TIME: Spring.
DESCRIPTION: Pseudobulbs are compressed, wrinkling when old and measure up to 6cm (2½"). Leaves are lanceolate-elliptic and up to 20cm (8") long. Erect inflorescence is up to 20cm (8") high. Flowers are 7.5cm (3") across.

Odontoglossum rossii

Odontoglossum stellatum

COMMON NAME: None.
COLOUR: Flowers bronze or purple with yellow apex and petals may be yellow-white. Labellum pink or white, tinted with mauve.
SIZE: Growing up to 20cm (8") high.
CLIMATE: Warm.
DISTRIBUTION: Native to Mexico and Guatemala.
FLOWERING TIME: Spring.
DESCRIPTION: Pseudobulbs are clustered, almost cylindrical, up to 5cm (2") high. Solitary leaf is narrowing and folding at the base and measures up to 15cm (6") long. Flowers are about 5cm (2") across.

Odontoglossum stellatum

ONCIDIUM
(on-sid-ee-um)

*O*ncidium comes from the Gk *onkos* (pad or mass) with reference to the fleshy, warty callus of the labellum. This is one of the largest and most cultivated of genera. At the same time it is very controversial, for the taxonomists who try to delineate between *Miltonia, Odontoglossum* and *Oncidium*. The latter is a genus of over seven hundred species, widespread from Florida (U.S.A.) to Mexico, and throughout tropical and subtropical America to Argentina, Brazil and the Andes of Colombia, Ecuador and Peru.

Oncidium is not an easy genus to describe. All segments of the plants are extremely variable. Primarily *Oncidiums* are epiphytic, with several lithophytic species growing on rock outcrops; while another group exists as pure terrestrials. Often the pseudobulbs are compressed, while other plants appear to be without pseudobulbs. The leaves may be papery, rigid, fleshy, coriaceous, distichous, flat, terete or deltoid. Inflorescence is usually from the base of the pseudobulb with one, two or several flowers. Their colours may be yellow and brown, or of a different hue such as white, magenta or red. The flower size also is quite variable from small to large, up to 7.5cm (5″) across. Sepals and petals are free and of various shapes. The labellum is tri-lobed and usually pandurate, but with many variations.

Culture: Compost in well-drained pots. Plants require humid conditions. Water frequently. They are most intolerant to stale conditions. Care must be taken with fragile new growth; do not allow water to lie around newly growing tips as rotting may occur. *Oncidium* is popular in collections.

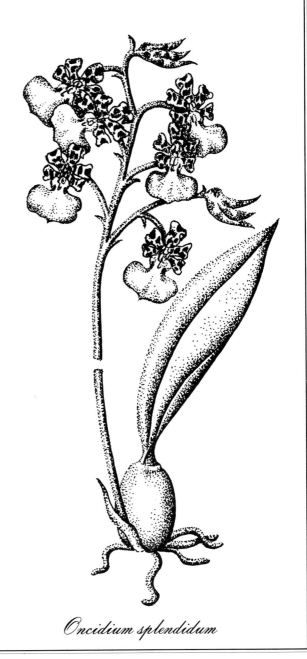

Oncidium splendidum

SOUTH AMERICA

Oncidium ampliatum

COMMON NAME: None.
COLOUR: Flowers yellow, spotted with red-brown. Labellum tri-lobed, white with red spots.
SIZE: Growing up to 50cm (20″) high.
CLIMATE: Intermediate to warm.
DISTRIBUTION: Native to Peru, Guatemala, Venezuela and Trinidad.
FLOWERING TIME: Spring.
DESCRIPTION: Pseudobulbs are clustered, compressed, ovoid, up to 12.5 cm (5″) high. Leaves are elliptic-oblanceolate, up to 38cm (15″) long. Inflorescence is erect, up to 1.2m (4′) long. Flower size is variable, about 2.5cm (1″) across. Labellum is tri-lobed.

Oncidium ampliatum

Oncidium barbatum

COMMON NAME: None.
COLOUR: Flowers yellow, marked red-brown. Labellum yellow, the crest spotted red.
SIZE: Growing up to 16.5cm (6½″) high.
CLIMATE: Intermediate.
DISTRIBUTION: Native to Brazil.
FLOWERING TIME: Spring.
DESCRIPTION: Pseudobulbs are compressed, clustered, oval-oblong, up to 6.5cm (2½″). Solitary leaf is linear to oval-oblong and up to 10cm (4″) long. Inflorescence is slightly panicled, up to 35cm (14″) long. Flowers are waxy and up to 4cm (1½″) long.

Oncidium barbatum

Oncidium carthagenense syn. *O. kymatoides*

COMMON NAME: None.
COLOUR: Flowers white or ochre yellow, blotched red-brown, lilac or red-purple.
SIZE: Growing up to 40cm (16″) high.
CLIMATE: Intermediate to warm.
DISTRIBUTION: Native to Mexico, Venezuela, Brazil, southern Florida (U.S.A.) and the West Indies. A common widespread epiphytic plant, growing from sea level to 1500m (4291′).
FLOWERING TIME: Spring to summer.
DESCRIPTION: Pseudobulbs are up to 2.5cm (1″) high and are covered by sheaths. Solitary leaf is apical lanceolate, oblong-elliptic, acute and up to 40cm (16″) long. Inflorescence is paniculate, erect with numerous flowers. Inflorescence is up to 2m (6′6″) long. Flowers are showy and 2.5cm (1″) across.

Oncidium carthagenense syn. *O. kymatoides*

Oncidium cavendishianum

COMMON NAME: None.
COLOUR: Flowers may be entirely yellow, but are generally yellow-green, spotted with red. Labellum yellow.
SIZE: Growing up to 60cm (2′) high.
CLIMATE: Warm.
DISTRIBUTION: Native to Mexico and Guatemala.
FLOWERING TIME: Winter to early spring.
DESCRIPTION: Pseudobulbs are small, borne from a robust rhizome. Leaves are oblong-lanceolate and up to 60cm (2′) high. Inflorescence is erect and up to 90cm (3′) long. Flowers are waxy, fragrant and about 4cm (1½″) across. Labellum is tri-lobed.

Oncidium cavendishianum

Oncidium crispum

COMMON NAME: None.
COLOUR: Flowers brown. Labellum brown-yellow, blotched red-brown.
SIZE: Growing up to 30cm (12″) high.
CLIMATE: Intermediate.
DISTRIBUTION: Native to Brazil.
FLOWERING TIME: Summer.
DESCRIPTION: Pseudobulbs are clustered, compressed, oblong, furrowed and ribbed on the flat side and are up to 10cm (4″) high. Leaves are lanceolate-oblong, acute, and grow up to 20cm (8″) long. Erect inflorescence are up to 90cm (3′) long, carrying as many as 80 blooms. Flowers are variable in size, but are about 7.5cm (3″) across.

Oncidium crispum

Oncidium enderianum syn. *O. crispum* var. *grandiflorum*

Oncidium enderianum syn. *O. crispum* var. *grandiflorum*

COMMON NAME: None.
COLOUR: Flowers brown, margins slightly edged with yellow. Labellum brown, splashed yellow; orange callus.
SIZE: Growing up to 30cm (12″) high.
CLIMATE: Intermediate.
DISTRIBUTION: Native to the southern mountains of Brazil.
FLOWERING TIME: Autumn.
DESCRIPTION: Pseudobulbs are compressed, ovate, furrowed and up to 10cm (4″) high. Leaves are broad-lanceolate, up to 20cm (8″) long. Inflorescence is branching, 90cm (3′) long with numerous flowers. Flowers are up to 6cm (2½″) across.

Oncidium longipes

Oncidium flexuosum

COMMON NAME: None.
COLOUR: Flowers deep yellow, generally with a red blotch at the base of segments.
SIZE: Growing up to 30.5cm (12″) high.
CLIMATE: Intermediate.
DISTRIBUTION: Native to Brazil, Paraguay and Uruguay.
FLOWERING TIME: Autumn to winter.
DESCRIPTION: Pseudobulbs are compressed, oblong-oval, up to 7.5cm (3″) high. Predominantly two leaves, linear to linear-lanceolate, acute and up to 23cm (9″) long. Inflorescence is up to 90cm (3′) long. Flowers are numerous and up to 3cm (1¼″) long.

Oncidium gravesianum

Oncidium gravesianum

COMMON NAME: None.
COLOUR: Flowers brown. Labellum blotched yellow.
SIZE: Growing up to 15cm (6″) high.
CLIMATE: Intermediate.
DISTRIBUTION: Native to Mexico and Panama.
FLOWERING TIME: Autumn.
DESCRIPTION: Pseudobulbs are compressed, up to 5cm (2″) high. Leaves are narrow-lanceolate and up to 15cm (6″) long. Inflorescence is basal and 45cm (18″) long. Flowers are large, showy, with variable colour and are up to 7.5cm (3″) across.

Oncidium flexuosum

Oncidium leaneri

COMMON NAME: None.
COLOUR: Flowers yellow with brown markings.
SIZE: Growing up to 50cm (20″) high.
CLIMATE: Intermediate.
DISTRIBUTION: Native to Brazil.
FLOWERING TIME: Autumn.
DESCRIPTION: Pseudobulbs are compressed, furrowed, conical, up to 15cm (6″) long. Leaves are strap-shaped, acute and up to 50cm (20″) long. Branching inflorescence is up to 1.5m (5′) and densely flowered. Flowers are 4cm (1½″) long.

Oncidium leaneri

Oncidium longipes

COMMON NAME: None.
COLOUR: Flowers yellow, blotched with brown. Labellum yellow, marked with red-brown.
SIZE: Growing up to 15cm (6″) high.
CLIMATE: Intermediate.
DISTRIBUTION: Native to Brazil.
FLOWERING TIME: Summer to autumn.
DESCRIPTION: Closely allied to *O. uniflorum*. Pseudobulbs are ovoid and up to 2.5cm (1″) high. One to two leaves are linear-lanceolate and up to 15cm (6″) long. Inflorescence is short. Flower is up to 4cm (1½″) long.

Oncidium ornithorhynchum

COMMON NAME: Bird Beak Orchid.
COLOUR: Flowers pink-lilac.
SIZE: Growing up to 35cm (14") high.
CLIMATE: Intermediate.
DISTRIBUTION: Native to Mexico, Costa Rica, El Savador and Guatemala.
FLOWERING TIME: Winter.
DESCRIPTION: Pseudobulbs are clustered, somewhat compressed, oblong-oval, and 12.5cm (5") high. Leaves are linear-lanceolate, acute and up to 30cm (12") long. Inflorescence is up to 60cm (2') long. Flowers are numerous, fragrant and 2cm (¾") long.

Oncidium ornithorhynchum

Oncidium papilio syn. *Psychopsis picta*

Oncidium papilio syn. *Psychopsis picta*

COMMON NAME: None.
COLOUR: Flowers yellow with orange-brown markings.
SIZE: Growing up to 25cm (10") high.
CLIMATE: Warm.
DISTRIBUTION: Native to Trinidad, Venezuela, Colombia, Ecuador and Peru. A widespread epiphytic plant, growing in the lower montane forests.
FLOWERING TIME: Throughout the year.
DESCRIPTION: Pseudobulbs are compressed, wrinkled, clustered, orbicular and up to 5cm (2") high. Leaves are oblong-elliptic, mottled maroon, obtuse and up to 20cm (8") long. Inflorescence is up to 90cm (3') long. Flowers are up to 10cm (4") long.

Oncidium rio grandense

COMMON NAME: None.
COLOUR: Flowers yellow.
SIZE: Growing up to 20cm (8") high.
CLIMATE: Cool to intermediate.
DISTRIBUTION: Native to Brazil.
FLOWERING TIME: Summer.
DESCRIPTION: A medium sized epiphytic plant. Pseudobulbs are cylindrical, slightly compressed, furrowed and up to 10cm (4") high. Bracts are sheathing for three-quarters of the length of the pseudobulbs. Leaves are apical, lanceolate and up to 10cm (4") long. Inflorescence rises from basal sheathing bracts, up to 25cm (10") long; raceme has up to 15 blooms or more. Flowers are 2.5cm (1") across.

Oncidium rio grandense

Oncidium sphacelatum

Oncidium sphacelatum

COMMON NAME: None.
COLOUR: Flowers variable, yellow, barred red-brown.
SIZE: Growing up to 75cm (30") high.
CLIMATE: Intermediate.
DISTRIBUTION: Native to Mexico, British Honduras, Guatemala, El Salvador and Honduras.
FLOWERING TIME: Spring.
DESCRIPTION: Pseudobulbs are compressed, almost oblong and up to 20cm (8") high. Leaves are linear, strap-shaped and grow up to 60cm (2'). Inflorescence is branched, up to 1.5m (5'). Numerous flowers are up to 3cm (1¼") across.

Oncidium splendidum

COMMON NAME: None.
COLOUR: Flowers yellow, spotted and blotched, red-brown. Labellum deep yellow.
SIZE: Growing up to 35cm (14″) high.
CLIMATE: Warm.
DISTRIBUTION: Native to Honduras and Guatemala.
FLOWERING TIME: Spring to early summer.
DESCRIPTION: Pseudobulbs are clustered, ovoid, somewhat compressed and up to 5cm (2″) high. Solitary leaf is oblong to oblong-elliptic, acute, keeled behind and up to 30cm (12″) long. Inflorescence is up to 120cm (4′) long. Flowers are showy and 7.5cm (3″) long.

Oncidium splendidum

Oncidium stipitatum

Oncidium stipitatum

COMMON NAME: None.
COLOUR: Flowers yellow, marked with red-brown.
SIZE: Growing up to 60cm (2′) high.
CLIMATE: Warm.
DISTRIBUTION: Native to Panama, Honduras and Nicaragua.
FLOWERING TIME: Summer.
DESCRIPTION: Pseudobulbs are very small, almost obsolete. Solitary leaf is terete, acuminate and up to 65cm (26″) long. Flowers are clustered, numerous, variable in size, about 2.5cm (1″) long.

Oncidium teres

Oncidium teres

COMMON NAME: None.
COLOUR: Flowers yellow with red-brown spots.
SIZE: Growing up to 60cm (2′) high.
CLIMATE: Warm.
DISTRIBUTION: Native to Panama.
FLOWERING TIME: Winter to spring.
DESCRIPTION: Pseudobulbs are very small. Solitary leaf is terete, acuminate and up to 65cm (26″) long. Flowers are clustered, numerous, variable in size, but about 1cm (½″) long. Inflorescence is up to 45cm (18″) long.

Oncidium wentworthianum

COMMON NAME: None.
COLOUR: Flowers yellow, blotched red-brown.
SIZE: Growing up to 40cm (16″) high.
CLIMATE: Intermediate.
DISTRIBUTION: Native to Mexico, Guatemala; growing at an altitude of 1500m (5000′).
FLOWERING TIME: Summer to autumn.
DESCRIPTION: Pseudobulbs are compressed, ovoid-ellipsoid, up to 10cm (4″) high. Leaves are strap-shaped, acute, up to 35cm (14″) long. Inflorescence is paniculate and up to 2m (6′6″) long. Flowers are numerous and 3cm (1¼″) across.

Oncidium wentworthianum

ORTHOCERAS
(or-tho-ser-as)

*O*rthoceras from the Gk *orthos* (straight, upright) and *ceras* (horn) with reference to the lateral sepals which spread like the horns of a buffalo. This genus of a single terrestrial species is found in Australia, New Zealand and New Caledonia. The genus is similar to *Diuris*, but differs from that genus in technical detail—the almost sessile flowers, the minute sessile petals and the erect filiform lateral sepals. Although cultivated by several Australian species growers, the genus is not found in many collections.

Culture: As for *Caladenia*, which is not easy to grow. Plants require rich, well-drained, free moving compost. In pots, use broken crock, granulated or crushed brick, topped with equal parts of shredded tree-fern, leaf mould, crumbled loam, sharp, gritty sand and sphagnum moss. Use liquid fertiliser regularly.

Orthoceras strictum

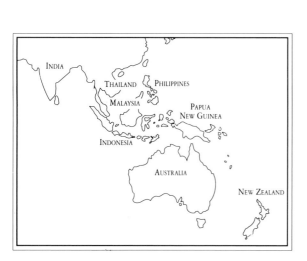

Orthoceras strictum

Orthoceras strictum

COMMON NAME: Bird Beak Orchid or Horned Orchid.
COLOUR: Flowers green-purple-brown.
SIZE: Robust terrestrial, up to 75cm (29½″) high.
CLIMATE: Cool.
DISTRIBUTION: Native to eastern Australia (Tasmania), New Zealand and New Caledonia; grows close to damp, swampy areas.
FLOWERING TIME: Late spring to early summer.
DESCRIPTION: Robust terrestrial, up to 75cm (30″) high. Leaves are radical, linear and channelled. The one to nine flowers are 2cm (¾″) long. Dorsal sepal has the appearance of a bird's beak.

PAPHIOPEDILUM
(paf-ee-oh-ped-i-lum)

*P*aphiopedilum from the Gk *paphos* (the island with a temple dedicated to Venus) and *pedilon* (sandal) meaning Venus' sandal or ladies' slipper. This is a genus of about one hundred species of terrestrial or occasionally epiphytic orchids. It is widespread from India, Burma, South-east Asia, China, Malaysia, Java, Borneo, the Philippines, Papua New Guinea to the Solomon Islands. *Paphiopedilums* are unique and unmistakable. They are stemless, pseudobulbless, sympodial plants, with fans of conduplicate coriaceous leaves. Each fan comprises six or more leaves. Flowers can be single or a few in number. The dorsal sepal is showy; lateral sepals are fused to form a symsepalum almost hidden by the labellum. The lateral petals are long and narrow, often with wavy margins and tufts of hairs. Because of the fusion of the sepals, the petals may be mistaken for sepals. The labellum is saccate, pouch-forming, with side lobes incurved. *Paphiopedilum* is closely related to *Cypripedium, Phragmipedium* and *Selenipedium*. All four are often referred to as '*Cyps*', having been treated in the past as one genus, *Cypripedium.*

In 1896, R. A. Rolfe established the following key to separate the genera: (a) Leaves plicate, alternate; rhizome prominent; leafy shoots with conspicuous internodes: (i) *Selenipedium* (three species). Leafy shoots often branching; inflorescence of numerous small flowers having trilocular ovaries; up to 3m (10′) tall; Central and South America. (ii) *Cypripedium* (about 28 species). Leafy shoots never branching; inflorescence of numerous small flowers with unilocular ovaries; up to 1m (40″) tall; temperate and subtropical America. (b) Leaves conduplicate, distichous; rhizomes present but condensed; leafy shoots without conspicuous internodes; often with lengthy axillary inflorescence: (i) *Paphiopedilum* (about 60 species). Sepals imbricate in bud; unilocular ovaries; South-east Asia. (ii) *Phragmipedium* (about 12 species). Sepals valvate in bud; trilocular ovaries; Central and South America.

Culture: Compost. Species such as *P. insigne* require 'cool-house' conditions and species such as *P. concolor* require 'warm-house' conditions. All species require humid conditions, shade from direct sunlight and good air movement. Water frequently as plants are unable to store water. Never allow plants to become dry.

Paphiopedilum ciliolare

Paphiopedilum acmodontum

COMMON NAME: None.
COLOUR: Flower a blend of white, pink and green with red-brown spots and vertical veins.
SIZE: Growing up to 25cm (10″) high.
CLIMATE: Intermediate.
DISTRIBUTION: Native to the Philippines (Visayan areas).
FLOWERING TIME: Late spring.
DESCRIPTION: Leaves are broad-ovate, tessellated with dark green or light green and are up to 30cm (12″) long. Flower scape is up to 30cm (12″) high and usually solitary. Labellum is pouched.

Paphiopedilum acmodontum

Paphiopedilum adductum

COMMON NAME: None.
COLOUR: Flowers white, with crimson vertical veins; petals white, blotched with crimson. Labellum white, veined, tinted with rose-pink.
SIZE: Growing up to 40cm (16″) high.
CLIMATE: Warm.
DISTRIBUTION: Native to Mindanao in the Philippines.
FLOWERING TIME: Summer.
DESCRIPTION: Leaves up to 45cm (18″) long. Flower scape bears up to five blooms. Pouched labellum.

Paphiopedilum adductum

Paphiopedilum appletonianum

COMMON NAME: None.
COLOUR: Flowers white with green and brown vertical veins. Petals marked with black-purple hairy warts. Labellum green-brown.
SIZE: Growing up to 15cm (6″) high.
CLIMATE: Cool to intermediate.
DISTRIBUTION: Native to Thailand, Himalayas, Assam and south-western Laos.
FLOWERING TIME: Late winter to early spring.
DESCRIPTION: Leaves are strap-shaped, up to 17.5cm (7″) long and faintly tessellated. Scape up to 45cm (18″) high. Solitary flower is about 10cm (4″) across.

Paphiopedilum appletonianum

Paphiopedilum argus

COMMON NAME: None.
COLOUR: Flower white with green vertical veins. Petals covered in black-purple hairy warts. Labellum brown-purple with green veins.
SIZE: Growing up to 25cm (10″) high.
CLIMATE: Cool to intermediate.
DISTRIBUTION: Native to the Philippines, Negros and Luzon. Growing at an altitude of 700 to 3000m (2300 to 10 000′).
FLOWERING TIME: Spring to early summer.
DESCRIPTION: Leaves are strap-shaped, dark green, tessellated with yellow-green and up to 30cm (12″) long. Flower scape is up to 60cm (2′) high. Flower is solitary and 10cm (4″) across.

Paphiopedilum argus

Paphiopedilum armeniacum

COMMON NAME: None.
COLOUR: Flower yellow.
SIZE: A small growing species.
CLIMATE: Intermediate.
DISTRIBUTION: Native to China—Bijiang, south Yunnan.
FLOWERING TIME: Spring.
DESCRIPTION: Leaves are oblong, up to 12.5cm (5″) long, with white tessellation and underside spotted with purple. Scape is up to 25cm (10″) high. Solitary flower has a pouched labellum.

Paphiopedilum armeniacum

Paphiopedilum barbatum

COMMON NAME: None.

COLOUR: Flower green-white, dark warts on petals, green and purple vertical stripes. Labellum brown-purple.

SIZE: Growing up to 25cm (10″) high.

CLIMATE: Intermediate.

DISTRIBUTION: Native to Peninsula Maylasia and coastal islands, Sumatra, Thailand and Mt Ophir, Singapore. Habitat is mountains at elevation of 200 to 1300m (1200 to 4000′). Preference for intermediate temperature and moist sheltered conditions.

FLOWERING TIME: Spring to autumn.

DESCRIPTION: Leaves are mottled, underside silver-green, and grow up to 30cm (12″) long. Scape is up to 35cm (14″) high. Flower is 10cm (4″) across.

Paphiopedilum barbatum

Paphiopedilum bellatulum syn. Cypripedium bellatulum

COMMON NAME: None.

COLOUR: Flower white, densely spotted with purple.

SIZE: Growing up to 30cm (12″) high.

CLIMATE: Cool to intermediate.

DISTRIBUTION: Native to Thailand, Burma (Moulmein); grows in limestone country at elevations of 1000 to 1600m (3300 to 5300′). Habitat varies from exposed cliff faces to moist mossy areas.

FLOWERING TIME: Spring to summer.

DESCRIPTION: Varied conditions affect leaf growth; they range from 20cm × 6cm (8″ × 2½″) wide in ideal conditions to 10cm × 3cm (4″ × 1¼″) in drier conditions. Leaves are narrow-elliptic, pale green mottled and under-surface is purple-maroon. Scape is short. Solitary flower is 8cm (3¼″) across.

Paphiopedilum bellatulum syn. *Cypripedium bellatulum*

Paphiopedilum birkii syn. P. sublaeve

COMMON NAME: None.

COLOUR: Flowers a blend of white, green and rose-pink. Labellum pouch rose-pink.

SIZE: Growing up to 25cm (10″) high.

CLIMATE: Intermediate to warm.

DISTRIBUTION: Native to western Malaysia, (Kedah Peak). It is a terrestrial liking warm conditions.

FLOWERING TIME: Summer.

DESCRIPTION: Leaves are up to 22.5cm (9″) long, are tessellated and lanceolate. Flower scape bears one to two blooms. Flowers are about 10cm (4″) across.

Paphiopedilum callosum

Paphiopedilum callosum

COMMON NAME: None.

COLOUR: Flower colour variable: white and green, purple-pink and green veins, black warts on petals. Labellum brown-purple.

SIZE: Growing up to 30cm (12″) high.

CLIMATE: Intermediate.

DISTRIBUTION: Native to Thailand and Cambodia. Grows at an altitude of 600 to 1200m (2000 to 4000′), lower slopes of mountains in moist areas.

FLOWERING TIME: Spring to summer.

DESCRIPTION: Leaves are tessellated and up to 22.5cm (9″) long. Scape is 40cm (16″) high. Flower is solitary and 9cm (3½″) across.

Paphiopedilum birkii syn. *P. sublaeve*

Paphiopedilum charlesworthii

COMMON NAME: None.

COLOUR: Dorsal sepal rose-pink, veins darker; rest of flower yellow-brown with darker veins.

SIZE: Growing up to 30cm (12″) high.

CLIMATE: Cool.

DISTRIBUTION: Native to Burma (Arakan Mountains), India (Bengal). Grows at an altitude of 1700m (5500′) on limestone mountains with westerly or north-westerly positions.

FLOWERING TIME: Autumn.

DESCRIPTION: Leaves are broad-linear, up to 20cm (8″) long and undersides are dotted with purple. Scape is up to 15cm (6″) high. Solitary flower is about 10cm (4″) across.

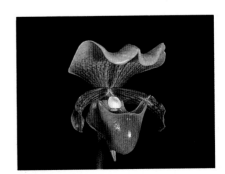

Paphiopedilum charlesworthii

Paphiopedilum ciliolare

Paphiopedilum ciliolare

COMMON NAME: None.
COLOUR: Flower blend of white and green with purple and green vertical veins, purple spots and warts. Labellum green-brown.
SIZE: Growing up to 25cm (10″) high.
CLIMATE: Intermediate.
DISTRIBUTION: Native to the Philippines (Luzon, Dinagat and Mindanao).
FLOWERING TIME: Spring to early summer.
DESCRIPTION: Broad, strap-shaped leaves with tessellation grow up to 17.5cm (7″) long. Scape is up to 30cm (12″) high. Solitary flower is about 10cm (4″) across.

Paphiopedilum concolor

Paphiopedilum concolor

COMMON NAME: None.
COLOUR: Flower colour variable, usually cream-yellow, spotted maroon-purple.
SIZE: Growing up to 30cm (12″) high.
CLIMATE: Intermediate.
DISTRIBUTION: Native to southern Thailand, southern Burma, Cambodia, Laos and Vietnam. Found growing at elevations of 300 to 1000m (1000 to 3300′) in limestone crevices near coastal areas, liking intermediate conditions.
FLOWERING TIME: Summer to autumn.
DESCRIPTION: Leaves are up to 15cm (6″) long, dark mottled green, underside spotted red-purple. Flower scape is up to 8cm (3″) long, bearing up to three blooms. Flower is up to 7.5cm (3″) across.

Paphiopedilum fairrieanum

Paphiopedilum delenatii

COMMON NAME: None.
COLOUR: Flower white tinted with pink. Labellum white and pink, tinted with lilac.
SIZE: Growing up to 15cm (6″) high.
CLIMATE: Warm.
DISTRIBUTION: Native to North and central Vietnam. Growing in crevices of limestone mountains, at low altitudes.
FLOWERING TIME: Spring to early summer.
DESCRIPTION: Leaves are rigid and thick with tessellation, underside green mottled with red-purple. Scape is up to 20cm (8″) high. Flower has a velvet texture. Labellum is almost rounded.

Paphiopedilum esquirolei

Paphiopedilum esquirolei

COMMON NAME: None.
COLOUR: Flower cream-green, with purple-brown suffusions and purple vertical veins and spots. Labellum cream-green, spotted with pink-purple.
SIZE: Growing up to 45cm (18″) across.
CLIMATE: Cool to intermediate.
DISTRIBUTION: Native to northern Thailand and southern China.
FLOWERING TIME: Spring.
DESCRIPTION: Leaves are notched apically, keeled, glossy green and 30cm (12″) long. Scape 20cm (8″) high. Flower is 14cm (5½″) across; labellum is helmet-shaped.

Paphiopedilum delenatii

Paphiopedilum fairrieanum

COMMON NAME: None.
COLOUR: Flower colour variable; blend of white and green with purple marks and veining. Labellum green with purple veins.
SIZE: Growing up to 30cm (12″) across.
CLIMATE: Cool.
DISTRIBUTION: Native to Himalayas, northern Burma, Bhutan and Assam in India. Grows on the edges of high river banks and forests at an altitude of 1200 to 3000m (4000 to 10 000′).
FLOWERING TIME: Late autumn.
DESCRIPTION: Leaves are channelled and up to 15cm (6″) long. Scape is up to 25cm (10″) high; usually has a solitary flower, 6cm (2½″) across.

Paphiopedilum fowliei

COMMON NAME: None.
COLOUR: Flower a blend of white, green, pink-purple with red-brown and green veining, dark warts. Labellum yellow-brown, veined dark brown.
SIZE: Growing up to 20cm (8″) across.
CLIMATE: Intermediate to warm.
DISTRIBUTION: Native to the Philippines and Palana Island. A lithophytic species, growing in leaf mould on limestone at an altitude of 700m (2300′).
FLOWERING TIME: Summer.
DESCRIPTION: Leaves are narrow elliptical, tessellated and up to 14 cm (5½″) long. Scape is up to 28cm (11″) high. Flower is about 10cm (4″) across.

Paphiopedilum fowliei

Paphiopedilum glaucophyllum

COMMON NAME: None.
COLOUR: Flowers pale green, stripes and marks brown. Labellum pouched, mauve-pink.
SIZE: Growing up to 40cm (16″) across..
CLIMATE: Warm.
DISTRIBUTION: Native to central Sumatra and Java. Habitat is rock pockets of humus on volcanic mountain slopes. Elevation 200 to 300m (660 to 1000′).
FLOWERING TIME: Spring to summer.
DESCRIPTION: Leaves are broad, strap-shaped, obtuse and 25cm (10″) long. Scape is up to 40cm (16″) high. Several flowers are 7cm (3″) across.

Paphiopedilum glaucophyllum

Paphiopedilum gratrixianum

COMMON NAME: None.
COLOUR: Flower blend of white, yellow-brown and green, spotted with brown-purple. Labellum cream-brown.
SIZE: Growing up to 22.5cm (9″) high.
CLIMATE: Cool to intermediate.
DISTRIBUTION: Native to central Vietnam.
FLOWERING TIME: Winter.
DESCRIPTION: Leaves are up to 22.5cm (9″) long. Solitary flower is similar in shape to *P. villosum*, but has a spotted dorsal sepal.

Paphiopedilum gratrixianum

Paphiopedilum haynaldianum

COMMON NAME: None.
COLOUR: Flower blend of yellow-green, pink with large brown apical spots, suffused with brown. Labellum helmet-shaped, yellow-green, suffused with brown-purple.
SIZE: Growing up to 30cm (12″) high.
CLIMATE: Warm.
DISTRIBUTION: Native to the Philippines (Luzon). Grows on mountain slopes at an altitude of over 1000m (3300′).
FLOWERING TIME: Spring to summer.
DESCRIPTION: Leaves are strap-shaped and up to 30cm (12″) long. Scape bears up to six blooms and is up to 50cm (20″) high. Flower is about 15cm (6″) across.

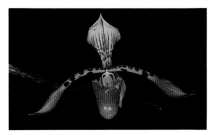

Paphiopedilum haynaldianum

Paphiopedilum hirsutissimum

COMMON NAME: None.
COLOUR: Flower blend of green and purple-pink, speckled with dark purple. Labellum helmet-shaped, green tinted and speckled with purple and tiny black warts.
SIZE: Growing up to 30cm (12″) high.
CLIMATE: Cool.
DISTRIBUTION: Native to Himalayas, Assam, Khasi Hills, Thailand and Burma. A terrestrial often found in epiphytic or lithophytic habitat. Grows at an altitude of 1000 to 1300m (3300 to 4300′).
FLOWERING TIME: Autumn to spring; early summer.
DESCRIPTION: Leaves are linear-oblong, keeled, acute and up to 30cm (12″) long. Flower scape is up to 30cm (12″) high. Solitary flower is up to 15cm (6″) across.

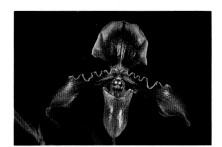

Paphiopedilum hirsutissimum

Paphiopedilum insigne

Paphiopedilum insigne

COMMON NAME: None.
COLOUR: Flower blend of white, light green with purple-brown spots and veining. Labellum helmet-shaped, yellow-green with brown marking.
SIZE: Growing up to 30cm (12″) high.
CLIMATE: Cool.
DISTRIBUTION: Native to Himalayas, Sylhet (Bangladesh), Nepal and Assam. Grows in exposed areas.
FLOWERING TIME: Autumn, winter, spring.
DESCRIPTION: Leaves are linear, acute and up to 30cm (12″) long. Scape is up to 27.5cm (11″) high. Solitary flower is about 10cm (4″) across. Labellum helmet-shaped. A common species of many varieties and prolific flowering.

Paphiopedilum insigne var. *Harefield Hall*

Paphiopedilum insigne var. Harefield Hall

COMMON NAME: None.
COLOUR: Flower purple-brown.
SIZE: Growing up to 30cm (12″) high.
CLIMATE: Cool.
DISTRIBUTION: Nepal, Assam.
FLOWERING TIME: Winter.
DESCRIPTION: Similar to *P. insigne*, but flower is much larger than the type form, 14cm (5½″) across. Flower is hairy and has shiny texture.

Paphiopedilum insigne var. *sanderae*

Paphiopedilum insigne var. sanderae

COMMON NAME: None.
COLOUR: Dorsal sepal light green with white margins, sparsely speckled with brown. Petals green. Labellum yellow-brown.
SIZE: Grows up to 30cm (12″) high.
CLIMATE: Cool.
DISTRIBUTION: Nepal, Assam.
FLOWERING TIME: Autumn, winter.
DESCRIPTION: Flower scape is up to 25cm (10″) high. Flower is about 12cm (5″) across. Labellum helmet-shaped.

Paphiopedilum javanicum var. *virens*

Paphiopedilum javanicum var. virens

COMMON NAME: None.
COLOUR: Flowers light green; petal base light green; lamina rose-pink with white margins. Labellum pale brown-green, lightly veined.
SIZE: Growing up to 30cm (12″) tall.
CLIMATE: Intermediate to warm.
DISTRIBUTION: Native to Mt Kinabalu, northern Borneo.
FLOWERING TIME: Autumn to winter.
DESCRIPTION: Closely allied to *P. virens*. Found growing in dense shade. Leaves 10 to 15cm (4 to 6″) long, pointed and coloured grey-green. Flower scape is up to 30cm (12″) high. Dorsal sepal is broad, pointed, light green with longitudinal dark striations and is horizontal. Petal bases are green, blade rose-pink with white margins. Petal margins are dotted with blackish warts and rose-purple ciliate. Labellum is pale brown-green and lightly veined. Staminode has green centre; upper margin white with three lobes; lower margin yellow-green with two lobes pointing downward.

Paphiopedilum malipoensis

COMMON NAME: None.
COLOUR: Flower green.
SIZE: Growing up to 15cm (6″) high.
CLIMATE: Intermediate.
DISTRIBUTION: Native to China.
FLOWERING TIME: Spring.
DESCRIPTION: Leaves are green, tessellated green, underside purple, margins wavy, broad-lanceolate and up to 15cm (6″) long. Inflorescence is up to 30cm (12″) high. Flower is solitary.

Paphiopedilum malipoensis

Paphiopedilum micranthum

Paphiopedilum micranthum

COMMON NAME: None.
COLOUR: Flower cream-white, tinted and veined with pink-purple.
SIZE: Growing up to 20cm (8″) across.
CLIMATE: Intermediate.
DISTRIBUTION: Native to China (south-east Yunnan).
FLOWERING TIME: Spring.
DESCRIPTION: A dwarf terrestrial. Leaves are oblong, obtuse with spotted underside. Erect scape is up to 22.5cm (9″) high. Solitary flower resembles *Cypripidium* and is about 6cm across. Labellum is elliptical-ovate.

Paphiopedilum moquetteanum

COMMON NAME: None.
COLOUR: Flower a blend of yellow-green, white, spotted and marked with red-purple. Labellum rose-pink.
SIZE: Growing up to 25cm (10″) high.
CLIMATE: Warm.
DISTRIBUTION: Native to West Java and Bogor.
FLOWERING TIME: Summer.
DESCRIPTION: Leaves are 25cm (10″) long and scape is up to 40cm (16″) high. Flower measures 11cm (4½″) across. Petal margins are undulate, twisted and cimiate.

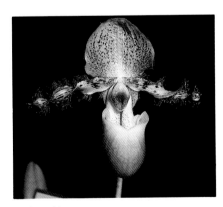

Paphiopedilum moquetteanum

Paphiopedilum niveum

Paphiopedilum niveum

COMMON NAME: None.
COLOUR: Flowers white, marked with fine purple spots.
SIZE: Growing up to 15cm (6″) high.
CLIMATE: Warm to hot.
DISTRIBUTION: Native to Thailand Peninsular, Malaysia, Satun, Borneo, Langkawi Island, Longcavi Island, and Tambulan Island.
FLOWERING TIME: Spring and summer.
DESCRIPTION: This dwarf species grows in crevices of limestone rocks close to the sea. Leaves are oblong, mottled green, underside purple, and grow up to 15cm (6″) long. Scape is short, 12cm (5″) high. Flowers are about 7cm (3″) across. Edges of dorsal sepal are waved.

Paphiopedilum parishii

COMMON NAME: None.
COLOUR: Flowers pale green; petals green turning red-purple towards the apex; margins with hairy, purple warts.
SIZE: Growing up to 30cm (12″) high.
CLIMATE: Cool to intermediate.
DISTRIBUTION: Native to Burma, Thailand and China. Found growing at elevations of 1200m (4000′).
FLOWERING TIME: Spring to summer.
DESCRIPTION: Leaves are 30 to 50cm (12 to 20″), arching, coriaceous with rounded tip. Inflorescence is up to 50cm (20″) high, branched with four to six flowers. Dorsal sepal is bent forward; petals are 12.5cm (5″) long, pendulous, twisted, with hairy warts along margins. Labellum is deep green tinged with purple. Staminode is pale yellow marbled with green. Similar in habit to *P. philippinense.*

Paphiopedilum sukhakulii

Paphiopedilum parishii

Paphiopedilum philippinense
(very similar to *P. roebbelenii*)

COMMON NAME: None.
COLOUR: Flowers a blend of white, yellow-green, veined purple-red. Labellum pouch cream-green.
SIZE: Growing up to 30cm (12″) high.
CLIMATE: Warm to hot.
DISTRIBUTION: Native to the Philippines, Guimares, Mindanao, Palawan to northern Borneo. Coastal terrestrial growing in association on the roots of *Vanda batemanii* in brightly lit positions, liking warm conditions.
FLOWERING TIME: Summer to autumn.
DESCRIPTION: Leaves are strap-shaped and up to 30cm (12″) long. Flower scape is up to 40cm (16″) long. Flowers are large. Petals are linear, pendulous, twisted and up to 15cm (6″) long.

Paphiopedilum sukhakulii

COMMON NAME: None.
COLOUR: Flower blend of white-cream and green, spotted with red-purple. Labellum green with purple veining.
SIZE: Growing up to 30cm (12″) across.
CLIMATE: Intermediate.
DISTRIBUTION: Native to Vietnam and north-eastern Thailand. Grows at elevations up to 1000m (3250′), in leaf litter at the base of a tree, usually along creek banks and humid places. Grows in association with *P. callosum* at lower altitudes.
FLOWERING TIME: Autumn to winter.
DESCRIPTION: Leaves 20cm by 4cm wide (8″ by 1½″) tessellated, mottled green, absence of blotches at base of leaf helps to distinguish this plant from its close relative *P. wardii.* Solitary flower is about 16cm (6½″) across. Labellum is helmet-shaped.

Paphiopedilum philippinense

Paphiopedilum superbiens

Paphiopedilum superbiens

COMMON NAME: None.
COLOUR: Flower white, veined with purple and green. Petals white-pink veined with purple and black warts. Labellum purple.
SIZE: Growing up to 15cm (6″) high.
CLIMATE: Warm.
DISTRIBUTION: Native to Java, Sumatra and the islands of Malacca Straits. Grows at an altitude of 300m (1000′).
FLOWERING TIME: Spring to summer.
DESCRIPTION: Terrestrial herb. Leaves up to 15cm (6″) long, tessellated and elliptic to oblong. Flower scape is up to 30cm (12″) long. Flower is solitary; dorsal sepal is 4cm (1½″) across.

Paphiopedilum urbanianum

COMMON NAME: None.
COLOUR: Flowers blend of white, green and purple.
SIZE: Growing up to 20cm (8″) high.
CLIMATE: Warm.
DISTRIBUTION: Native to the Philippines (Mindoro). Semi-terrestrial growing at elevations of 500 to 800m (1600 to 2600′).
FLOWERING TIME: Autumn.
DESCRIPTION: Leaves are mottled, narrow-elliptic and up to 20cm (8″) long. Flower scape grows up to 25cm (10″) high. Flowers measure 12cm (5″) across.

Paphiopedilum urbanianum

Paphiopedilum venustum

Paphiopedilum venustum

COMMON NAME: None.
COLOUR: Flower blend of white with green, pink with dark warts.
SIZE: Growing up to 25cm (10″) across.
CLIMATE: Cool.
DISTRIBUTION: Native to Assam and Nepal. Growing at elevations of 1000 to 1500m (3300 to 5000′) in sheltered valleys.
FLOWERING TIME: Winter.
DESCRIPTION: Leaves are mottled, strap-shaped, elliptic and 15cm (6″) long. Flower scape grows up to 25cm (10″) high. Flower is 12cm (5″) across.

Paphiopedilum villosum

COMMON NAME: None.
COLOUR: Flower blend of white, green and maroon.
SIZE: Growing up to 35cm (14″) high.
CLIMATE: Cool.
DISTRIBUTION: Native to Thailand, Laos, Assam and Burma. Grows at elevations of 1200 to 1600m (4000 to 5200′). Found growing in decaying leaf mould and moss.
FLOWERING TIME: Autumn.
DESCRIPTION: Leaves are up to 35cm (14″) long and narrow-lanceolate. Flower scape is about 30cm (12″) high and flower about 12cm (5″) wide.

Paphiopedilum villosum

Paphiopedilum virens

Paphiopedilum virens

COMMON NAME: None.
COLOUR: Flower pale green with dark mottled marking.
SIZE: Growing up to 15cm (6″) high.
CLIMATE: Intermediate to warm.
DISTRIBUTION: Native to Mt Kinabalu and northern Borneo.
FLOWERING TIME: Spring, summer to autumn.
DESCRIPTION: Leaves are 10 to 12.5cm (4 to 5″) long. Flower grows to 10cm (4″) across. Closely allied to *P. javanicum*; the two main differences are the shape of the staminodes and the much lighter leaves. In *P. virens*, the staminode is wide, pink with a marble green centre. Upper incisure is v-shaped with lower margins having four incisions. In *P. javanicum*, the staminode is light green, darker markings in centre, white mark below upper margin, with two incisions on lower margin forming three lobes pointing downwards. Habitat is in semi-shade conditions.

PAPILIONANTHE
(pa-pil-ee-oh-nan-thee)

Papilionanthe from the Lat. *papilio* (butterfly) *anthos* (a flower) with reference to the resemblance of some flowers to a butterfly. This is an epiphytic, monopodial genus of some eleven species. It was first established in 1915 when Schlechter separated *Vanda teres* from other *Vanda* species creating a new genus *Papilionanthe*. The separation was based on the intermediate characteristics of *V. teres*, between *Vanda* and *Aerides*. This segregation was ignored by many and overlooked by others. On re-examining Schlechter's criteria of limitations, Leslie Garay agreed and added another ten species to the genus *Papilionanthe*. *Papilionanthe* differs from both *Vanda* and *Aerides* in the spur of the labellum and the structure of the column foot. *Papilionanthe* species are characterised by a short, stout, non-pyramidal column extending with a long prominant foot.

Culture: Compost. As for *Vanda*. Use large, well-drained pots or baskets. Pots and bench soon become overgrown because of strong aerial root growth.

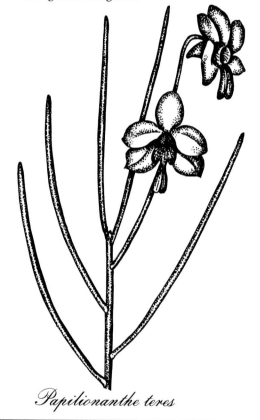

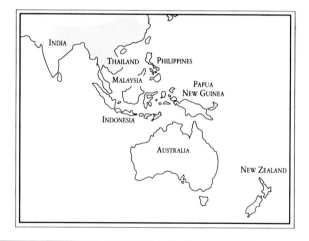

Papilionanthe teres

Papilionanthe teres syn. *Vanda teres*

Papilionanthe teres syn. *Vanda teres*

COMMON NAME: None.
COLOUR: Petals deep rose-pink, sepals white, tinged with rose-pink. Labellum yellow, outer lobe rose-pink, veined.
SIZE: Climbing.
CLIMATE: Warm.
DISTRIBUTION: Native to India and Burma.
FLOWERING TIME: Summer.
DESCRIPTION: Plant is large and showy. Leaves alternate terete and grow up to 20cm (8″) long. Labellum is large and tri-lobed. Flower measures up to 10cm (4″) across.

PESCATOREA
(pess-ka-tor-ee-ah)

Pescatorea is named after V. Pescatore of Chateau Cella St Cloud near Paris, who owned a very fine collection of orchids. *Pescatorea* is a small genus of about fifteen pseudobulbless epiphytic species, distributed from Costa Rica to Colombia. These spectacular orchids are closely allied to *Chondrorhyncha*, *Huntleya* and *Zygopetalum*. The distinguishing technical features are: (a) *Chondrorhyncha* lacks a conspicuous clawed labellum; (b) *Huntleya* has broad projecting apical column wings; (c) *Zygopetalum* has pseudobulbs. *Pescatorea* is an erect, tufted herb without pseudobulbs. Leaves are plicate, distichous and fan-shaped. Inflorescence is short and axillary. Flowers are large, showy and fragrant. Sepals and petals are fleshy and concave. The labellum is tri-lobed, fleshy with conspicuous linguate claw and the callus is deeply ribbed. These large, showy, wax-like, fragrant orchids are increasingly evident in collections and at orchid shows.

Culture: Compost as for *Zygopetalum*. Plants require shade and roots must be kept moist continually in perfectly drained pots.

Pescatorea cerina

SOUTH AMERICA

Pescatorea cerina

Pescatorea cerina

COMMON NAME: None.
COLOUR: Flower white. Labellum yellow.
SIZE: Growing up to 60cm (2′) high.
CLIMATE: Warm.
DISTRIBUTION: Native to Panama and Costa Rica.
FLOWERING TIME: Autumn.
DESCRIPTION: Leaves are clustered in a loose fan arrangement, are linear-lanceolate and grow up to 60cm (2′) long. Flower scape is 10cm (4″) high. Flower is 7.5cm (3″) across.

PHAIUS
(fay-us)

Phaius from the Gk *phaios* (dusky) with reference to the flowers which turn dark with age or if damaged. This is a genus of about thirty species. It is widespread throughout Africa, Madagascar, Asia, Indonesia, Papua New Guinea, Australia and the Pacific Islands. *Phaius* is a genus of robust sympodial terrestrial plants closely allied to *Calanthe*. Plants have pseudobulbs or stem-like pseudobulbs, each having up to eight large petiolate, plicate, grooved leaves. Inflorescence is from the base or is lateral on the pseudobulb, or emerges part way up the thickened stem. Flowers are often many, conspicuous, showy, moderately large, opening successively, remaining in bloom for a long period of time. Sepals and petals are fleshy and spreading. The labellum is tubular, extending into a basal spur, erect, convolute, spreading at the apex. Flower colours occur in a wide range of hues.

Culture: Coarse compost as for larger terrestrials, in perfectly drained pots. Roots need to be kept moist, not wet. Plants require shady cool conditions, with much less water once growth is complete. Excessive watering causes leaves to 'damp off'; so when watering avoid wetting leaves, otherwise they will go black.

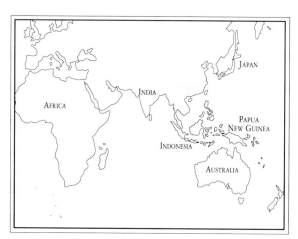

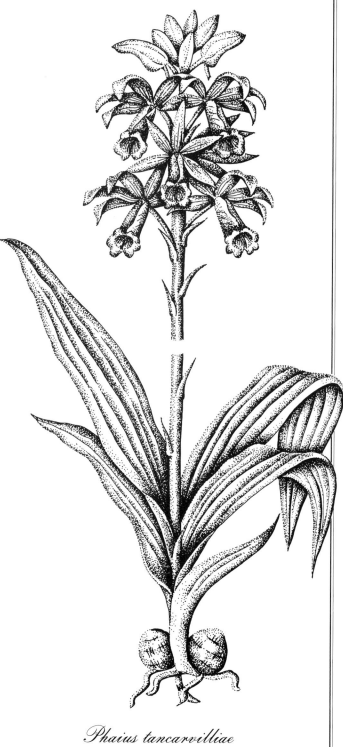

Phaius tancarvilliae

Phaius australis

COMMON NAME: Swamp Orchid.
COLOUR: A blend of red-brown and white.
SIZE: Growing up to 60cm (25″) high.
CLIMATE: Cool to intermediate.
DISTRIBUTION: Native to eastern Australia in moist areas.
FLOWERING TIME: Spring.
DESCRIPTION: Robust terrestrial species. Pseudobulbs are small and ovate. Leaves are large, ovate-lanceolate and fluted. Inflorescence is erect and up to 1.5m (5′) long. Flowers are fragrant, showy, large and numerous

Phaius australis

Phaius graffii

Phaius graffii

COMMON NAME: None.
COLOUR: Flowers yellow; petals and sepals reverse side white. Labellum throat white.
SIZE: Growing up to 75cm (30″) high.
CLIMATE: Warm.
DISTRIBUTION: Native to Fiji.
FLOWERING TIME: Late winter to spring.
DESCRIPTION: Pseudobulbs are conical and grow up to 5cm (2″) high. Leaves are sheathing at the base, plicate, broad lanceolate and 75cm (30″) high. Inflorescence is 1m (40″) high with numerous blooms. Flowers are up to 10cm (4″) across. Labellum is tubular and spreading at the apex.

Phaius tancarvilliae syn. *P. tankervilliae*

Phaius tancarvilliae syn. P. tankervilliae

COMMON NAME: Swamp Orchid.
COLOUR: A blend of red-brown and white.
SIZE: Growing up to 90cm (3′) high.
CLIMATE: Intermediate to warm to hot.
DISTRIBUTION: Native to Australia, the Pacific Islands, Malaysia, Indonesia, southern China and is naturalised in Panama, Hawaii, Cuba and Jamaica.
FLOWERING TIME: Spring to summer.
DESCRIPTION: A robust species closely allied to *P. australis*. *P. australis* differs from *P. tancarvilliae* in that the column is superior; at no time is it enclosed within the labellum tube. Only the base of the labellum embraces the foot of the column.

PHALAENOPSIS

(fal-en-op-siss)

*P*halaenopsis from the Gk *phalaina* (moth) *opsis* (appearance) with reference to the delicate, moth-like white flowers; this 'moth orchid' is considered by many authors as the most beautiful of all. Possibly the first discovery of *Phalaenopsis* was by Rumphius in 1750 on the island of Amboina when he mis-identified a plant as *Angraecum*. In 1825, Blume officially established the genus and since then *Phalaenopsis* has been revised several times. In about 1969, the genus was divided into nine sections. The sixty species of the genus extend from the Himalayas through Burma, Malaysia, Formosa, Borneo, the Philippines to Indonesia, Papua New Guinea and Australia.

Phalaenopsis species have very short stems. Leaves are stem clasping, distichous, coriaceous, up to 60cm (20″) long and either shiny or mottled green. Inflorescence is lateral, erect, arching or pendulous. Flowers are small to large, showy, white, pink, or violet in colour with red-brown or yellow markings. Sepals and petals are free and spreading. The labellum is tri-lobed and jointed; lateral lobes are erect and parallel to the column; the mid-lobe or lamina is of various shapes, entire or forked, or without appendages (antennae or tendrils). The type species is *Phalaenopsis amabilis*.

Culture: Compost should be 5cm (2″) coarse. Pot in baskets where roots can grow and be exposed to the air. If in pots, allow the roots to escape over the side of the pot. Plants require shade, warmth and humidity. Water frequently. Check with your local nursery for advice on a fertiliser program.

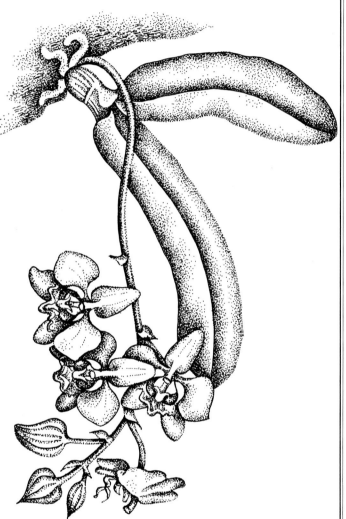

Phalaenopsis amabilis

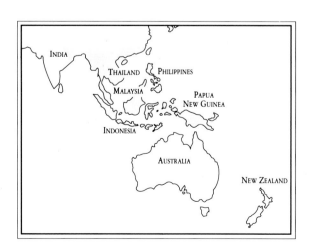

Phalaenopsis amabilis syn. P. amabilis var. *papuana* and syn. var. *rosenstromii*

COMMON NAME: White Moth Orchid.
COLOUR: Flowers white. Labellum marked with yellow.
SIZE: Growing up to 45cm (18″) across.
CLIMATE: Hot.
DISTRIBUTION: Native to northern Australia, Indonesia, Papua New Guinea and New Britain.
FLOWERING TIME: Spring to summer.
DESCRIPTION: A tropical epiphyte. Leaves are few, oblong-ovate and about 35cm (14″) long. Inflorescence is up to 90cm (3′) long. Flowers are showy and up to 10cm (4″) across.

Phalaenopsis amabilis syn. *P. amabilis* var. *papuana* and syn. var. *rosenstromii*

Phalaenopsis amboinensis

COMMON NAME: None.
COLOUR: Flowers pale yellow, blotched and barred with red-brown. Labellum white marked with yellow.
SIZE: Growing 25cm (10″) high.
CLIMATE: Hot.
DISTRIBUTION: Native to Ambon Island, Papua New Guinea and Indonesia.
FLOWERING TIME: Winter.
DESCRIPTION: An epiphytic plant. Leaves are elliptic-oblong and grow up to 20cm (8″) long. Flower measures up to 5cm (2″) across.

Phalaenopsis amboinensis

Phalaenopsis aphrodite

COMMON NAME: None.
COLOUR: White with lip-disc marked red.
SIZE: Growing up to 40cm (16″) across.
CLIMATE: Hot.
DISTRIBUTION: Native to the Philippines.
FLOWERING TIME: Winter to early spring.
DESCRIPTION: Closely allied to *P. amabilis*, the major differences being that the lip-disc is marked with red and the mid-lobe is nearly triangular in shape. Flowers are smaller, measuring about 7.5cm (3″) across.

Phalaenopsis aphrodite

Phalaenopsis cornu-cervi

COMMON NAME: None.
COLOUR: Flowers yellow-green, marked with brown. Labellum white.
SIZE: Growing up to 25cm (10″) high.
CLIMATE: Hot.
DISTRIBUTION: Native to Thailand, Sumatra, Malaysia, Borneo, Java and Burma.
FLOWERING TIME: Throughout the year (especially spring to autumn).
DESCRIPTION: Leaves are oblong, obtuse, coriaceous and up to 25cm (10″) long. Flower spike bears six to twelve blooms, each growing to 5cm (2″) across.

Phalaenopsis cornu-cervi

Phalaenopsis equestris var. *apparri* syn. *P. rosea* var. *apparri*

COMMON NAME: None.
COLOUR: Flowers rose-pink. Labellum deep rose.
SIZE: Growing up to 15cm (6″) high.
CLIMATE: Hot.
DISTRIBUTION: Native to the Philippines.
FLOWERING TIME: Autumn to winter.
DESCRIPTION: Leaves are oval and grow to 15cm (6″) long. Arching inflorescence grows up to 30cm (12″) long. Numerous flowers are up to 3cm (1¼″) across. Labellum is 2.5cm (1″) across.

Phalaenopsis amboinensis

Phalaenopsis equestris var. *apparri* syn. *P. rosea* var. *apparri*

Phalaenopsis fasciata

Phalaenopsis fasciata

COMMON NAME: None.
COLOUR: Flowers green-yellow, barred red-brown. Labellum marked yellow and pink.
SIZE: Growing up to 25cm (10″) across.
CLIMATE: Hot.
DISTRIBUTION: Native to the Philippines.
FLOWERING TIME: Summer to autumn.
DESCRIPTION: A rather robust epiphytic plant. Stems are short and enclosed by leaf sheaths. Leaves grow up to 20cm (8″) long and are distichous, elliptic-ovate. Inflorescence bears a few flowers which are usually waxy, fleshy and about 5cm (2″) across. Flowers open one to two at a time. Labellum is yellow and marked with red.

Phalaenopsis hieroglyphica

Phalaenopsis hieroglyphica

COMMON NAME: None.
COLOUR: Flowers cream-white spotted with brown. Labellum white flushed with pink-purple.
SIZE: Growing up to 30cm (12″) high.
CLIMATE: Hot.
DISTRIBUTION: Native to the Philippines (Polillo and Palawan only).
FLOWERING TIME: Spring.
DESCRIPTION: Leaves are oblong-lingulate and grow up to 30cm (12″) long. Inflorescence grows up to 32cm (12½″) long. Numerous flowers are long lasting. Labellum is tri-lobed, short clawed, truncate, with a central ridge. Mid-lobe is erose toward the apex, fleshy, centre hairy with a pair of long appendages in front.

Phalaenopsis X *intermedia*

Phalaenopsis X intermedia

COMMON NAME: None.
COLOUR: Petals and sepals white, speckled with deep pink at the base. Labellum violet, mid-lobes speckled with crimson, with middle lobe crimson.
SIZE: Growing up to 30cm (12″) across.
CLIMATE: Hot.
DISTRIBUTION: Native to the Philippines.
FLOWERING TIME: Winter to spring.
DESCRIPTION: A natural hybrid, *P. aphrodite* X *P. equestris*. Flower measures 5cm (2″) across. Leaves are green, oblong-elliptic with the underneath purple.

Phalaenopsis lindenii

Phalaenopsis lindenii

COMMON NAME: None.
COLOUR: Flowers white suffused with pink and dots at the base. Labellum pink and white, speckled with yellow and purple lines.
SIZE: Growing up to 25cm (10″) high.
CLIMATE: Hot.
DISTRIBUTION: Native to the Philippines.
FLOWERING TIME: Winter to autumn.
DESCRIPTION: Leaves are lanceolate to oblong, mottled and up to 25cm (10″) long. Flowers measure up to 3cm (1¼″) across.

Phalaenopsis lueddemanniana

Phalaenopsis lueddemanniana

COMMON NAME: None.
COLOUR: Flowers variable in colour, usually purple transverse bars on white-cream background.
SIZE: Growing up to 25cm (10″) high.
CLIMATE: Warm to hot.
DISTRIBUTION: Native to the Philippines.
FLOWERING TIME: Spring.
DESCRIPTION: Leaves are waxy and elliptic, but variable in shape and growing up to 25cm (10″) long. Flowers generally measure less than 5cm (2″) across. Five varieties of *P. lueddemanniana* are illustrated showing the colour variants: var. *bartonii*, var. *deltonii*, var. *luzon*, var. *purpurea* and var. *ochracia* syn. *P. ochracia*.

Phalaenopsis lueddemanniana var. *bartonii*

Phalaenopsis lueddemanniana var. *deltonii*

Phalaenopsis lueddemanniana var. *luzon*

Phalaenopsis lueddemanniana var. *ochracia* syn. *P. ochracia*

Phalaenopsis leuddemanniana var. *purpurea*

Phalaenopsis pallens

COMMON NAME: None.
COLOUR: Flowers white or lemon with brown lines. Labellum white and yellow.
SIZE: A dwarf epiphytic.
CLIMATE: Hot.
DISTRIBUTION: Native to the Philippines.
FLOWERING TIME: Winter to spring.
DESCRIPTION: Drooping leaves are distichous, elliptic to ovate and up to 18cm (7″) long. Inflorescence is sparsely flowered and about 18cm (7″) long. Flowers measure up to 5cm (2″) across.

Phalaenopsis pallens

Phalaenopsis pantherina

COMMON NAME: None.
COLOUR: Flowers lemon-green, barred and blotched red-brown.
SIZE: Growing up to 10cm (4″) high.
CLIMATE: Hot.
DISTRIBUTION: Native to Borneo.
FLOWERING TIME: Throughout the year.
DESCRIPTION: A robust epiphytic plant. Leaves are fleshy, oblong-oblanceolate and grow up to 25cm (10″) long. Inflorescence is compressed with angled, fleshy bracts, usually bearing solitary blooms. Flowers are waxy, fleshy and 4cm (1½″) long. *P. pantherina* is considered rare and is similar to *P. cornu-cervi*, differing in lateral sepal markings. With *P. pantherina*, lateral sepals are fully barred and all perianth segments are broader; also the plant tends to be more robust, while in *P. cornu-cervi* the lateral sepals carry only a marginal line of barring.

Phalaenopsis pantherina

Phalaenopsis parishii var. lobbii

COMMON NAME: None.
COLOUR: Flowers white. Labellum barred with yellow-orange to brown.
SIZE: Spreading to 15cm (6″) across.
CLIMATE: Warm.
DISTRIBUTION: Native to India and Burma, growing at elevations of 400 to 500m (1300 to 1660′).
FLOWERING TIME: Spring.
DESCRIPTION: Leaves are broad-elliptic and up to 7.5cm (3″) long. Raceme is shorter than the leaves. Flowers are up to 2.5cm (1″) across. Labellum is tri-lobed. The species is often deciduous in nature.

Phalaenopsis parishii var. *lobbii*

Phalaenopsis sanderiana

COMMON NAME: None.
COLOUR: Flowers white-pink to pink-purple.
SIZE: Growing up to 40cm (16″) across.
CLIMATE: Hot.
DISTRIBUTION: Native to the Philippines, growing at low altitudes.
FLOWERING TIME: Throughout the year.
DESCRIPTION: An epiphytic species with short stems. Leaves are elliptic-oblong, fleshy with the underneath purple-green. Inflorescence is long, bearing few to numerous flowers, each up to 7.5cm (3″) across.

Phalaenopsis sanderiana

Phalaenopsis sanderiana var. alba

COMMON NAME: None.
COLOUR: Flowers white. Labellum throat marked with yellow, spotted purple at the base.
SIZE: Growing up to 40cm (16″) across.
CLIMATE: Hot.
DISTRIBUTION: Native to the Philippines.
FLOWERING TIME: Throughout the year.
DESCRIPTION: An epiphytic species. Leaves are green, elliptic-oblong, fleshy, with the underneath purple-green. Inflorescence is long with few to numerous flowers, each growing to 7.5cm (3″) across.

Phalaenopsis sanderiana var. *alba*

Phalaenopsis schilleriana

COMMON NAME: Tiger (in the Philippines).
COLOUR: Flowers variable in colour, lilac to white. Labellum white with yellow and crimson markings.
SIZE: Growing up to 45cm (18″) high.
CLIMATE: Warm to hot.
DISTRIBUTION: Native to the Philippines. Grows at 750 to 900m (2500 to 3000′).
FLOWERING TIME: Spring.
DESCRIPTION: Leaves are dark green, oblong-elliptic and up to 45cm (18″) long. Inflorescence is up to 90cm (3′) long. The numerous flowers are variable in size and colour, but are generally about 6.5cm (2½″) across.

Phalaenopsis stuartiana

Phalaenopsis schilleriana

Phalaenopsis stuartiana

COMMON NAME: None.
COLOUR: Petals white lightly spotted, purple at the base. Sepals white, lateral sepals lemon on the inner half and spotted at the base with red. Labellum yellow, margins white, marked with purple.
SIZE: Growing up to 35cm (14″) high.
CLIMATE: Hot.
DISTRIBUTION: Native to the Philippines.
FLOWERING TIME: Autumn to spring.
DESCRIPTION: Small epiphyte. Leaves are grey-green, mottled when young, growing up to 35cm (13½″) long, with a purple underside at maturing. Inflorescence is up to 90cm (3′) long. Flowers are numerous and up to 5cm (2″) across. Labellum has double horns at the tip.

Phalaenopsis veitchiana syn. P. X gertrudes

COMMON NAME: None.
COLOUR: Flowers variable pink. Labellum white-purple, spotted purple at the base.
SIZE: Short and spreading.
CLIMATE: Hot.
DISTRIBUTION: Native to the Philippines.
FLOWERING TIME: Spring.
DESCRIPTION: This epiphytic species is a natural hybrid between *P. equestris* and *P. schillariana*. Leaves are silver-green and elliptic-oblong. Inflorescence is simple. Flowers are variable in size, but usually about 5cm (2″) across. Labellum is tri-lobed.

Phalaenopsis veitchiana syn. *P. X gertrudes*

Phalaenopsis violacea

Phalaenopsis violacea

COMMON NAME: None.
COLOUR: Flower colour variable green-white with violet markings. Labellum yellow and violet.
SIZE: Growing up to 25cm (10″) high.
CLIMATE: Hot.
DISTRIBUTION: Native to Peninsula Malaysia, Borneo and Sumatra. Growing at low altitudes in shady position along rivers.
FLOWERING TIME: Spring to summer.
DESCRIPTION: Leaves are variable, oblong-elliptic, obovate and up to 23cm (9″) long. Inflorescence is stout, flexuose and up to 12.5cm (5″) long. Flowers are up to 7.5cm (3″) across.

PHRAGMIPEDIUM
(frag-mi-pee-dee-um)

Phragmipedium from the Gk *phragma* (a fence, division or partition) *pedion* (slipper) with reference to the divisions of the trilocular ovary and the slipper-like shape of the labellum. This is a genus of about 12 to 20 either terrestrial or epiphytic species. They come from Panama, south to Brazil, Bolivia, Peru, Venezuela and Costa Rica. This genus forms part of the complex group often referred to as 'Cyps'. R. A. Rolfe separated the tropical American species from *Paphiopedilum* in about 1896. (See *Paphiopedilum*.) *Phragmipedium* species are sympodial herbs with short stems, fibrous roots, having tufted fans of six to eight coriaceous dark green leaves, growing up to 90cm (3′) long. Inflorescence is erect, axillary, with a many-flowered raceme. Flowers are large and showy, with up to 15 blooms. The dorsal sepal is free; lateral sepals unite for the full length into a synsepalum. Petals are free spreading. The labellum is sac- or slipper-shaped. (The ovary is tri-celled.) The species *P. lindenii* is of notable interest in that the labellum is replaced by a third petal; initially, it was described as a new genus, but after much discussion it remains in *Phragmipedium*.

Culture: As for *Paphiopedilum*. Compost in pots. Fertilise monthly. Plants require humidity, shade from direct sunlight, good air movement, plenty of water and perfect drainage.

Phragmipedium schlimii

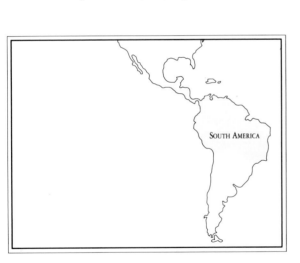

SOUTH AMERICA

Phragmipedium schlimii

COMMON NAME: None.
COLOUR: Flower colour variable, white mottled with pink. Labellum rose-pink.
SIZE: Growing to 30cm (12″) high.
CLIMATE: Intermediate.
DISTRIBUTION: Native to Colombia, growing at an altitude of 1500 to 1800m (5000 to 6000′) in moist areas.
FLOWERING TIME: Mostly spring.
DESCRIPTION: Leaves are strap-shaped, acute and up to 30cm (12″) long. Inflorescence is up to 60cm (2′) high with five to eight blooms. Flower is up to 5cm (2″) across.

Phragmipedium schlimii

PLEIONE
(play-oh-nee)

Pleione is named after Pleione, mother of the pleiades (the seven daughters of Atlas) in Greek mythology, who were transformed into a cluster of stars by Zeus. *Pleione* comprises a small group of about twenty species of epiphytic, or on occasions lithophytic or terrestrial, plants closely allied to *Coelogyne*. They are found in the Himalayas through Burma, southern China to Formosa. This genus is well known in European collections. It is a dwarf plant often occurring in clusters. Stems are thickened to pseudobulbs. Leaves are plicate and deciduous. Flowers appear after leaf-fall, are attractive, large and delightfully showy. The labellum is tri-lobed, frilled or incised, trumpet-shaped, rather like the *Cattleyas.*

Culture: Compost. It is important to remember these plants grow from 1000 to 3000m (3000 to 11 000′), so require shade, 'cool-house' humid conditions, and repotting in small pots or shallow pans after flowering.

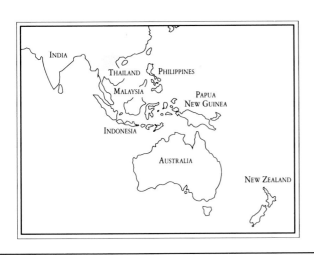

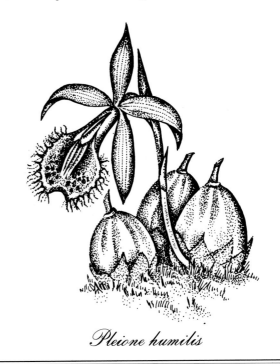

Pleione humilis

Pleione bulbocodiodies
syn. *P. pricei, P. formosana*

COMMON NAME: None.
COLOUR: Flowers pink to deep pink. Labellum white to pink, spotted and marked pink-purple to soft brown.
SIZE: Growing up to 50cm (20″) high.
CLIMATE: Cool.
DISTRIBUTION: Native to China, Taiwan, Tibet, Thailand and Burma. Growing on mossy rocks and trees at 700 to 2900m (2300 to 9500′) in altitude.
FLOWERING TIME: Spring.
DESCRIPTION: A variable epiphytic or lithophytic species. Pseudobulbs are small, pear-shaped, clustered and up to 2.5cm (1″) high. Leaves are linear, elliptic-lanceolate and grow up to 50cm (20″) long. Inflorescence is up to 20cm (8″) long, appearing at the same time as immature leaves. Flowers are large, showy and up to 8cm (3¼″) across. Labellum is tri-lobed, sub-ovate with side lobes erect and mid-lobe margins erose.

Pleione bulbocodiodies syn. *P. pricei, P. formosana*

PORPHYROGLOTTIS
(por-feer-oh-glott-is)

Porphyroglottis from the Gk *porphyros* (purple) *glottis* (mouth of wind-pipe) with reference to the labellum's dark purple throat. This is a single species genus. This most unusual plant comes from Sarawak, Borneo. *Porphyroglottis* is almost unknown in collections.

Culture: As for *Dendrobiums*. Compost in a basket or on a tree-fern slab for this pendulous variety. Consult your local orchid society for the care of the plant.

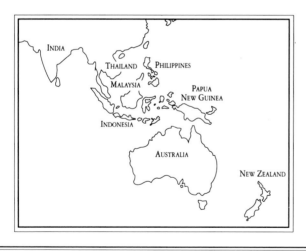

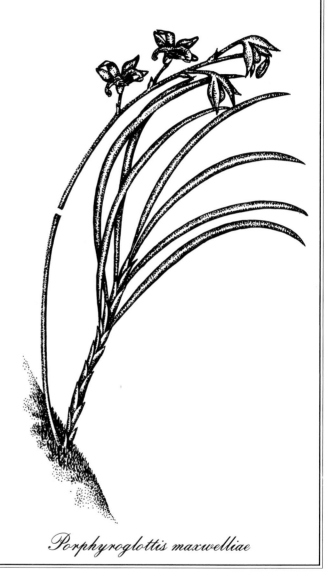

Porphyroglottis maxwelliae

Porphyroglottis maxwelliae

COMMON NAME: None.
COLOUR: Sepals and petals white-pink (rose colour). Labellum dark purple-brown with yellow blotch towards tip.
SIZE: Growing up to 90cm (3') high.
CLIMATE: Hot.
DISTRIBUTION: Native to Borneo (Sarawak) and Johor.
FLOWERING TIME: Spring.
DESCRIPTION: Stems are long. Leaves are linear, acute and up to 50cm (20") long. Inflorescence grows up to 1.5m (5') long, flowering in succession with two to three blooms at a time. Flowers are up to 4cm (1½") long with sepals and petals reflexed. Vegetatively identical to a small *Grammatophyllum speciosum*.

Porphyroglottis maxwelliae

PRASOPHYLLUM
(praz-oh-fill-m)

Prasophyllum from the Gk *pason* (leek) *phyllum* (a leaf) with reference to the leek-like leaf which sometimes exceeds the flower spike in length. This genus of about 80 species is confined to Australia and New Zealand. At present, the genus is divided into two sections: (a) *Euprasophyllum* in which the labellum is either sessile at the base of the column, or connected to a short rigid claw but not moveable; and (b) *Micranthum* in which the labellum is articulate and moveable on a claw attached to the column foot.

This glabrous terrestrial has a root system of globular tubers. It has a single, leek-like leaf. There are several flowers in a terminal raceme or spike. Flower colour is inconspicuous, but is usually greenish white or purple. The flower is reversed, in that the labellum stands above the column. The dorsal sepal is erect or concave, curved about the column and is often recurved. Lateral sepals are as large as the dorsal sepal.

Petals are usually shorter. The labellum is oval, oblong or lanceolate, but divided; margins are crisped, ciliate, denticulate or entire.

Culture: As for *Caladenia*. Use rich, well-drained, free-moving compost. In pots, use broken crock, crushed brick, topped with equal parts of shredded tree-fern, leaf mould, crumbled loam, sharp gritty sand and sphagnum moss. Apply liquid fertiliser regularly.

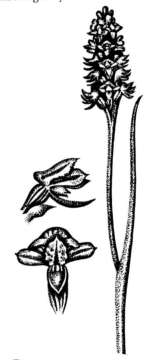

Prasophyllum cucullatum

Prasophyllum elatum

Prasophyllum elatum

COMMON NAME: Tall Leek Orchid.
COLOUR: Flowers yellow-brown, yellow-green or purple-black. Labellum white and green, but may be green to purple-black.
SIZE: A robust terrestrial, up to 1.3m (52″) high.
CLIMATE: Cool.
DISTRIBUTION: Native to Australia (coastal and nearby tablelands).
FLOWERING TIME: Spring.
DESCRIPTION: Solitary leaf is sheathing at the base. Inflorescence is up to 1.2m (4′) high. Flowers are inverted, large and numerous, forming a dense spike.

PTEROSTYLIS

(ter-o-stye-liss)

P*terostylis* from the Gk *pteron* (a wing) *stylos* (a column) with reference to the wing of the column. This genus of over 70 species is native to Australia, extending to Papua New Guinea, New Caledonia and New Zealand. 'Green Hoods,' as they are affectionately known, are not well represented in collections, although the number of collectors exhibiting Australian natives is increasing. The distinguishing feature of this genus is the manner in which the dorsal sepal and the petals appressed to it form a galea or hood surrounding the column. In several species the lateral sepals are reflexed, exposing the labellum. The column is elongated and curved within. The galea is winged on both sides.

Culture: As for *Caladenia*. Use rich, well-drained, free-moving compost. In pots, use broken crock, crushed brick, topped with equal parts of shredded tree-fern, leaf mould, crumbled loam, sharp gritty sand and sphagnum moss. Apply liquid fertiliser regularly.

Pterostylis nutans

Pterostylis grandiflora

Pterostylis grandiflora

COMMON NAME: Cobra Greenhood.
COLOUR: Flowers white with green and red markings.
SIZE: Small terrestrial up to 35cm (14″) high.
CLIMATE: Intermediate.
DISTRIBUTION: Native to Australia and New Zealand.
FLOWERING TIME: Autumn to winter, later in Tasmania.
DESCRIPTION: Plant has radical leaves. Leaves are basal. Large elegant blooms, galea 6cm (2½″) around the curve.

RENANTHERA

(ren-ann-ther-a)

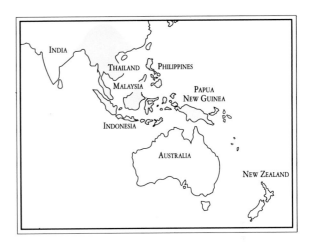

*R*enanthera from the Gk *renes* (kidney) *anthera* (anther) with reference to the kidney-shaped anthers, a characteristic which helps in the separation of *Renanthera* from *Vanda* and *Aerides*. This genus of about 15 species of robust monopodial epiphytic orchids comes from Burma, Peninsula Malaysia, Indonesia and Papua New Guinea to the Pacific Islands. Stems grow up to 4.5m (15′) and become almost woody with age. Leaves are coriaceous and unevenly lobed at apex. Inflorescence is axillary in the upper leaves, paniculate, many-flowered (up to 150 flowers). Individual flower spikes are up to 1.2m (4′) long. Flowers are showy, predominantly red or yellow, and measure 6 to 9 cm (2.5 to 3.5″) across. Dorsal sepal and petals are similar, free and spreading. The lateral sepals are the largest segment of the flower. The labellum is tri-lobed with a sack-like basal spur. Lateral lobes are erect and the mid-lobe is reflexed. The small callus is lamellate and directly below stigmatic surface. **Culture:** Compost in pots. Plants require humid conditions and plenty of indirect sunlight. Fertilise each month.

Renanthera imschootiana

Renanthera matutina

COMMON NAME: None.
COLOUR: Flowers dark red with dark spots, may be tinted with yellow. Labellum chrome yellow, white and spotted red.
SIZE: Scrambling plant, up to 2m (6'6") high.
CLIMATE: Hot.
DISTRIBUTION: Native to Sumatra, Java and Peninsula Malaysia.
FLOWERING TIME: Autumn.
DESCRIPTION: Leaves are oblong-linear and emarginate. Inflorescence is branched with numerous flowers and is up to 60cm (2') high. Flowers measure about 5cm (2") across.

Renanthera monachica

Renanthera matutina

Renanthera monachica

COMMON NAME: None.
COLOUR: Flowers yellow-orange, spotted red.
SIZE: An erect epiphytic plant 50cm (20") high.
CLIMATE: Warm.
DISTRIBUTION: Native to the Philippines.
FLOWERING TIME: Late winter to spring.
DESCRIPTION: Leaves are strap-shaped, unequally emarginate, up to 12.5cm (5") long. Inflorescence is densely flowered, up to 17.5cm (7") long. Flowers are 2.5cm (1") across.

Renanthera storiei

Renanthera storiei

COMMON NAME: None.
COLOUR: Flowers scarlet, mottled red. Base of labellum mid-lobe white.
SIZE: Growing up to 3m (10') high.
CLIMATE: Hot.
DISTRIBUTION: Native to the Philippines. A tropical lowland species.
FLOWERING TIME: Summer.
DESCRIPTION: Stems are up to 3m (10') long. Leaves are oblong, emarginate and up to 20cm (8") long. Inflorescence is paniculate. Numerous flowers measure up to 4.5cm (1¾") across. Closely related species *Renanthera coccinea*.

RHINERRHIZA

(rye-ner-rye-za)

Rhinerrhiza from the Gk *rhis* (snout) *rhiza* (root) with reference to the raspy tuberculate roots which give rise to the common name 'Raspy Root'. This genus of a single epiphytic species is confined to eastern Australia. Originally it was included in *Sarcochilus,* but it differs in the thick raspy roots and the filiform segment of the perianth. The inflorescence has as many as six to eight racemes, up to 90cm (3') long, each with up to 40 or more fugacious flowers. These flowers open simultaneously overnight, so by dawn, a somewhat unattractive plant has been transformed into a showy blaze of red and orange blooms which last but a few days. The flower wilts when picked and the colours fade quickly. This genus is rare in collections, although it responds well to cultivation. *Rhinerrhiza* is a must for growers of unusual botanical orchids.

Culture: As for the smaller *Vanda.* Plants respond well when mounted on a tree-fern slab. They require light shade (indirect sunlight), water, drainage and light dressings of fertiliser.

Rhinerrhiza divitiflora

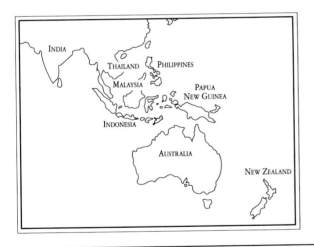

Rhinerrhiza divitiflora

COMMON NAME: Raspy Root Orchid.
COLOUR: Flowers orange marked with red-brown.
SIZE: Epiphytic plant growing up to 17.5cm (7″) high, supported by flat raspy roots.
CLIMATE: Cool.
DISTRIBUTION: Native to north-eastern Australia (coastal and nearby ranges).
FLOWERING TIME: Autumn.
DESCRIPTION: Leaves are oblong, corrugated and grow up to 18cm (7″). Inflorescence is up to 90cm (3') long. Flowers are numerous with as many as 80 blooms; they are spider-like in appearance. Petals are up to 3cm (1¼″) long.

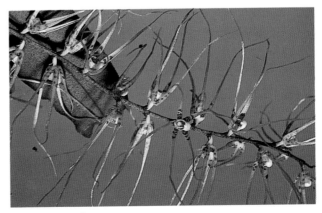

Rhinerrhiza divitiflora

RHYNCHOSTYLIS
(rink-oh-stye-liss)

Rhynchostylis from the Gk *rhynchos* (a beak) *stylos* (a pillar) with reference to the beaked column (although the beaked column is not exclusive to the genus). This genus of about four species was originally described as *Saccolobium*, a closely allied genus, but later was renamed *Rhynchostylis*. Its distribution ranges from India, Sri Lanka, Burma, South-east Asia, Malaysia, the Philippines, Borneo and Indonesia. These species are often called Fox-tail Orchids because of the erect or pendulous inflorescence of densely crowded, small, colourful flowers. The plant is a stout, short-stemmed monopodial epiphyte. Leaves are coriaceous, with a distinct keel and unequal apical lobes. The many flowers are showy, are 2 to 2.5cm (¾ to 1″) across and are coloured white with pink, blue or purple markings. Sepals and petals are spreading and waxy. The labellum is short, adnate to the base of the column foot, compressed, deeply saccate or with a sac-like spur at base. The genus is freely inter-fertile with numerous hybrids.

Culture: Compost. Pot in a hanging basket, allowing the numerous aerial roots to hang freely. Plants require high humidity, shade and lots of frequent watering while growing. Apply less water when roots show signs of inactivity.

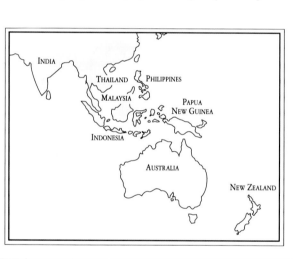

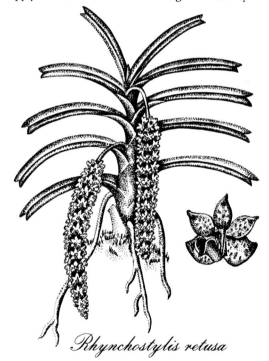

Rhynchostylis retusa

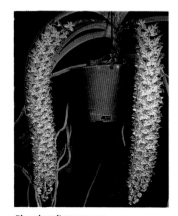

Rhynchostylis praemorsa

Rhynchostylis praemorsa

COMMON NAME: One of the Fox-tail Orchids.
COLOUR: Flower colour variable, usually white, spotted pink-lilac; may be pink or purple.
SIZE: Growing up to 60cm (2′) high.
CLIMATE: Warm.
DISTRIBUTION: Native to the Philippines.
FLOWERING TIME: Summer to autumn.
DESCRIPTION: A variable epiphytic plant. Robust stems are up to 60cm (2′) high. Leaves are lingulate, arching, coriaceous and up to 50cm (20″) long. Inflorescence is pendulous, up to 60cm (2′) long and many-flowered. Flowers are fragrant, waxy and about 2cm (¾″) across. This species is consistently confused with *Rhynchostylis retusa*.

ROBIQUETIA
(roe-bi-quet-ee-ah)

Robiquetia is named after Pierre Robiquet, a French chemist who discovered caffeine and morphine. This genus has about 25 species of pendulous, monopodial, epiphytic orchids. It is widespread in Indonesia, Malaysia, the Philippines, Papua New Guinea, Australia and the Pacific Islands to Fiji. Leaves are distichous. Inflorescence is racemose, pendulous and many-flowered. Flowers are small. Sepals and petals are free. The labellum is joined to the column, is tri-lobed and spurred, but the spur lacks appendages within; side lobes are small and fleshy. The spur is long and bent or flattened.

Culture: Mount on a tree-fern slab or may be grown in pans. Plants require humidity, reasonable shade and plenty of water while growing. *Robiquetia* are rare in collections; these plants are attractive and deserve more attention from growers.

Robiquetia wassellii

Robiquetia cerina syn. *R. merrillii*

Robiquetia cerina syn. R. merrillii

COMMON NAME: None.
COLOUR: Flowers purple and yellow.
SIZE: Growing up to 15cm (6″) high.
CLIMATE: Warm.
DISTRIBUTION: Native to the Philippines. Growing at 350 to 3200m (1200 to 10 500′) in altitude, on rocks of mountain slopes.
FLOWERING TIME: Throughout the year.
DESCRIPTION: An epiphytic or lithophytic plant. Leaves are oblong, strap-shaped, unequally emarginate, overlapping and up to 20cm (8″) long. Inflorescence grows up to 12.5cm (5″) long. Flowers are numerous, small and up to 1.5cm (1½″) across. Labellum is spurred.

Robiquetia tierneyana syn. Saccolabium tierneyanum

COMMON NAME: None.
COLOUR: Flowers pale green-yellow, mottled brown.
SIZE: A large robust epiphyte, growing up to 60cm (2′) high.
CLIMATE: Warm.
DISTRIBUTION: Native to Australia (north-eastern Queensland).
FLOWERING TIME: Autumn.
DESCRIPTION: Roots are thick, creeping or aerial. Leaves are oblong, emarginate and up to 14cm (5½″) long. Raceme is short. Numerous flowers are up to 2cm (¾″) across.

Robiquetia tierneyana syn. *Saccolabium tierneyanum*

Robiquetia wassellii

COMMON NAME: None.
COLOUR: Flowers green. Spur yellow.
SIZE: Pendulous epiphytic.
CLIMATE: Hot.
DISTRIBUTION: Native to Australia (northern Queensland rainforest).
FLOWERING TIME: Spring.
DESCRIPTION: Leaves are up to 14cm (5½″) long and narrow-oblong and unequally emarginate at apex. Raceme is pendulous. Numerous flowers are small.

Robiquetia wassellii

ROSSIOGLOSSUM

(ross-ee-o-gloss-um)

*R*ossioglossum is named after John Ross, an orchid collector in Mexico (1830–1840). This is a very small genus of six species which originates from Mexico to Panama. Originally these species were in the genus *Orchis*. In 1916, they were considered to be a section of the genus *Odontoglossum*. In 1976, Garay and Kennedy showed that these species do not conform to the taxonomic key of the genera *Odontoglossum*, thus giving rise to the genus *Rossioglossum*. The difference is that the labellum of *Rossioglossum* is free, at right angles to the column, the side lobes are auriculate, and the mid-lobe is large and pandurate. This medium to large epiphytic plant has short rhizomes. Pseudobulbs are ovoid. It has two leaves at apex which are large and petiolate. Flowers are large, showy and yellow with red markings. Sepals and petals are free and spreading. The labellum is free, pandurate, the mid-lobe is large and the callus fleshy.

Culture: As for *Odontoglossum* and *Oncidium*. Compost in well-drained pots. Provide humid conditions and frequent watering. Take care with fragile new growth; don't allow water to sit around newly growing tips as they may rot.

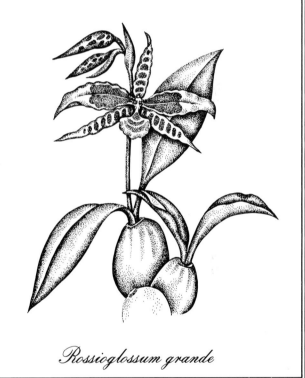

Rossioglossum grande

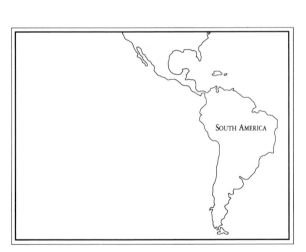

SOUTH AMERICA

Rossioglossum grande syn. *Odontoglossum grande*

Rossioglossum grande syn. *Odontoglossum grande*

COMMON NAME: None.
COLOUR: Flowers yellow, barred and marked red-brown.
SIZE: Growing up to 50cm (20″) high.
CLIMATE: Intermediate to warm.
DISTRIBUTION: Native to Mexico and Guatemala.
FLOWERING TIME: Autumn.
DESCRIPTION: Pseudobulbs are clustered, compressed, ovoid and up to 10cm (4″) high. Leaves are lanceolate to elliptic, acute and up to 40cm (16″) long. Inflorescence is up to 30cm (12″) long. Flowers are large, showy and measure about 10cm (4″) across. Labellum is pandurate and tri-lobed; side lobes are auriculate; mid-lobe is shortly clawed and emarginate; disc is bi-lobed with callus between the lobes.

SARCOCHILUS

(sar-kok-i-lus)

Sarcochilus from the Gk *sarx* (flesh) *chilos* (lip) with reference to the fleshy labellum. This was once a large genus, but over the last several decades many species have been reclassified and transferred to other genera, especially the Asian and Indonesian species which differ from the Australian species. There is now a small number of species. Most of the transferred species went to *Pteroceras. Sarcochilus* is now a genus of about a dozen epiphytic or lithophytic plants found in northern and eastern Australia. Roots are smooth and fleshy. The base of stems is covered with persistent scarious leafy-bases. The few leaves are channelled and the apex is unequally bi-lobed. The few to many flowers are showy and often fragrant. Sepals and petals are free, with the lateral sepals adnate to the column foot for a distance. The labellum is tri-lobed, articulate to apex of column foot, shallowly saccate. The large side lobes are erect and curved. The mid-lobe is small and fleshy and is attached to a short spur which is often poorly developed. The basal sac or disc is almost filled by callus thickenings.

Culture: Most species do best on tree-fern fibre slab or pans filled with gravel. All species require high humidity and moderate shade.

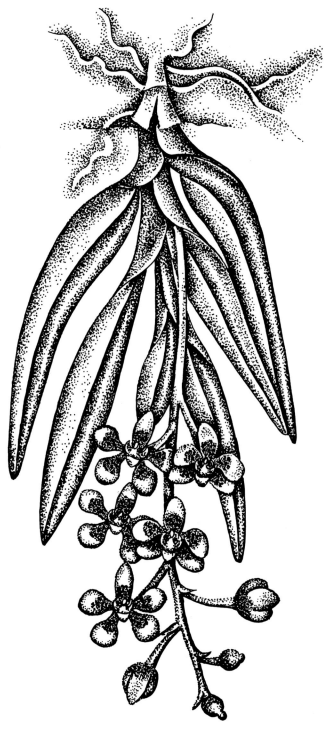

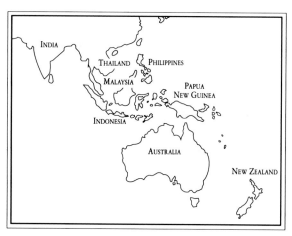

Sarcochilus ceciliae

COMMON NAME: Fairy Bells.
COLOUR: Flowers pink, mauve-pink or purple.
Labellum white.
SIZE: Growing up to 10cm (4″) high.
CLIMATE: Cool.
DISTRIBUTION: Native to Australia (eastern coast
and nearby mountains), growing in clumps on
rocks.
FLOWERING TIME: Late spring to summer to early
autumn.
DESCRIPTION: A variable species in growth and
flower form. Stems are erect. Leaves are linear to
lanceolate and grow up to 12.5cm (5″) long.
Inflorescence is in the form of a loose raceme.
Flowers measure about 1.5cm (½″) across.

Sarcochilus ceciliae

Sarcochilus falcatus

COMMON NAME: Orange Blossom Orchid.
COLOUR: Flowers white. Labellum marked with
orange, having a crimson-purple stripe.
SIZE: Growing up to 15cm (6″) high.
CLIMATE: Cool.
DISTRIBUTION: Native to Australia (eastern
rainforests).
FLOWERING TIME: Spring.
DESCRIPTION: Small, very fragrant epiphytic herb,
growing on trunks and limbs of softwood trees.
Leaves are flat, oblong-lanceolate and falcate,
measuring up to 15cm (6″) long. Flower scape
carries three to twelve blooms. Flower is about
2.5cm (1″) across with a showy display.

Sarcochilus fitzgeraldii

Sarcochilus fitzgeraldii

COMMON NAME: Ravine Orchid.
COLOUR: Flowers white, spotted pale purple-
pink. Labellum with yellow-orange markings.
SIZE: Growing up to 17.5cm (7″) high.
CLIMATE: Cool.
DISTRIBUTION: Native to eastern Australia
(rainforest areas). A prostrate epiphyte and
lithophyte growing chiefly on rocks in deep
shady ravines.
FLOWERING TIME: Spring.
DESCRIPTION: Leaves are falcate, channelled and
up to 17.5cm (7″) long. Inflorescence is
racemose with numerous flowers measuring up
to 3cm (1¼″) across.

Sarcochilus falcatus

Sarcochilus hartmannii

COMMON NAME: Hartmann's Orchid.
COLOUR: Flowers white with red blotches.
Labellum tri-lobe marked with yellow.
SIZE: Growing up to 10cm (4″) high.
CLIMATE: Cool.
DISTRIBUTION: Native to eastern Australian coast
and nearby mountains, growing on cliffs and
rocks.
FLOWERING TIME: Spring.
DESCRIPTION: Stems are erect, stout and up to
10cm (4″) high. The six to eight leaves are up to
17.5cm (7″) long, are oblong-lanceolate, falcate
and channelled. Inflorescence is erect to
arching and is 20cm (8″) long. Flowers measure
up to 2.5cm (1″) across.

Sarcochilus hartmannii

Sarcochilus moorei

COMMON NAME: None.
COLOUR: Flowers ochre-yellow, spotted and
blotched with brown.
SIZE: A pendulous epiphyte, up to 45cm (18″)
long.
CLIMATE: Hot.
DISTRIBUTION: Native to Australia (northern
Queensland) and Papua New Guinea.
FLOWERING TIME: Winter to spring.
DESCRIPTION: Leaves are up to 30cm (12″) long,
are narrow-oblong and unequally emarginate.
Raceme is pendulous and up to 45cm (18″)
long. Numerous flowers measure 2.5cm (1″)
across.

Sarcochilus moorei

SCHOMBURGKIA
(shom-berg-kee-a)

Schomburgkia is named after Dr Richard Schomburgk, a German botanist who explored and collected with his elder brother Sir Robert, in British Guiana (Guyana). In 1865, at the age of 54, he became director of Adelaide Botanic Gardens in Australia. Unfortunately, many taxonomists do not consider *Schomburgkia* a valid genus, so include it within *Laelia*. *Schomburgkia* has recently been divided into two sections: (a) *Schomburgkia*: pseudobulbs are fusiform, resembling those of *Cattleya*, but with a stalked base; leaves coriaceous, long and narrow. Inflorescence up to 15 flowers and up to 1.8m (6') long, e.g. *S. undulata*. Found in South America, Venezuela and Guyana. (b) *Chaunoschomburgkia*: pseudobulbs are thick, cylindrical or conical, yellow-green, becoming hollow with age, and a favourite nesting place for a certain species of ant; leaves short and broad, e.g. *S. tibicinis*. Found in Central America and West Indies, Mexico to Costa Rica.

Schomburgkia is a genus of about twelve species from central and northern South America. Pseudobulbs are fusiform or conical and are often hollow. Leaves are coriaceous and spreading. Inflorescence is erect and very long. The flowers are large, showy and cream, red-brown, red-purple or wine-purple in colour. Sepals and petals are similar and free with undulating margins. Labellum is tri-lobed with side lobes erect on either side of the column; the mid-lobe is spreading with five longitudinal keels. *Schomburgkias* are distinguishable from *Laelia* by the beautiful undulate sepals and petals, and the labellum which does not enclose the column.

Culture: Compost in well-drained pots as for *Cattleya* and *Laelia*. Both the fusiform and hollow pseudobulb groups require plenty of water while growing, as well as shade with plenty of light. The hollow pseudobulb group require a longer dry period once growth and flowering is complete. Avoid frequent repotting.

SOUTH AMERICA

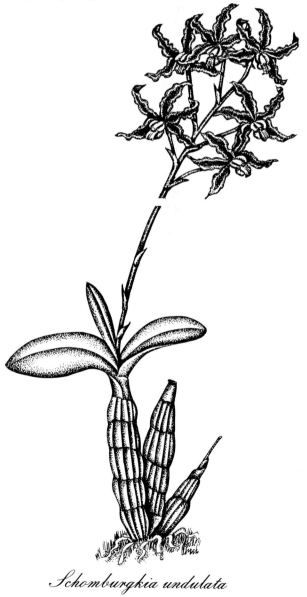

Schomburgkia undulata

Schomburgkia superbiens syn. *Laelia superbiens*

Schomburgkia superbiens syn. *Laelia superbiens*

COMMON NAME: None.

COLOUR: Flowers purple, variegated with yellow.

SIZE: A large epiphyte or terrestrial plant, growing up to 5m (16′) high.

CLIMATE: Intermediate.

DISTRIBUTION: Native to Mexico, Guatemala and Honduras. Growing at altitudes up to 2000m (6600′) in rainforests; uncommon in the open.

FLOWERING TIME: Autumn.

DESCRIPTION: Pseudobulbs are oblong-fusiform, furrowed and up to 3m (10′) high. Leaves stem from the apex, are oblong-lanceolate and up to 30cm (1′) long. Inflorescence measures up to 80cm (32″) long. Flowers are numerous, large, showy, with sepals up to 7.5cm (3″) long and petals up to 5cm (2″) long. Labellum is tri-lobed and 5cm (2″) long. Margins are convolute and enfold the column. Side lobes are short-oblong and the apex is crisp. Mid-lobe is obovate and the disc has five or six prominent, crisp, longitudinal lamellae.

SOBRALIA
(so-bral-ee-a)

Sobralia is named after Dr Francisco Sobral, a Spanish physician and botanist. This is a genus of about 35 terrestrial, lithophytic and epiphytic species. They are wide-spread from Mexico to Brazil in South America. This group of interesting, vegetative orchids has reed-like short to very long stems with few coriaceous or papery, plicate, distinctly nerved leaves. The flowers are large and spectacular. Their beauty often excels that of the *Cattleyas*. The single, successive flowers bloom over a period of many weeks; each bloom is short-lived, lasting not more than a day or two. The labellum is tri-lobed or entire, with the base adnate to the column, the basal half tubular then spreading and the disc with or without calli. The glorious beauty of these handsome orchids always makes them a centre of attraction.

Culture: Compost in well-drained pots. Plants require careful watering with moderate shade. As a note of warning, these plants are susceptible to toxic fumigants! Before importing any species of this genus discuss this problem with your customs and quarantine officers. Other than that concern, *Sobralias* are not difficult to grow if careful attention is given to their requirements.

Sobralia macrantha

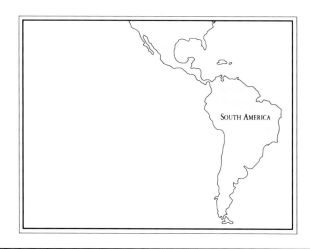

SOUTH AMERICA

Sobralia decora

COMMON NAME: None.
COLOUR: Flowers white. Labellum flushed with lilac.
SIZE: Growing up to 75cm (30″) high.
CLIMATE: Intermediate to warm.
DISTRIBUTION: Native to Mexico, British Honduras, Honduras, Costa Rica, Guatemala and Nicaragua.
FLOWERING TIME: Spring to summer.
DESCRIPTION: Stems are cane-like, clustered and up to 75cm (30″) high. Leaves are linear-lanceolate, acute and up to 23cm (9″) long. Inflorescence is terminal with few blooms. Flowers are fragrant and grow up to 10cm (4″) across.

Sobralia xantholeuca

Sobralia xantholeuca

COMMON NAME: None.
COLOUR: Flowers yellow. Labellum marked orange.
SIZE: Growing up to 2m (6′6″) high.
CLIMATE: Warm.
DISTRIBUTION: Native to central America, liking warm conditions.
FLOWERING TIME: Late spring to summer.
DESCRIPTION: Leaves alternate on reed-like stem and are linear-lanceolate. Flowers bloom in succession for as long as the season lasts and measure up to 15cm (6″) across.

Sobralia decora

Sobralia macrantha

COMMON NAME: None.
COLOUR: Flower colour is variable, generally rose-purple. Labellum marked with white and yellow. A white form has been recorded.
SIZE: Growing up to 2.4m (8′) high.
CLIMATE: Intermediate.
DISTRIBUTION: Native to Mexico through to Costa Rica.
FLOWERING TIME: Spring to autumn.
DESCRIPTION: Stems are clustered and grow up to 2.4m (8′). Leaves are sheathing, lanceolate and up to 30cm (12″) long. Flowers open singly over a long period. Flowers are large, but size is variable.

Sobralia macrantha

SOPHRONITIS
(sof-roe-nye-tis)

Sophronitis from the Gk *sophronia* (modest) with reference particularly to *Sophronitis cernua*. This is a very small genus of less than ten species found in eastern Brazil and Paraguay. As recently as 1977, J. A. Fowlie set the taxonomic limits of this genus. *Sophronitis* is a genus of dwarf epiphytic or lithophytic sympodial plants. The pseudobulbs are small, ovoid, thickly clustered on a rhizome, each pseudobulb having a single, erect, apical, coriaceous, shiny or grey-green leaf. Inflorescence is terminal with one or many flowers. These flowers are showy and scarlet or orange-red in colour which is quite vivid at times. Sepals and petals are alike in shape, with petals slightly broader. The labellum is tri-lobed, with the lateral lobes partially encircling the column; the mid-lobe is smaller with a yellow disc; the spur is adnate to the ovary.

Culture: Mount on a tree-fern fibre slab. Plants require humidity; *never* allow them to become dry, but be careful with watering. Provide moderate shade.

SOUTH AMERICA

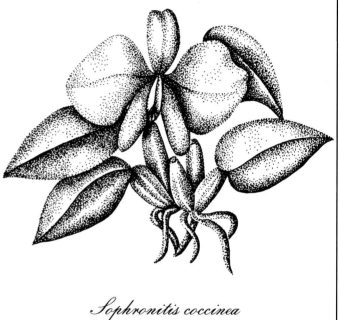

Sophronitis coccinea

Sophronitis coccinea

COMMON NAME: None.

COLOUR: Flower colour variable, generally scarlet. Labellum yellow-orange marked with scarlet.

SIZE: Growing up to 12.5cm (5″) high.

CLIMATE: Intermediate.

DISTRIBUTION: Native to Brazil.

FLOWERING TIME: Autumn to winter.

DESCRIPTION: Pseudobulbs are clustered, fusiform and grow up to 4cm (1½″) high. Solitary leaf is oblong-lanceolate and up to 7.5cm (3″) long. Flowers are usually solitary with variable size.

Sophronitis coccinea

SPATHOGLOTTIS
(spath-oh-glot-is)

Spathoglottis from the Gk *spathe* (a spath) *glotta* (a tongue) with reference to the broad lamina of the labellum. This genus of about 40 species is found from India across South-east Asia, China, Indonesia, Papua New Guinea, to the Pacific Islands, with two species in Australia. The largest number of species is found in Papua New Guinea. Covered with dry leaf sheaths, the pseudobulbs look more like *Gladiolus* corms. Closely allied to *Calanthe* and *Phaius*, *Spathoglottis* are quite handsome terrestrials, gaining popularity yearly. The pseudobulbs are green with up to four plicate, ribbed, lanceolate leaves, each up to 60cm (2') long. Racemes are erect with up to 25 blooms in a tight cluster. Flower segments are free and showy. Sepals and the floral stem are covered with soft hairs. Petals are larger than sepals. Flowers vary in colour from yellow to red-purple. The labellum is tri-lobed; lateral lobes are narrow and erect. The mid-lobe is interestingly narrow in the middle and flared at each end; the basal third is bi-lobed with two ear-like projections or appendages covered with fine, soft hairs. The lamina is apically bi-lobed.

Culture: Compost is three parts peat, one part sand and one part sphagnum moss. Plants can be grown in full sunlight, though moderate shade is desirable. Water and fertilise frequently.

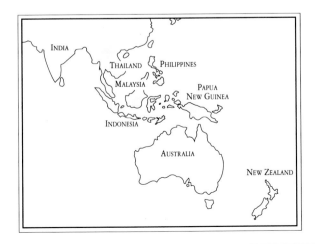

Spathoglottis paulinae

Spathoglottis pacifica

COMMON NAME: Known as 'Varavara' in Fiji.
COLOUR: Flowers pink, mauve or rarely white.
SIZE: Growing up to 1.5m (5′) high.
CLIMATE: Warm to hot.
DISTRIBUTION: Native to Fiji.
FLOWERING TIME: Throughout the year.
DESCRIPTION: A common terrestrial orchid.
Pseudobulbs are conical and up to 10cm (4″)
high. Leaves are ribbed, broad-lanceolate and
1.5m (5′) long. Inflorescence is basal, up to 2m
(6′6″) high, with a dense head of flowers
opening in succession. Flowers measure 3.5cm
(1½″) across.

Spathoglottis pacifica

Spathoglottis paulinae

Spathoglottis paulinae

COMMON NAME: None.
COLOUR: Flowers light purple. Labellum deep
purple.
SIZE: Terrestrial herb growing up to 60cm (2′)
high.
CLIMATE: Warm.
DISTRIBUTION: Native to Australia (far north-
east).
FLOWERING TIME: Winter to end of summer,
peaking in early summer.
DESCRIPTION: Leaves are plicate and strongly
ribbed. Flowers on slender scape, measure
2.5cm (1″) across. Similar to *S. plicata*, but
S. plicata has larger, and more, flowers opening
at one time. The labellum side lobes are at right
angles in *S. plicata* and at 45 degrees in
S. paulinae.

Spathoglottis plicata

COMMON NAME: Solomon Islands Orchid.
COLOUR: Flowers pink, mauve, purple or white.
SIZE: A terrestrial species up to 90cm (3′) high.
CLIMATE: Warm to hot.
DISTRIBUTION: Native to South-east Asia,
Indonesia, India, the Philippines to Papua New
Guinea, Solomon Islands, Fiji and Australia
(north-east).
FLOWERING TIME: Spring to autumn.
DESCRIPTION: Pseudobulbs are covered in old
leaf fibres, are ovoid and are up to 5cm (2″)
high. Leaves are fine, plicate, linear-lanceolate,
acuminate and 30 to 120cm (1 to 4′) long.
Inflorescence is lateral and up to 90cm (3′)
long. Flowers measure 3cm (1¼″) across.

Spathoglottis plicata

Spathoglottis vanoverberghii

Spathoglottis vanoverberghii

COMMON NAME: None.
COLOUR: Flowers yellow, usually sparsely
spotted crimson on the mid-lobe of the
labellum.
SIZE: Growing up to 45cm (18″) high.
CLIMATE: Intermediate.
DISTRIBUTION: Native to the Philippines, Luzon,
growing at high elevations.
FLOWERING TIME: Late winter to spring.
DESCRIPTION: Pseudobulbs are ovoid-cylindrical
and grow up to 4cm (1½″) high. Leaves are
plicate, lanceolate and up to 38.5cm (15″).
Inflorescence is erect and is usually shorter than
the leaves.

STANHOPEA
(stan-hope-ee-a)

Stanhopea was named in honour of the Right Honorable Philip Henry, Fourth Earl of Stanhope, President of the London Medico-Botanical Society. This genus of about 50 species of interesting and fascinating orchids extends from Mexico (where it is affectionately known as 'el toro', the bull) to the tropics of northern South America, Peru and Brazil. At first, species were described by colour, but with further work, colour variation was no longer valid as an indicator of species differentiation. *Stanhopea* is allied to *Coryanthus*, differing in that the epichile of the labellum of the former does not have the saccate of the latter.

Pseudobulbs are deeply ribbed and in tight clusters, each with a single apical leaf. This leaf is plicate and deeply veined beneath. Inflorescence arises from the base of the pseudobulb and is pendulous, burrowing down through the leaf litter and debris in the crutch of the tree or rock crevice and into the open, forming a raceme of one to ten short-lived flowers. The flowers, which emerge from large, inflated buds which open with an audible click, are fleshy and exceedingly fragrant. Sepals and petals are alike in colour, are subsimilar, free, spreading and reflexed; petals often have wavy margins. The labellum is the extraordinary segment of the flower; it is fleshy, waxy and is divided into three distinct sections. The basal third, the hypochile, is usually hollow, calceiform or shoe-shaped where it joins the column. The middle third, the mesochile, is divided, having two prominent horn-like projections. The upper third, the epichile, is articulated to the mesochile and is very variable in shape, from cordate to oblong. The column is long, with the wings extending almost to the apex of the labellum; they are gracefully arched.

Culture: In a basket, use a compost of tree-fern fibre and sterilised bark. Use a 1:1:1 ratio fertiliser monthly. Plants require high humidity, regular water and moderate shade. The most commonly cultivated species is *S. nigroviolace* which is often wrongly named *S. tigrina*.

Stanhopea tigrina

Stanhopea eburnea

Stanhopea nigroviolacea

SOUTH AMERICA

Stanhopea anfracta

COMMON NAME: None.
COLOUR: Flowers orange to yellow, spotted purple-red. Column white; spotted. Hypochile eye spot is often in varying colours.
SIZE: Growing up to 40cm (16").
CLIMATE: Intermediate.
DISTRIBUTION: Native to Panama, Peru and Ecuador. A forest epiphytic growing at altitudes of 1100 to 1200m (3500 to 4000').
FLOWERING TIME: Spring to summer to early winter.
DESCRIPTION: Pseudobulbs are ovoid-conical and grow up to 6cm (2½") high. Leaves are petioled at base, are plicate and broad-elliptic. Inflorescence is pendulous, carrying five to twelve blooms. Flowers are fragrant and up to 7.5cm (3") across.

Stanhopea anfracta

Stanhopea candida

COMMON NAME: None.
COLOUR: Flowers white. Labellum interior spotted purple.
SIZE: Epiphytic plant growing up to 30cm (12") high.
CLIMATE: Intermediate.
DISTRIBUTION: Native to Mexico, Panama, Peru, Colombia and Brazil.
FLOWERING TIME: Summer.
DESCRIPTION: Pseudobulbs are ovoid-conical and up to 6cm (2½") high. Leaves are plicate, broad-elliptical and up to 45cm (18") long. Inflorescence is pendulous, bears three to seven blooms, each up to 7.5cm (3") across.

Stanhopea candida

Stanhopea embreei

COMMON NAME: None.
COLOUR: Flowers ivory-white to rich cream. Sepals and petals may be spotted maroon. Labellum orange-yellow; hypochile with a maroon eye spot on either side.
SIZE: Growing up to 55cm (22") high.
CLIMATE: Intermediate.
DISTRIBUTION: Native to Guatemala, Panama and Ecuador.
FLOWERING TIME: Spring.
DESCRIPTION: Pseudobulbs are ovoid-conical and up to 6cm (2½") high. Leaves are plicate, broad-elliptical and grow up to 45cm (18") long. Inflorescence is pendulous, usually a raceme of three to seven blooms. Flowers are large and showy, measuring 12.5cm (5") across. The orange-yellow hypochile of the labellum is squared, flat-based with a maroon eye spot on either side of the hypochile. Column and epichile are spotted maroon.

Stanhopea embreei

Stanhopea inodora

Stanhopea graveolens

COMMON NAME: None.
COLOUR: Flowers yellow-gold, spotted red-maroon.
SIZE: Growing up to 60cm (2') tall.
CLIMATE: Cool to intermediate.
DISTRIBUTION: Native to Mexico, Guatemala and Honduras in forests up to 2700m (9000') altitude.
FLOWERING TIME: Summer.
DESCRIPTION: An epiphytic or lithophytic plant. Pseudobulbs are ovoid-conical, somewhat depressed and are 5 to 7.5cm (2 to 3") long. Leaf is apical and elliptic-lanceolate. Inflorescence is pendulous with three to nine flowers. Flowers are showy, but have a foul smell. Sepals are concave and petals recurved. Labellum is 5cm (2") long; hypochile is short, saccate and toothed at base; mesochile horns are porrect; and epichile is ovate to revolute. Column is up to 5cm (2") long. Species is closely allied to, and often mistaken for, *Stanhopea wardii.*

Stanhopea graveolens

Stanhopea inodora

COMMON NAME: None.
COLOUR: Flowers ice green-white. The hypochile is partly tinted gold.
SIZE: This epiphytic plant is one of the largest and most vigorous of the *Stanhopeas.*
CLIMATE: Intermediate to warm.
DISTRIBUTION: Native to Mexico and Nicaragua.
FLOWERING TIME: Spring to summer.
DESCRIPTION: Pseudobulbs are ovoid-conical, furrowed, clothed with large sheaths, and grow up to 8cm (3¼") high. Leaves are very broad, elliptic, acute, cuneate near the base and are up to 50cm (20") long. Inflorescence is lateral, basal and pendulous. Raceme has six to ten blooms. Flowers are large, about 10cm (4") long.

Stanhopea insignis

COMMON NAME: None.

COLOUR: Flowers cream to orange-yellow, covered with purple blotches. Labellum white, spotted with dark and light purples.

SIZE: Growing up to 60cm (2') high.

CLIMATE: Intermediate.

DISTRIBUTION: Native to Peru and Brazil.

FLOWERING TIME: Autumn.

DESCRIPTION: Pseudobulbs are clustered, ovoid and up to 7.5cm (3") high. Leaves are plicate, oblong, acute and up to 45cm (18") long. Inflorescence is pendulous and grows up to 25cm (10") long. Flower measures up to 12.5cm (5") long.

Stanhopea insignis

Stanhopea nigroviolacea

Stanhopea nigroviolacea

COMMON NAME: None.

COLOUR: Flowers lemon-yellow with maroon blotches and spots. Labellum white, spotted purple. *S. tigrina* is spotted with two small blotches, but is not blotched.

SIZE: Growing up to 60cm (2') high.

CLIMATE: Intermediate.

DISTRIBUTION: Native to Mexico. Grows up to 2000m (7000') in altitude.

FLOWERING TIME: Summer.

DESCRIPTION: This epiphytic species has been mistakenly identified for many years as *S. tigrina.* Pseudobulb is ovoid with corrugated grooves and is up to 5cm (2") long. Leaves are petiolate, broad, acute and up to 60cm (2') long. Inflorescence is pendulous and fragrant flowers are large and showy, each measuring up to 15cm (6") long. In *S. nigroviolaceae* the hypochile is deeper and the horns broader than *S. tigrina.*

Stanhopea oculata

COMMON NAME: None.

COLOUR: Flower colour variable, generally yellow with red-purple spots.

SIZE: Growing up to 50cm (20") high.

CLIMATE: Intermediate.

DISTRIBUTION: Native to Mexico, Honduras, British Honduras, Guatemala, Costa Rica and Panama.

FLOWERING TIME: Summer.

DESCRIPTION: *S. ocullata* is distinguished from its close ally *S. Wardii* by the hypochile being transversely cleft below, which forms a hump below the mesochile. Pseudobulbs are obliquely ovoid and are up to 6.5cm (2½") high. Leaves are elliptic, petiolate, acute and grow up to 45cm (18") long. Inflorescence is pendulous with three to six blooms. Flowers are fragrant, each up to 12.5cm (5") across.

Stanhopea oculata

Stanhopea wardii

Stanhopea wardii

COMMON NAME: None.

COLOUR: Flowers lemon to cream, spotted with red-purple. Hypochile of the labellum maroon or orange-yellow with purple spots on either side.

SIZE: Growing up to 52.5cm (21") high.

CLIMATE: Intermediate to warm.

DISTRIBUTION: Native to Mexico and Panama.

FLOWERING TIME: Autumn.

DESCRIPTION: Closely allied to *S. oculata,* but differing in the structure of the hypochile as described in that species. Pseudobulbs are ovoid-conical, angled, somewhat compressed and grow up to 7.5cm (3") long. Leaves are elliptic-lanceolate, plicate and are up to 45cm (18") long. The one to six blooms are showy, fragrant and 12.5cm (5") across.

STENOGLOTTIS

(sten-oh-glott-is)

Stenoglottis from the Gk *stenos* (narrow) *glotta* (a tongue) with reference to the narrow irregular lobes of the labellum. This genus of three species comes from eastern, central and southern Africa. Two of the three species are well known in choice collections, but *S. zambesiaca* from Nyasaland (Malawi) is exceedingly rare. These terrestrial herbs have fleshy, tuber-like roots, short stems, and the leaves form a basal rosette. Inflorescence is erect and many-flowered. The flowers are interesting and are coloured pink with dark spots. Sepals are adnate to the column and labellum for a short length, then are spreading. Petals are wider than sepals and are erect. The labellum is united to the column with or without the spur; it is wedge-shaped with three to seven lobes or tails.

Culture: Compost in small well-drained pots. Plants require moist, shady conditions. The leaves die back during and after flowering. Supply a little water until new growth appears.

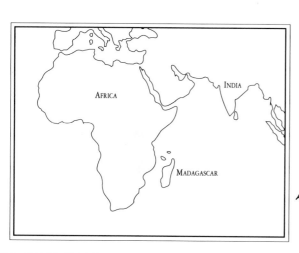

Stenoglottis longifolia

Stenoglottis longifolia

Stenoglottis longifolia

COMMON NAME: None.
COLOUR: Flowers mauve or rarely white. Labellum spotted purple.
SIZE: Growing up to 20cm (8″) high.
CLIMATE: Intermediate.
DISTRIBUTION: Native to South Africa, Zululand.
FLOWERING TIME: Autumn.
DESCRIPTION: A terrestrial or lithophytic or epiphytic species. Leaves are linear-oblong, acuminate, margins undulate, up to 18cm (7″) and form a dense basal rosette. Inflorescence is erect, up to 50cm (20″) long with a densely flowered raceme.

THELYMITRA

(thel-ee-mye-tra)

Thelymitra from the Gk *thelys* (female) *mitra* (head-dress or headband) with reference to the ornate wings that decorate the head of the column. This genus of over 80 species of terrestrial orchids is indigenous principally to Australia, with several species scattered through the Philippines, Indonesia, Papua New Guinea, the Pacific Islands and New Zealand. They are commonly known as Sun Orchids, because of their habit of opening only in bright sunlight. These species are true terrestrial herbs with a root system of two underground tubers. The solitary leaf is fluted and narrow. Inflorescence is a tall raceme of one or many wide open un-orchid-like blooms. Flowers are graceful; all segments of the perianth are similar and spreading. They open only in warm sunshine. The column is complex; it is erect with lateral wings united in front at the base and extending upwards at side of anther into plumed, brush-like appendages.

Culture: As for *Caladenia*. In Australia cultivated *Thelymitra* hybrids are freely available from nurseries specialising in Australian native species. These nurseries will also supply complete information on cultivating *Thelymitra*.

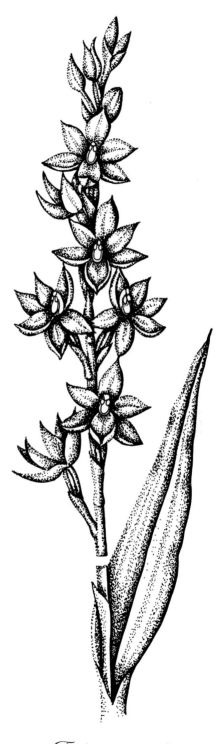

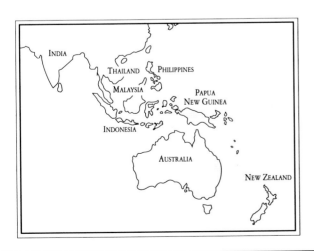

Thelymitra nuda

Thelymitra aristata

COMMON NAME: Scented Sun Orchid.

COLOUR: Flowers pink, blue or mauve.

SIZE: A variable terrestrial plant up to 90cm (3') high.

CLIMATE: Cool.

DISTRIBUTION: Native to Australia (moist areas) in close association with *Dendrobium kingianum.*

FLOWERING TIME: Spring.

DESCRIPTION: Leaves are sheathing, broad, lanceolate and 15 to 25cm (6 to 10") long. Inflorescence 1 to 35 blooms, up to 90cm (3') high. Flowers are fragrant, each measuring to 3.5cm (1½") across.

Thelymitra aristata

Thelymitra ixioides

Thelymitra ixioides

COMMON NAME: Spotted Sun Orchid.

COLOUR: Flowers blue-mauve with dark blue spots, rarely pink.

SIZE: A robust terrestrial 20 to 60cm (8 to 24") high.

CLIMATE: Cool.

DISTRIBUTION: Native to Australia and New Zealand (dry areas).

FLOWERING TIME: Spring.

DESCRIPTION: Leaves are channelled and 12.5 to 20cm (5 to 8") long. Flowers are in a terminal raceme, are numerous or solitary and about 3 to 6cm (1¼ to 2¼") across.

Thelymitra venosa

COMMON NAME: Veined Sun Orchid.

COLOUR: Flowers blue with darker veins.

SIZE: A slender terrestrial. Grows to 75cm (30") high.

CLIMATE: Cool.

DISTRIBUTION: Native to Australia (common in alpine moss beds and moist swampy areas).

FLOWERING TIME: Summer.

DESCRIPTION: Leaves are narrow to broad-lanceolate and deeply channelled. Terminal raceme with one to three flowers, each 2 to 5cm (¾ to 2") across.

Thelymitra venosa

THUNIA
(too-nee-a)

Thunia is named in honour of Count von Thun Hohenstein of Tetschin, Bohemia. This is a small genus of less than ten very beautiful terrestrials from India, Burma, South-east Asia and China. In early times *Thunia* was included in *Phaius*, however, it lacks pseudobulbs. The leaves are deciduous. Inflorescence is terminal on thick, clustered, leafy stems or cane-like pseudobulbs, often 5cm (2″) thick, racemose and drooping. Flowers are large, attractive and white or purple-magenta in colour. Sepals and petals are free. The labellum is tubular or bell-shaped, entire. The front margin is fringed and has yellow markings with a short, obtuse spur at the base of the labellum.

Culture: Compost. As for *Phaius*. Once the flowers fade and die, the leaves turn yellow and drop. Any repotting may be carried out once all the leaves have fallen. This genus is very easily grown and grows best in pots. Plants require moderate shade.

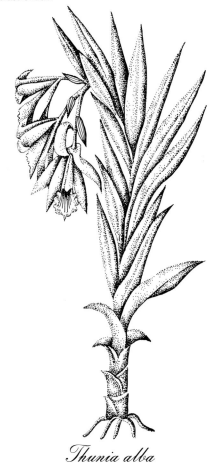

Thunia alba

Thunia marshalliana

COMMON NAME: Orchid of Burma.
COLOUR: Flower white. Labellum marked with yellow.
SIZE: Growing up to 90cm (3′) high.
CLIMATE: Intermediate.
DISTRIBUTION: Native to Burma.
FLOWERING TIME: Summer.
DESCRIPTION: Pseudobulbs are terete, stem-like, robust and up to 90cm (3′) high. Leaves are lanceolate. Inflorescence is arching and clustered. Flower measures 12½cm (5″) across.

Thunia marshalliana

TRICHOPILIA
(trik-o-pill-ee-a)

Trichopilia from the Gk *tricho* (hair) *pilos* (of felt, such as in a hat or cap) with reference to the fringed margin or hood of the column. This genus of about 30 species of large fragrant flowers is widespread throughout central and South America, from Mexico and the West Indies to Peru and Brazil. It is a small to medium epiphytic, sympodial orchid. The pseudobulbs are almost flattened and are clustered along a creeping rhizome. The single leaf is apical, oblong to lanceolate and coriaceous. Inflorescence is a spike from the base of the pseudobulb with one to many blooms. Flowers are exceptionally attractive; individual flowers measure up to 15cm (6″) across, are free flowering and have a wide range of colours. They somewhat resemble *Cattleya*. Sepals and petals are similar in shape, size and colour. The labellum is tri-lobed, fused at base to column, is trumpet-shaped or tubular-involute, is spreading above, with wavy margins and is sweetly fragrant. The column is usually hidden. The orchid's distinguishing feature is the ciliated hood of the anther cap.

Culture: Mount on a tree-fern fibre slab. Water well. Be careful how you use fertiliser as foliage is subject to burn. Plants require humidity and moderate shade.

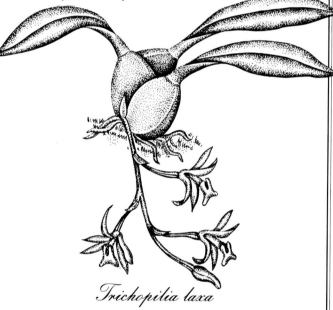

Trichopilia laxa

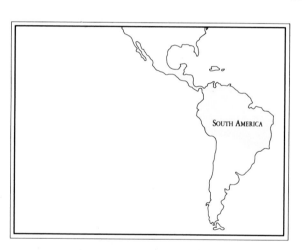

SOUTH AMERICA

Trichopilia suavis

Trichopilia suavis

COMMON NAME: None.
COLOUR: Flower colour variable, usually white to cream, spotted with pink. Labellum marked with yellow.
SIZE: Growing up to 25cm (10″) high.
CLIMATE: Warm.
DISTRIBUTION: Native to Costa Rica, Peru and Colombia.
FLOWERING TIME: Spring.
DESCRIPTION: An epiphytic plant. Pseudobulbs are clustered, broad, oblong-ovoid and compressed. Leaves are solitary, apical, broad ovate, coriaceous and about 20cm (8″) or more long. Flower spike is short. Flowers are fragrant and grow up to 10cm (4″) across. Labellum margins are frilled.

VANDA
(van-da)

Vanda comes from the Sanskrit word describing the plant we today know as *Vanda tesselata* from Bengal, (India), Sri Lanka and Burma. It was discovered in 1795 by Sir W. Jones. This genus of over 70 species of monopodial epiphytic orchids extends from India to South-east Asia and Borneo, and south to Indonesia, Papua New Guinea and Australia. Vandas are as popular as *Cattleyas, Cymbidiums, Dendrobiums, Laelias, Oncidiums, Paphiopedilums* and *Phalaenopsis*, being found in most collections. *Vanda* is divided into two main groups: (a) *Vanda tricolour:* with strap-like, distichous, stem-clasping leaves, keeled, green above and light beneath, the apex erose; (b) *Vanda teres:* with terete leaves about as thick as a pencil. The base of these leaves encircle the stems.

The plant's inflorescence is axillary, erect, racemose, with few to many flowers. In group (b) the inflorescence is on the side of the stem opposite the leaf. Flowers are showy, with a wide range of colours. Sepals and petals are subsimilar, free and spreading. The labellum is tri-lobed, the base is spurred or saccate and is adnate to the column; lateral lobes may be small or long auricle appendages, almost encircling column. The spur is conical; the mid-lobe is porrect, varying in size with the fleshy disc.

Culture: Compost in large well-drained pots or baskets. Because of their habit of strong aerial root growth, pots and bench soon become overgrown. *Vandas* do exceptionally well on large tree-fern slabs, and on trees in the open garden.

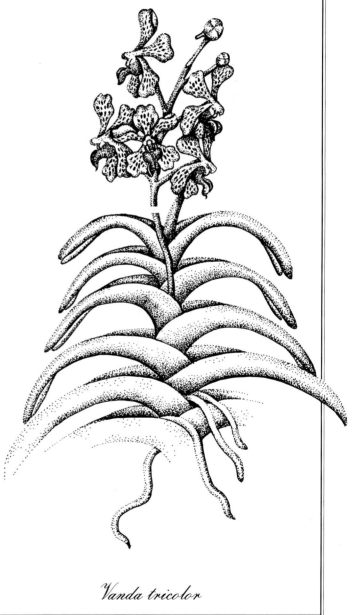

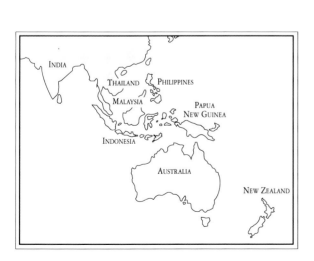

Vanda tricolor

Vanda coerulea

COMMON NAME: Blue Vanda.

COLOUR: Flowers blue. Labellum tri-lobed with front lobe deep blue.

SIZE: Monopodial, growing up to 90cm (3') high.

CLIMATE: Intermediate.

DISTRIBUTION: Native to Thailand, Burma and northern India at high elevations.

FLOWERING TIME: Autumn.

DESCRIPTION: Blue is considered a rare colour in orchids. Leaves are coriaceous, distichous, strap-like and 7.5 to 25cm (3 to 10″) long. Inflorescence is erect or suberect, with 6 to 20 flowers, each up to 10cm (4″) across. Sepals and petals equal. Labellum is small, tri-lobed, with small lateral lobes, and the mid-lobe has ridges terminating in bituberculate apex. Conical spur.

Vanda coerulea

Vanda cristata

Vanda cristata

COMMON NAME: None.

COLOUR: Flowers yellow to green-yellow. Labellum green underneath, tawny above, spotted with deep red stripes.

SIZE: Growing up to 30cm (12″) high.

CLIMATE: Intermediate.

DISTRIBUTION: Native to Bhutan, Nepal and Sikkim. Growing at high elevations.

FLOWERING TIME: Spring to summer.

DESCRIPTION: Plant erect, with coriaceous leaves which are 15cm (6″) long. Flowers are waxy and fragrant. Labellum is tri-lobed: lateral lobes erect and deltoid shaped; mid-lobe subpandurate; spur short and conical.

Vanda dearei

COMMON NAME: None.

COLOUR: Flowers cream, floral segment tips generally flushed with buff-brown. Labellum marked with lemon, streaked with crimson.

SIZE: A robust plant reaching height of up to 2.4m (8').

CLIMATE: Hot.

DISTRIBUTION: Native to Borneo, growing at low elevations.

FLOWERING TIME: Mainly summer, but throughout the year.

DESCRIPTION: Leaves are broad, and compact. Inflorescence is short with few blooms. Flower is fragrant and about 5cm (2″) across. Labellum is tri-lobed.

Vanda dearei

Vanda denisoniana

Vanda denisoniana

COMMON NAME: None.

COLOUR: Flower colour variable from white-green to white. Labellum has a basal yellow blotch.

SIZE: Growing up to 45cm (18″) high.

CLIMATE: Intermediate.

DISTRIBUTION: Native to Burma and Arakan Mountains, growing at elevations of 600 to 750m (2000 to 2500').

FLOWERING TIME: Spring.

DESCRIPTION: Stems are leafy throughout. Leaves are linear, emarginate and up to 30cm (12″) long. Flower is fragrant, measuring about 5cm (2″) long.

Vanda hindsii syn. *V. whiteana*

COMMON NAME: None.
COLOUR: Flower colour variable, usually red-brown with yellow margins, or may have yellow-brown flecks. A rare pure yellow form exists.
SIZE: Growing up to 90cm (3') high.
CLIMATE: Hot.
DISTRIBUTION: Native to far north-eastern Australia and Papua New Guinea.
FLOWERING TIME: Late spring to summer.
DESCRIPTION: Stems are up to 90cm (3') high. Leaves are strap-like, distichous, compact and grow up to 40cm (16") long. Raceme is about 30cm (12") long with up to seven blooms. Flowers measure up to 3.5cm (1½") across.

Vanda hindsii syn. *V. whiteana*

Vanda lamellata

Vanda lamellata

COMMON NAME: None.
COLOUR: Flowers lemon with brown markings.
SIZE: A dwarf species.
CLIMATE: Warm.
DISTRIBUTION: Native to the Philippines and northern Borneo.
FLOWERING TIME: Winter.
DESCRIPTION: Leaves are slender, coriaceous, recurved and strap-like. Plant has a profusion of flowers. Flower measures about 5cm (2") across.

Vanda pumila

COMMON NAME: None.
COLOUR: Flowers cream or yellow. Labellum streaked with purple.
SIZE: A small epiphytic species with short stout stem.
CLIMATE: Intermediate.
DISTRIBUTION: Native to Himalayas, India (Sikkim), Bhutan and Thailand, growing at altitudes of 600m (1000').
FLOWERING TIME: Winter.
DESCRIPTION: Leaves are strap-shaped, curved, emarginate and grow up to 20cm (8") long. Inflorescence is erect, as long as the leaves and is axillary. Flower is fragrant, showy and up to 6cm (2½") across.

Vanda pumila

Vanda roeblingiana

Vanda roeblingiana

COMMON NAME: None.
COLOUR: Flowers yellow, striped irregularly with red-brown. Labellum yellow-cream streaked with red-brown.
SIZE: Growing up to 90cm (3') high.
CLIMATE: Intermediate.
DISTRIBUTION: Native to the Philippines, Luzon, growing at elevations of 1200 to 1500m (4000 to 5000').
FLOWERING TIME: Summer.
DESCRIPTION: Erect stems grow to about 90cm (3') high. Leaves are linear, unequally emarginate, acuminate and up to 20cm (8") long. Inflorescence grows up to 30cm (12") long. Flowers measure 5cm (2") across and are fragrant. Labellum is tri-lobed.

Vanda stangeana

COMMON NAME: None.
COLOUR: Flowers golden-green, tessellated with red-brown. Labellum white, marked and spotted red, tip gold-green.
SIZE: Growing up to 45cm (18″) high.
CLIMATE: Intermediate.
DISTRIBUTION: Native to India, Assam and Nepal, growing between 1200 to 1500m (4000 to 5000′) in altitude.
FLOWERING TIME: Spring.
DESCRIPTION: Stems are erect, robust and grow up to 45cm (18″) high. Leaves are distichous, strap-like, emarginate, recurved and up to 15cm (6″) long. Inflorescence is usually erect and about 12.5 cm (5″) long. Flowers are almost 6cm (2½″) long with undulate margins.

Vanda stangeana

Vanda tricolor

COMMON NAME: None.
COLOUR: Flower colour variable, usually pale yellow, spotted and flecked red-brown. Labellum white, streaked red-brown and tinted purple and mauve.
SIZE: A large erect epiphytic, lithophytic or terrestrial, growing up to 1.2m (4′) high.
CLIMATE: Warm.
DISTRIBUTION: Native to Java, Bali and Laos.
FLOWERING TIME: Autumn to winter.
DESCRIPTION: Leaves are imbricate, strap-like, curved, unequally emarginate and grow up to 45cm (18″) long. Inflorescence is shorter than the leaves. Flower measures up to 7.5cm (3″) across, is fragrant, large and showy.

Vanda tricolor

Vanda tricolor var. insignis

COMMON NAME: None.
COLOUR: Flowers yellow-green, blotched brown. Mid-lobe of labellum red-purple.
SIZE: Growing up to 1.2m (4′) high.
CLIMATE: Same as type.
DISTRIBUTION: Native to Mollucas, Timor and Alor Islands.
FLOWERING TIME: Usually autumn, but may flower three times annually.
DESCRIPTION: Same as type, except labellum is wider.

Vanda tricolor var. *insignis*

Vanda tricolor var. *suavis*

Vanda tricolor var. suavis

COMMON NAME: None.
COLOUR: Flowers white, spotted and flecked, red-purple.
SIZE: Same as type form.
CLIMATE: Warm.
DISTRIBUTION: Native to Java.
FLOWERING TIME: Autumn to winter.
DESCRIPTION: Differing from its type form by having a longer inflorescence with more numerous flowers. Labellum is slightly more linear with reflexed margins.

VANDOPSIS

(van-dop-sis)

*V*andopsis from the Gk *opsis* (appearance; resembles) with reference to a resemblance to the genus *Vanda*. *Vandopsis* is a genus of less than ten species of very robust monopodial epiphytic orchids. They are widespread, occurring from Burma, through South-east Asia to Borneo, the Philippines, Indonesia and Papua New Guinea. *Vandopsis* was probably first recognised as a genus by Gaudichaud in about 1817; from then until about 1850 various species were continually being shifted from one genus to another and at about that time Pfitzer established *Vandopsis* as a recognised genus. The plants are erect. Leaves are distichous, coriaceous yet fleshy, strap-like and keeled. Inflorescence is axillary, up to 1.8m (6′) long and many-flowered with up to 22 blooms. Flowers are fleshy, thick-textured like a banana skin, or coriaceous, remaining open over a long period of time (*V. lissochiloides* for as long as four months). Sepals and petals are subsimilar. The labellum is tri-lobed; lateral lobes are joined across the base of the mid-lobe by a fleshy bridge. The mid-lobe is elongated, fleshy and keeled from the apex almost to the base. Flowers are yellow with purple or brown markings or blotches.

Culture: As for *Vanda*, use coarse compost in well-drained pots, or better still, mount on a large tree-fern slab.

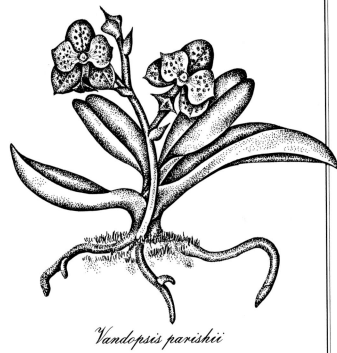

Vandopsis parishii

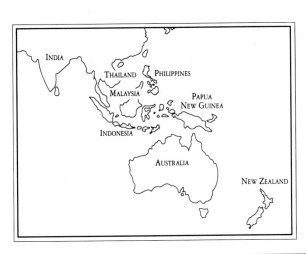

Vandopsis lissochiloides

COMMON NAME: None.
COLOUR: Flowers yellow marked with purple and red-purple underneath.
SIZE: Growing up to 1.8m (6′) high.
CLIMATE: Warm.
DISTRIBUTION: Native to the Philippines.
FLOWERING TIME: Spring to summer.
DESCRIPTION: Is often mistaken for *V. batemani*. Numerous flowers, each up to 7.5cm (3″) across.

Vandopsis lissochiloides

VANILLA
(va-nil-la)

Vanilla from the Spanish *vainilla*, a diminutive of the Spanish *vaina* (meaning a pod or sheath) with reference to the slender pod-like fruit. Several species of the genus are grown in various countries of the world as a commercial agricultural crop. This tall climbing monopodial herb is widely distributed throughout the tropics and subtropics of the world. It is closely related to *Pogonia*. *Vanilla* is a genus of over 100 species of terrestrial or epiphytic plants branching with leaves and roots at each nodes. Roots attach to bark or twigs for support. Species of the genera *Vanilla* and *Galoelia* are the only orchids to have developed the climbing habit so well. Leaves are alternately large or reduced to scale-like appendages, thus giving the plant an appearance of a leafless vine. Inflorescence is axillary, clustered with few or many flowers which do not open fully.

They are 7.5cm (3″) long, are fleshy and often showy. Sepals and petals are equal in shape, colour and size; segments are free. The labellum is tri-lobed or entire with the distinct claw adnate to the column, with lateral lobes encircling the column; the mid-lobe is flaring at the apex and the margins are wavy having appendages. The column is long, slender and often pubescent. The fruit is a long fleshy pod, not necessarily dehiscent.

Culture: Compost in a large pot with plenty of support or in a well-drained flower bed. The growing stems need to be supported with a tree-fern trunk or can be grown along a wall or with wires. Plants require humidity at all times with shade. Generally the flowers do not appear until the plant is well grown.

Vanilla planifolia

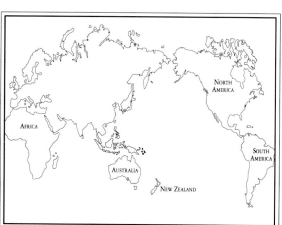

Vanilla pompona

Vanilla pompona

COMMON NAME: Vanilla Orchid.
COLOUR: Flowers green-yellow. Labellum white to yellow-orange.
SIZE: Climbs up to 6m (20′) high.
CLIMATE: Warm.
DISTRIBUTION: Native to Mexico, throughout Central America to Peru, Bolivia and Brazil.
FLOWERING TIME: Summer.
DESCRIPTION: A climbing, succulent, robust plant. Leaves are fleshy, ovate-oblong and grow up to 30cm (12″) long. Inflorescence is axillary with numerous, clustered flowers. Flowers are shy openers, are fragrant and measure up to 9cm (3¾″) long.

ZYGOPETALUM
(zye-go-pet-a-lum)

Z*ygopetalum* from the Gk *zyon* (a yoke, occurring as a pair) *petalon* (a petal) with reference to the yoke-like callus on the base of the labellum, which appears to hold the petals together. This genus of almost twenty species is found in tropical South America from Paraguay, Peru, Bolivia, the Guyanas and south to Brazil. It is a genus of sympodial epiphytes.

Pseudobulbs are ovoid, short, stout, distinctly sheathed, wrinkling with age. It has two or more leaves which are apical, distichous, glossy, plicate, veined and becoming deciduous. Inflorescence from the base of the pseudobulb is a raceme of three to twelve flowers. Flowers are showy and interesting. Sepals and petals are usually alike in size and colour, are green with brown or purple blotches, with undulating margins. The labellum is tri-lobed, with a small spur attached to the base of the column. Lateral lobes are erect and small, encircling the column. The mid-lobe is broad with a wavy margin. Disc has an entire fleshy callus. The flower is often highly perfumed.

Culture: Compost. Best treated as a terrestrial, so plant in large well-drained pots. Plants require humid conditions and shade. Provide plenty of water while growing and far less once bulbs are fully grown.

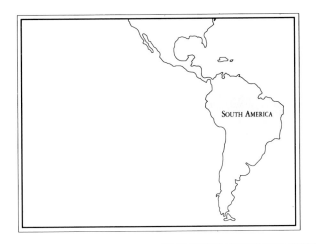

SOUTH AMERICA

Zygopetalum intermedium

Zygopetalum mackayi

COMMON NAME: None.
COLOUR: Petals and sepals green, blotched with green-brown. Labellum has violet stripes.
SIZE: Growing up to 55cm (22″) high.
CLIMATE: Intermediate.
DISTRIBUTION: Native to Brazil.
FLOWERING TIME: Autumn.
DESCRIPTION: Pseudobulbs are 10cm (4″) high. Leaves grow up to 45cm (18″) long. Flower scape bears five to ten flowers, each up to 7.5cm (3″) across and very fragrant.

Zygopetalum mackayi

Pests and Diseases

By far the most damaging of orchid diseases are caused by virus infection. Although much work has been done, no cure has been discovered. Most growers burn all affected plants, a safe precaution considering the ease with which viruses spread through plant collections. When an orchid is infected with a virus, the disease affects all parts of the plant, and cannot be eliminated by tissue culturing the *meristematic* tissue, as is done with some other types of plants. However the seed is not affected and can be used for propagation providing the pod is allowed to dry and split, ejecting the seed onto a sterile surface.

More than fifty different viruses have been identified in orchids but only two are easily detected by growers and are our concern here: Cymbidium Mosaic Virus (C.M.V.) and Tobacco Strain 'O' Virus (often called *Odontoglossum Ring Spot Virus*).

Plants may be infected with either of these viruses, or with any of the viruses, without showing any signs of the disease. It is only when some abnormality occurs that a virus is detected, unless tests are carried out in a laboratory on an indicator plant. Tests on healthy plants are usually undertaken when a plant is to be mericloned or used as a seed carrying parent.

HOW TO DETECT A VIRUS

Cymbidium Mosaic Virus can infect any genera of orchid, but as the name suggests, it is found mostly in *Cymbidiums*. It is usually detected by the leaves becoming streaked with broken lines of a paler colour. The flowers will often be deformed or have variations of colour, but the leaves are the main clue in detecting the disease.

Tobacco Strain 'O' Virus is detected in a wider range of genera, but particularly in *Odontoglossum, Cattleya* and *Dendrobium*. One symptom is a distinct ring spot, that is, an outer ring of necrotic black tissue, with some green tissue inside and then a necrotic black spot in the centre. Several such spots may occur on a single leaf. It is often called 'colour break virus' because the flowers are marked with irregular colour patterns. A third sign is the appearance of shallow dimples on the leaves. These signs and any other abnormality should be regarded as suspect and plants should be destroyed. If not destroyed, then plants should be isolated completely from the rest of the collection.

As viruses are seldom detected early, all plants must be regarded as possible carriers of the disease. As the disease is spread by innoculating one plant with the sap of another, we can reduce the spreading by simply using sterile tools and by using only sterilised pots. Likewise do not re-use potting material and thoroughly wash hands after working on each plant. Practising these simple procedures will not eliminate the spread of the disease, but it will certainly help keep your collection healthy.

FUNGAL AND BACTERIAL DISEASES

Other diseases affecting orchids are usually of fungal or bacterial origin, and they too can be reduced by good housekeeping practices—keep the growing area clean and free from unnecessary debris and allow for plenty of fresh air to circulate around the plants. However, sometimes problems occur in the cleanest houses. For practical purposes it is best to regard fungi problems in two categories: (a) Those that affect the plant above the potting mix; and (b) Those that affect the root area.

If the problem is in the pseudobulb or leaf area then it is best to use a contact fungicide. Some growers use these fungicides regularly as a preventative measure. Mancozeb is very good, but before using check to see if its use in your area is prohibited.

If the disease is in the root area, it will usually be found when the new leads appear; they will suddenly die, leaving a soft squashy mess, called damp-off. This can be controlled with a systemic fungicide. Benomyl or Furalaxy are good, but again check to see if its use is prohibited.

Bacterial diseases are usually not identified as such, but are thought to be of fungal origin until it is found that fungicides do not control the problem. There are relatively few bacteriacides on the market, but your local nursery may offer a product to help with your problem. Regulations vary from state to state and from country to country, so consult your local nursery or orchid society. However the writers use 'Physan 20' when necessary.

PESTS

Pests in orchids are numerous and destructive but all can be controlled to acceptable levels with proper treatment. Of the insect pests which cause ugly disfiguration of both plant and flower, the Red Spider Mite (*Tetranychus urticae*) is the most difficult to eradicate. Their favourite host plant is the *Cymbidium*, where they feed on the underside of the leaves. Regularly inspect your *Cymbidiums*. The mite is just visible to the naked eye and a build-up can be rapid. With a heavy infestation the leaves turn yellow, and a network of fine webs will be seen on the underside of the leaves. Control can be effected by the use of azobenzene fumigation, followed by an alternate treatment using a malathion aerosol spray. These chemicals do not kill eggs, so a follow up of three or four applications about ten days apart will be necessary. As a note of caution, remember that chemicals affect humans as well as insects. Read and follow instructions carefully.

False mite (*Brevipalpus russulus*) is red and attacks many plants, but seems to prefer *Phalaenopsis*. It causes pitting on the upper surface of the leaves. If treatment is neglected, a fungal infection will quickly develop, defoliating the plant. Here, again, a fumigation followed by a malathion aerosol spray should give complete control.

Brown or soft scales (*Diaspis boisluvalii* or *Coccus hesperidum*) are protected by a dome-shaped hard shell which resists chemical sprays. Likewise the Mealy Bug (*Pseudococcus longispinus*) is protected from sprays by a white waxy substance. Since both are sap-sucking pests, a systemic insecticide makes the plant toxic, thus the pests can be controlled with three applications, each about ten days apart. Should only several plants be affected, then paint the infection with methylated spirits using a small paint brush.

Aphids (*Cerataphis lantaniae*) attack young buds and tender new growth. There are several commercial sprays available for the treatment of Aphids. Check with your supplier or nursery. Liquid derris spray is usually most effective. Slugs and snails can be controlled by using common garden-snail baits. Most of the other insect pests, such as thrips, caterpillars, etc., can be controlled with the well-known and recommended garden insecticides.

As with fungal diseases, insect pests and other problems can be reduced considerably with good housekeeping. Close your houses as much as possible against insect entry. Keep overgrown grass and weeds away from the outside and, above all, check newly acquired plants carefully so you don't introduce new problems; treat new plants properly before introducing them to your collection.

Government regulations may prohibit dangerous chemicals, so always check with your local nursery or orchid society; they will recommend the best available legal sprays and chemicals if you are confronted with pests or diseases.

Clubs and Organisations

For the novice and professional alike, orchid and general gardening societies can prove valuable sources of information. Most countries throughout the world have orchid societies which amateurs can join.

The American Orchid Society is a large organisation which publishes a monthly magazine *The Orchid Digest*. Botanical gardens throughout the world are also helpful, especially when trying to identify a plant.

For both interest and competition, orchid shows are held throughout the year in numerous countries. On a large scale, international orchid shows are conducted in Asia with entries from all over the world.

American Orchid Society Inc.
84 Sherman Street
Cambridge, Massachusetts 02140
United States of America

Orchid Society of South-East Asia
Phoon Yoon Seng
22 Tosca Street
Singapore 1545

Honolulu Orchid Society Inc.
1710 Pali Highway
Honolulu Hawaii 96813

Royal Horticultural Society
Vincent Square
London SW1P 2PE United Kingdom

Orchid Society of Great Britain
9 Harlands Close
Haywards Heath, West Sussex
RHY16 1PS, England

Sydney Orchid Society
75 Quigg Street
Lakemba NSW 2195
Australia

ORCHID HYBRIDS

There is a special procedure for registering hybrids. Application forms must be completed and submitted with The Royal Horticultural Society in England for the cross to be officially recognised. All new hybrid names are published in an English journal called *The Orchid Review*. Every three years an international list is published in the *Sanders List of Orchid Hybrids*.

GLOSSARY

Actinomorphic: radially symmetrical.

Acuminate: tapering to a point.

Acute: sharp point.

Adnate: attached along the whole length to a part of unlike kind (e.g. of a petal attached to a column).

Aerial: exposed to the atmosphere as adventurous from tree or stem.

Ancipital: two-edged, as stem of plant.

Anterior: on the side of an organ farthest from the axis or stem on which it grows.

Antero-lateral: anterior and at the side.

Anther: the part of the stamen that holds pollen.

Anticous: on the anterior side.

Apetalous: without petals.

Apex: (Plural apices): tip.

Apical: at or pertaining to the tip of any structure.

Apiculate: tipped with a short and abrupt point.

Apomixis: reproduction which replaces or serves as a substitute for sexual reproduction; reproduction from cells other than ovules.

Arcuate: arched.

Aromatic: fragrant.

Articulate: jointed.

Ascending: growing upward.

Asexual: sexless, without sex involvement.

Auricle: ear-like lobe at the base of lamina.

Awn: a stiff bristle-like appendage (eg. a beard of barley)

Axil: the angle formed by a leaf or bract with the branch or stem.

Axillary: arising from the axil of a leaf or bract.

Axis: the main stem or the central column from which organs originate.

Back bulb: old pseudobulb.

Bicalcarate: two-spurred

Bidentate: having two teeth.

Bifarious: into two rows.

Bifid: divided by a deep cleft into two parts.

Bifurcate: branched into, or twice forked.

Bilobate: having two lobes.

Bipartite: divided into two parts.

Bisexual: of a flower containing both stamens and pistil.

Boss: swelling.

Botryoidal: resembling a bunch of grapes.

Bract: modified leaf or a flowering stem.

Bracteate: having bracts.

Bracteole: a small bract below an individual flower.

Calceiform: shoe-shaped or shoe-like.

Calceolate: slipper-shaped.

Callosities: alternative term for calli especially in *Microtis*.

Callosity: a hard lump.

Callus: (plural calli) thickened region, especially of labellum.

Campanulate: bell-shaped.

Canaliculate: with a longitudinal groove.

Capillary: hair-like.

Capitulum: inflorescence with sensile flowers compacted into a dense cluster, as in daisies; also known as a head.

Capsule: the fruit or seed case of most orchids.

Carinate: with a keel.

Cauda: a tail-like appendage; adjective caudate.

Caudicle: a star-like structure connected with the pollinia of orchids.

Cauline: attached to or pertaining to the stem (e.g. leaves on the stems).

Cavate: hollowed out.

Chelate: shaped like a lobster's claw.

Cilia: (singular cilium) fine hair-like structures usually around the margins of an organ.

Circinate: coiled into a tight spiral.

Clavate: club-shaped.

Claw: the stalk-like base of the petal, sepal or labellum.

Clinandrium: the depression on the top of the column on which the anthers rest.

Clone: a group of individuals (each a ramet) produced asexually from a single parent, normally of uniform genetic identity.

Column: the central organ of the orchid flower, formed by the fusion of the stamens and pistils.

Complicate: folded upon itself.

Confluent: running together.

Conical: cone-shaped.

Connate: of parts of like kind, closely united at their bases.

Connivent: converging but not fused.

Convolute: rolled together so margins overlap, furled like an umbrella

Cordate/Cordiform: heart-shaped.

Coriaceous: of leathery texture.

Corolla: the second lower-most whorl of sterile parts in a flower; each member is termed a petal.

Corymb: a racemose inflorescence in which the lower flowers are at more or less the same height.

Corymbiform: with the shape of a corymb.

Crassinode: nodes swollen in shape, thick and thin.

Crenulate: with tiny rounded teeth along the margins.

Cruciform: shaped like a cross.

Cucullate: arched into a hood.

Cuneate: wedge-shaped; broadest at apex.

Cuspidate: terminating in a sharp rigid point.

Cymbiform: boat-shaped.

Decurrent: extending downwards from the place of insertion; applied to leaves when their blades continue down the stem, forming raised lines.

Decurved: curved downwards.

Deflexed: bent downwards.

Deltoid: triangular with corners rounded.

Dentate: with outward facing acute teeth along the margins.

Denticulate: finely dentate.

Depressed: flattened down.

Dichotomous: forked in pairs; repeatedly dividing into branches.

Dilatation: a widening into a blade.

Disc: in orchids, the face or upper surface of the middle portion of the labellum.

Distal: towards the free end of an organ.

Distichous: arranged in two ranks, as leaves on opposite sides of stem.

Divaricate: widely diverging.

Dorsal: relating to the back of a structure; that is, the side facing away from the axis; but note that most orchid flowers twist around as they develop so that the dorsal side becomes the side *towards* the axis.

Dorsiventral: having distinct surfaces on both sides.

Dorsum: the back of an organ, that is, the side facing away from the axis.

Ellipsoid: compressed sphere; an elliptic solid.

Elliptic: shaped like an ellipse.

Emarginate: notched at the apex.

Endemic: confined to a particular region.

Ensiform: shaped like a sword blade.

Entire: without any division or irregularity (used especially of leaf margins or labellum).

Epichile: the terminal part of the jointed labellum of some orchids.

Epigeal: on or above the surface of the soil.

Epiphyte: a plant which grows upon trees, but which does not derive nourishment from their tissue.

Equitant: of leaves, arranged in such a way that each leaf is folded along its length and encloses the leaves younger than it.

Erect: upright.

Erose: jagged; as though bitten or gnawed off.

Evanescent: soon vanishing.

Exserted: protruding.

Eye: the incipient bud of a growth, particularly in sympodial orchids.

Falcate: sickle or scythe shaped.

Farinaceous: resembling flour; containing starch.

Flabelliform: fan-shaped.

Flagelliform: whip-like; long and slender like a lash.

Faucet gland: a tap-like gland that drips fluid.

Filiform: thread-like.

Fimbriate: fringed with long hairs or thread-like outgrowth; noun fimbria.

Flexuose: zig zag.

Foliaceous: leaf-like in appearance.

Foveolar: having pits or small depressions.

Fugacious: soon withering.

Furcate: forked into two.

Furfuraceous: scruffy; scaly or flaky.

Fused: amalgamated into one whole.

Fusiform: spindle-shaped.

Galea: a helmet-shaped structure, such as is formed in the flowers of *Pterostylis* in the fused dorsal sepal and lateral petals.

Gammate: shaped like the Greek capital letter *gamma* (i.e. upside down L).

Genus: the smallest natural group of species having certain essential characteristics in common. The first word in the botanical name of a plant is the genus to which it belongs.

Gibbous: with a swollen spur.

Glabrous: without hairs; having a smooth surface.

Globose: almost round.

Gynostemium: alternate name for column.

Hastate: spear shaped.

Herbaceous: without woody tissue.

Hirsute: covered with rough, fairly long hairs; pubescent.

Hydroponic: method of growing plants using nutrient solutions alone.

Hispid: with strong hairs or bristles.

Hypochile: lower or basal section of jointed labellum of some orchids.

Imbricate: overlapping, especially in bud.

Incumbent: lying upon a surface; distinct from erect.

Incurved: curved inwards; of the margins of the lamina of a leaf, curving towards the upperside or the side facing the axis.

Indent: notched.

Indigenous: native.

Inferior: describing the ovary when it is situated beneath the perianth, as in all orchids.

Inflexed: turned or bent sharply inwards.

Inflorescence: arrangement of the flowers on a plant; the flowers and shoot on which they are borne.

Inrolled: rolled inwards on the upper side.

Insectiform: insect-like in appearance

Inverted: turned upside down; reverse position.

Involute: rolled inwards on the upperside.

Irritable: sensitive to touch.

Keiki: a plantlet produced as an offshoot from a plant. (A Hawaiian term used by orchidists.)

Labellum: the lip-like petal of orchids, usually very distinct in appearance.

Lamellate: composed of thin plates.

Lamina: a flattened expansion of an organ, e.g. a leaf blade or the broad middle part of the labellum.

Laminate: blade-like.

Lanceolate: shaped like the head of a lance or a spear and broadest below the middle.

Lateral: at the side, as in the two lateral sepals of an orchid flower.

Leaf-fistula: the opening in a hollow leaf, through which the stem emerges.

Lenticular: lens-shaped.

Linear: long and narrow, having parallel sides.

Lingulate: strap-shaped.

Linear: long and narrow, having parallel sides.

Linguiform: tongue-shaped.

Lithophytic: growing on rocks; noun lithophyte.

Lobe: a division in the leaf or petal.

Lobule: a small lobe.

Lorate: strap-like.

Membranaceous: thin; more or less translucent.

Mentum: a chin; a pouch-like extension formed by the union of the column foot and bases of lateral sepals.

Mericlone: a plant produced by meristem propagation.

Meristem: the growing tissue made up of actively dividing cells, particularly at the tips of roots and at the apex of the vegetative or floral shoot.

Mesial: towards or on the middle line of a part.

Mesochile: middle section of jointed labellum of some orchids.

Monopodial: a form of growth in which there is a single vegetative shoot which continues to grow from year to year from its terminal bud.

Monotypic: of a genus having a single species.

Mucro: a sharp, abrupt terminal point.

Mucronate: having a mucro.

Mutation: a sudden departure from the parent type due to change in a gene or chromosome (a sport).

Nomenclature: a system of names and naming.

Obclavate: Club-shaped; widest at the base.

Obfalcate: Inversely sickle-shaped; that is, sickle-shaped but broadest above the middle.

Oblanceolate: lance-shaped in reverse, widest at the apex.

Oblong: moderately elongate but blunt at each end.

Obovate: tapering to both ends, about one-and-a-half times as long as broad, and widest above the middle.

Obtuse: bluntly pointed or rounded at the apex.

Operculate: like or funished with a cap or lid.

Orbicular: circular or almost circular.

Orifice: the mouth of a cavity.

Ovary: the lowest part of the pistil containing the ovules; when fertilised becomes the fruit.

Ovate: shaped like a lengthwise section of an egg; more or less elliptical but broader below the middle.

Ovoid: of three-dimensional objects, shaped like an egg.

Ovule: an unfertilised seed in the ovary.

Panicle: an inflorescence in which the axis is divided into branches, both bearing a group of flowers.

Papilla: (plural papillae) minute wart-like glands or protuberances.

Papillose: having papillae.

Patelliform: shaped like a saucer.

Patent: spreading.

Pectinate: resembling the teeth of a comb.

Pedicel: the stalk of an individual flower of an inflorescence.

Peduncle: stalk of a flower cluster, or individual flower when flower is the sole member in an inflorescence.

Peltate: the stalk is attached at the back and in the centre of the leaf.

Pendulous: hanging.

Penicillate: ending in a tuft of hairs.

Perianth: single term for calyx and corolla.

Persistent: not withering or falling.

Petals: an individual member of the corolla; orchids have three petals.

Petaloid: resembling a petal, as a petal-like sepal.

Petiole: the leaf-stalk.

Pistil: in an orchid, the fertile part of the flower consisting of ovary, styles and stigma.

Placenta: parts of the ovary to which the ovule or ovules are attached.

Plicate: folded like a fan.

Plumose: feathery or feather-like.

Pollinium: (plural pollinia) A pollen mass formed by aggregation of individual pollen grains.

Porrect: directed forward and downwards.

Posterior: the parts of an organ closest to an axis or stem on which it grows.

Praemorse: bitten off at the apex.

Process: any projecting appendage or extension.

Procumbent: trailing over the ground without rooting.

Proliferation: producing offshoots; growing by multiple division.

Prostrate: lying on or trailing over the ground.

Protocrom: a tuber-like structure formed in an early stage of a plant's development, prior to the production of leaves and roots.

Proximal: part nearest the axis;

Pseudobulb: the swollen bulb-like part of the stems of many epiphytic orchids.

Pubescent: having soft short downy hairs.

Pulvinate: cushion- or pad-shaped.

Pyriform: pear-shaped, but broadest below the middle.

Quadrate: rectangular or square.

Raceme: an indefinite inflorescence with undivided axis and equally pedicellate flowers; adjective racemose.

Radical: springing from the root or near the junction of the stem and root.

Ramet: individual of a clonal line or group.

Reclinate: turned or bent downwards from the apex.

Recomplicate: folded back on itself, then folded again.

Recurved: curved backwards or downwards.

Reflexed: suddenly bent backwards.

Reniform: kidney-shaped.

Resupinate: having the flower reversed by a 180 degree twist of the pedical during development.

Reticuate: net-like.

Retinaculum: the attachment of stipitate pollinia to the rostellum.

Retracted: drawn back.

Retroflex: bent or turned backwards.

Retuse: a shallow notch in a rounded apex.

Reversed: of the flower, without a twisted pedicel; not resupinate.

Revolute: the margins of leaves rolled back towards the mid-rib.

Rhizome: a prostrate or subterranean stem.

Rhombic: of a lamina, nearly square, with petiole at one of the acute angles.

Rosette: a cluster of radiating leaves.

Rostellum: a structure on the column of the orchid; an extension of the upper edge of the stigma.

Rostrate: beaked.

Rostrum: a beak or beak-like extension.

Rugose: wrinkled.

Rugulose: somewhat wrinkled.

Runcinate: sharply incised with teeth pointing backwards.

Saccate: short and rounded like a little bag.

Sagittate: arrow-head shaped.

Saprophyte: a plant which lives upon dead organic matter.

Scape: a stalk from the base of the plant bearing flowers, not leaves.

Scarious: dry, thin, more or less transparent, and usually brownish as if scorched.

Sclerophyll forest: a forest dominated with sclerophyllous trees such as eucalypts.

Sclerophyllous: a plant with hard textured leaves.

Scutiform: shield-shaped.

Secund: with the flowers or other organs all directed to one side; often applied to an inflorescence.

Semilunar: shaped like a half moon.

Sepal: an individual calyx segment; orchid flowers have three sepals.

Septate: divided by partitions (septa).

Serrate: toothed like a saw.

Serrulate: minutely serrate.

Sessile: without stalk.

Seta: (plural setae) stiff hair or bristle.

Sigmoid: S-shaped.

Sinuate: wavy margins.

Sinus: a cavity or gap.

Solitary: occurring singly.

Spathulate: spoon-shaped.

Spicate: disposed in a spike or resembling a spike.

Spike: an unbranched inflorescence having the youngest flowers at the top and all sessile.

Spreading: diverging outwards.

Spur: a hollow, horn-like extension of a petal.

Stamen: male organ in a flower, consisting of a fertile, pollen bearing anther attached to a sterile filament.

Stem-clasping: leaf basal clasping around stem.

Stigma: the top of the pistil which is the receiving surface for the pollen.

Stipe: (plural stipitate) stalked, applied to the ovary.

Stoma: (plural stomata) a pore, usually on the underside of leaves, through which gaseous exchange takes place.

Striate: marked with parallel lines.

Subtend: to be positioned immediately below.

Subulate: narrow and tapering to a fine point; awl shaped.

Suffusion: an overspread of colour.

Sympodial: having an axis or stem which simulates a simple stem, but which is made up of the bases of a number of axes which rise as branches one from another.

Taxonomy: the science of classification.

Terete: almost rounded; cylindrical, not angular.

Terminal: situated at the tip.

Terrestrial: growing in the earth or on the ground.

Tessellate: divided or marked into small squares, like a mosaic.

Tetragonal: four sided.

Tomentose: covered in matted hairs.

Trapezoid: four-sided figure with two sides parallel.

Trapeziform: shaped like a four-sided figure with no pair of sides parallel.

Tridentate: three toothed.

Trifid: divided into three parts by clefts or notches.

Trilobate: having three lobes.

Trullate: trowel shaped.

Truncate: blunt-ended, as if cut off abruptly.

Tuber: a swollen, underground stem used for food storage.

Tuberculate: beset with little tubercles or knobby projections.

Tumid: swollen or inflated.

Turbinate: top shaped like an inverted cone.

Umbel: an inflorescence in which all flowers arise from the apex of the peduncle, similar to the spokes of an umbrella; adjective umbellate.

Uncinate: hooked or barbed at the apex.

Undulate: wavy sides.

Unguiculate: clawed.

Unilocular: having one cavity or chamber.

Urceolate: like a pitcher or urn.

Valvate: opening by valves; of members of a whorl of floral parts, arranged in the bud so that the margins of each are pressed against those of the next, without overlapping.

Venation: the way the veins of the leaves are arranged.

Verrucose: covered with wart-like projections.

Villous: covered with long soft hairs.

Viscid: sticky.

Whorl: a set of organs coming from the same node and arranged in a circle round the axis.

Wings: the membranous margin of the seed or fruit; also applied to the two lateral petals of pea flowers.

Zygomorphic: divisible into two halves in one plane only; bilaterally symmetrical.

BIBLIOGRAPHY

Bechtel, Helmut & Phillip Cribb & Edmund Launert *The Manual of Cultivated Orchid Species* London, Blandford Press, 1981.

Bennett, Keith S. *The Tropical Asiatic Slipper Orchids* Sydney, Angus & Robertson, 1984.

Hawkes, Alex D. *Encyclopaedia of Cultivated Orchids* London, Faber and Faber Limited, 1965.

Hodgson, Margaret & Roland Paine *Field Guide to Australian Orchids* Sydney, Angus & Robertson, 1988.

Lavarack, P. S. & B. Gray *Tropical Orchids of Australia*, Melbourne, Thomas Nelson, 1985.

Millar, Andree *Orchids of Papua New Guinea* Canberra, Australian National University Press, 1978.

Pottinger, Mollie *African Orchids* Berkshire, H. G. H. Publications 1983.

Schweinfurth, Charles *Orchids of Peru* Chicago, Natural History Museum, 1970.

Sheehan, Tom & Marion *Orchid Genera Illustrated* New York, Comstock Publishing Associated, a division of Cornell University Press, 1979.

Shuttleworth, Floyd S. & Herbert S. Zim and Gorden W. Dillon *A Golden Guide to Orchids* New York, Golden Press, 1970.

Williams, Mark L. Isaac *An Introduction to the Orchids of Asia* Sydney, Angus & Robertson, 1988

Valmayor, Helen *Orchidiana Philippiniana* USA, Eugenio Lopaz Foundation, 1984.

INDEX OF COMMON NAMES

INDEX OF
BOTANICAL NAMES